Liz Grist has a PhD in biochemistry, has been Medical Correspondent for *Options* since 1983, and writes for a number of other medical periodicals. She is a regular contributor on medical subjects to *New Scientist* and *General Practitioner*, and her articles have appeared in the *Daily Telegraph*, the *Sunday Times*, the *Observer*, the *Guardian*, the *Daily Express*, *Woman* and *Parents*. This is her first book. She lives in Sussex with her husband and two small children.

Liz Grist

A Woman's Guide to Alternative Medicine

Fontana/Collins

First published by Fontana Paperbacks 1986

Set in Linotron Plantin

Made and printed in Great Britain by
William Collins Sons & Co. Ltd, Glasgow

For Duncan and Beatrice

Contents

Acknowledgements

I should like to thank the following people for their advice, help and encouragement at various stages along the way: my former colleague Steve Parker, with whom I first discussed the idea for the book – it was his initial enthusiasm that confirmed my belief that it *should* be written; my agent Caradoc King of A. P. Watt Ltd, who convinced me, despite my initial doubts about combining objective science and the largely subjective experience of alternative medicine, that it *could* be written; and my editor Helen Fraser, who gave me much help and contributed a number of useful suggestions.

I'm also indebted to everyone who talked, or wrote to me, during the research stage of the book. Strictly 'orthodox' doctors, those with an 'alternative' bent, and non-medical practitioners alike – hardly any turned down my requests for information, and most spent a considerable amount of time discussing the cons as well as the pros of their approach. In particular, I'd like to thank Dr Iain Chalmers, Dr Ronald Davey, Dr Anita Davies, Dr Stephen Davies, Dr Alec Forbes, Jo Garcia, Dr Alan Grant, Jeremy Kenton, Dr George Lewith, Simon Mills, Dr Dorothy Rowe, Celia Wright and Hein Zeylstra, who all, in their different ways, contributed to my greater understanding of the place of alternative medicine in women's health.

A special word of thanks is due to Dr Chalmers, who agreed to review the chapter on pregnancy, and to Dr Norma Williams, who read the entire manuscript. Any errors, of course, remain my responsibility.

I'm grateful to all the woman who wrote to me and whom I can't acknowledge individually here: some asked that their real names not be used and so I decided the fairest thing was to quote them all pseudonymously, apart from those who had previously had accounts of their experiences published elsewhere. Without their help, the book would have been the poorer. Whilst I agree with the many critics of alternative medicine that such 'anecdotal' reports tell us nothing about the *scientific* validity of the methods, they do tell us that the treatment – for whatever reason – can work; and that's what we, the patients, want to know.

This book would not have been written without the input from several friends, who started the ball rolling by telling me about their own dissatisfaction with orthodox medicine. 'Isn't there anything else?' they asked me as they battled on with heavy periods, bad backs and the like. Ironically, though, conventional treatment usually did – eventually – solve their problems! Which is another reason why I still believe, after writing this book, that one should never be too hasty about rejecting it.

My most heartfelt thanks go to my husband, Roger, who supported me – in part financially, but mostly emotionally – throughout. If writing a book is hard work, keeping the author sane is even harder! And, whenever my journalistic fervour threatened to get the better of my objectivity, it was he, as another scientist, who helped me keep the balance. If this book achieves its aim, it's as much to his credit as it is to mine.

A word on the book itself: I deliberately chose not to provide references for every source that I consulted while researching this book, since I thought too many references would be distracting to the general reader. I decided, therefore, only to cite those books or articles which elaborate upon the more surprising or controversial points I have made.

Finally, I'd like to acknowledge permission to quote passages from copyright material as follows: Drs Ann McPherson and Anne Anderson and Oxford University Press for *Women's Problems in General Practice*; Professor David Smail and J. M. Dent and Sons Ltd for *Illusion and Reality: the Meaning of Anxiety*; Lillian B. Rubin and

Fontana Paperbacks for *Intimate Strangers*; Lucy Goodison for *Women and Migraine*; Dr Michael Colgan and Muller, Blond and White Ltd for *Your Personal Vitamin Profile*; Dr Dorothy Rowe and John Wiley and Sons for *The Construction of Life and Death*; Dr Barbara North, Penelope Crittenden and Thorsons Publishers for *Stop Herpes Now!*; Rosetta Reitz and George Allen and Unwin Ltd for *Menopause. A Positive Approach*; Professor Michael Baum and Oxford University Press for *Breast Cancer. The Facts*; and Lawrence LeShan and Thorsons Publishers for *You Can Fight for Your Life*.

Introduction

Few people today – I hope – still believe that women are the weaker sex. Yet there's no getting away from the fact that even though, on average, we live longer than men, we do tend to have more health problems than they do. Surveys have shown that women consult their doctors up to twice as frequently. One reason is that women ask their doctor's advice on behalf of other members of their families, particularly their children. At the same time, women consult more often in their own right. They are, or so surveys of general practice suggest, more likely to have problems with their reproductive organs, their urinary tracts, their hormones – and with their mental well-being. They also suffer twice as much as men from what one study described as 'symptoms and ill-defined complaints' – that is, those feelings of unwellness that doctors find difficult to diagnose and treat.

Then, of course, there's contraception and pregnancy. Most forms of contraception are designed for the woman rather than the man and need to be prescribed and/or fitted (in the case of the intra-uterine device and the diaphragm) by a doctor. And every woman who's pregnant needs antenatal care.

Women not only see more of their doctors but they also, in the words of Dr Ann McPherson, co-editor of *Women's Problems in General Practice*,[1] 'consume a diet rich in pills'. 'The General Household Survey, for instance,' she writes, 'showed that in a fortnight previous to the survey, half the women and a third of the men reported that they had taken prescribed medicine, and another study showed that twice as many women as men had treated themselves.' Small wonder then, as Helen Roberts reports in her book *The*

Patient Patients,[2] a study of women and their doctors, that 'women, when questioned, admit to feeling unhealthy more often then men do . . .'

But what are the doctors doing to help us – apart, that is, from prescribing pills? The answer is: not as much as they'd like. Roberts suggests that doctors find their female patients the most troublesome and that it's those vague but common complaints which cause them the greatest frustration. The premenstrual syndrome and some of the psychological problems associated with the menopause are typical examples.

Is this frustration inevitable? Is it really necessary for doctors to fall back – as a number of them still do – on trite and unhelpful explanations such as 'I'm afraid that's the price you pay for being female' or 'It's your age, dear' or 'With two small children, you're bound to feel below par'? And what about more obvious conditions such as painful or heavy periods, menopausal hot flushes – and cancer? Conventional medicine does have some answers to these but they're not always very satisfactory ones. Yet they've remained popular with doctors – partly because until recently they had nothing else to offer and partly because, most being male, they had little idea of women's real feelings about their treatment. As Helen Roberts says in her book: 'Doctor and patient normally agree that the doctor defines the situations, and defines what is and what is not acceptable as appropriate for the patient to talk about . . . Even if doctors are not omnipotent,' she points out, 'if we are ill and afraid it is sometimes nice to believe they are.'

But things are changing. More doctors are realizing that there's much more to medicine than hormones, drugs and surgery. And they are at last getting the message that we want to be involved in treatment decisions. A number of them are beginning to offer alternatives as well as, or instead of, their usual treatments. In this country a group of them has formed the British Holistic Medical Association, which is aimed at promoting the care of patients as people, not as mere collections of symptoms. With this approach, it doesn't matter whether the treatment is orthodox or alternative.

The important thing is whether it helps the patient.

The essence of alternative medicine is self-help. This means taking responsibility for our own bodies and not letting others decide what's best for us. It's about making choices – not just about whether to take or leave the doctor's pills, but about choosing a healthy lifestyle which can help prevent disease. It's true that alternative methods can be used to treat conditions that seem to have beaten ordinary medics, but we also must realize that these complaints might never have cropped up had we paid more attention to diet and tackled our stress levels before they became overwhelming. In fact, alternative medicine is turning out to be less of a rival than an ally to conventional treatment. All medicine is about *healing* and it doesn't matter how this is achieved. The two approaches – alternative and orthodox – can be used side by side, to complement each other. That's why many practitioners prefer the term *complementary* or *holistic* medicine.

But as with anything different – and exciting – there's a danger of going overboard. Alternative medicine is no exception. Not all the claims made for it are justified. Nor should one seek an alternative remedy for all one's ills. As with conventional medicine, the treatment may not be appropriate. Nor may the practitioner be as well-trained as he or she might be.

This is why this book has been written. I believe that every woman has the right to know as much as possible about *any* treatment she's being offered and whether it's likely to help her. And that's why, although I've included a number of personal accounts from women themselves, I've also tried to look objectively at the scientific evidence for the efficacy of the various treatments. This hasn't been easy because there's so little good research on alternative medicine. Nor has it been possible to confirm – as many of its practitioners claim – that it's always safe. As you'll discover, I have serious reservations about the safety of one or two of the methods, either because of the techniques themselves or because of the way they are practised.

So this book won't necessarily make it any easier for you to decide whether alternative medicine could help you. I hope, though, that if and when you do make that decision, you'll have a more realistic idea of what to expect.

1. Alternative Therapies

As I explained in the introduction, my aim in this book is to examine how some of the better-known alternative therapies may be used to treat women's health problems. For reasons of space, it hasn't been possible to include every alternative therapy now practised in this country. In general, therefore, I've discussed only therapies which are widely available and/or those which have a reasonable following among medically qualified practitioners. This, I feel, allows you, the consumer, the greatest possible choice when you start looking for a therapist.

No doubt some readers who have already tried alternative medicine will feel that I've been too selective, that I've excluded some excellent techniques simply because they're less well-known or are too esoteric to appeal to the increasing number of doctors who are now interested in alternatives. But this book is intended to be a practical guide to women's health, and not a comprehensive treatise on alternative medicine – of which there are several already – and one has to draw the line somewhere.

Similarly, in this chapter on the therapies themselves, I've avoided going into too much detail. Many readers will already have a nodding acquaintance, either from other books or from talking to friends who have tried them, with, for example, acupuncture, osteopathy and homoeopathy. And further information can be found in some of the books listed in the bibliography. Some therapies are either not discussed at all in this chapter or mentioned only briefly. This is because they're covered in some detail elsewhere in the book. Nutritional medicine, for example, comes into Chapter 2 on healthy eating, whilst psychotherapy appears in Chapters 4, 11, 13 and 14.

As to the scientific basis, or lack of it, of alternative treatment – some of the evidence for its efficacy in a particular condition is mentioned in the appropriate chapter. In the following section, however, I'll be discussing briefly some additional results which have been obtained with some of the individual therapies. And, later in the chapter, I'll be talking about some of the principles involved in testing alternative medicine.

THE THERAPIES

Acupuncture

This technique came to the West from China, where it forms part of a system of medicine thousands of years old which also includes the prescription of herbs. Acupuncture – the Latin for needle puncture – is the use of needles to puncture the skin at carefully defined points to restore the balance of energy believed to be necessary for good health. Acupuncture points are said to lie on *meridians*, which are the channels through which this energy flows. Acupuncturists sometimes also use *shiatsu* or *acupressure* – where, instead of needles, pressure from the fingers is used to stimulate the acupuncture points. Points may also be treated with *moxibustion*, the burning of a herb known as moxa, over the point.

Non-medical acupuncturists who are trained according to the traditional Chinese method adhere strictly to the age-old techniques for diagnosis and treatment, including pulse diagnosis: there are said to be twelve pulses – six in each wrist – which are believed to give the therapist invaluable information about the patient's state of health. Medically trained acupuncturists, on the other hand, have tended to dispense with many aspects of the Chinese system; they don't believe meridians exist and many of them have abandoned pulse diagnosis. In medical hands, acupuncture treatment is often stripped to its basic essentials – the needling of points.

There is now quite a bit of evidence that acupuncture does work – at least in the relief of pain. This is backed by experiments which show that acupuncture results in changes in the levels of endorphins, the body's natural painkillers, and in other chemicals involved in the transmission of nerve impulses. But there is also good evidence that the needling of *any* point will produce considerable pain relief. It seems however that stimulation of the traditional points, rather than just sticking needles in anywhere, has greater and more long-lasting effects.

There is so far very little research to support the use of acupuncture in conditions which aren't painful. Even the most sceptical of medical acupuncturists however concede that good results are possible – it's just that we haven't yet discovered how these are brought about.

Chiropractic

Chiropractors specialize in mechanical disorders of the joints, particularly those of the spine, and their effects on the nervous system. Chiropractic – together with osteopathy (see below) – may be used to treat not only pains in the back and neck themselves but also *referred* pains such as headaches, and leg and arm pain, which may originate in the spine. X-rays are often used to aid diagnosis, and treatment usually involves manipulation of the spine.

Clinical ecology

Practitioners of clinical ecology believe that diseases may be caused by a sensitivity to foods and/or chemicals in a person's environment. Their aim is to pinpoint these substances and treat the sensitivity. This may be done either by advising the patient to avoid these particular substances or by making her less sensitive to them. Clinical ecology, though now practised by a number of doctors, remains highly controversial – not least because the diagnosis and treatment of sensitivity is often made by methods which the ecologists admit have no known scientific basis, and which are both unreliable and difficult to interpret. These include *cytotoxic* testing, where the patient's white blood cells are mixed with the suspect substances, *sublingual* drop testing, and *intradermal* skin testing, where dilutions of the substances are placed under the patient's tongue or into her skin respectively, in an attempt to bring on her symptoms. To 'switch off' her symptoms, she is then given increasing dilutions of the same solution until one is found that does not provoke them (for further details of this method, see Chapters 5 and 13).

Clinical ecology has three other big credibility problems. The first is that conventional medical methods for testing and treating true allergies – for example to pollen and house dust – often give negative results when used on patients who appear sensitive to food and chemicals. By this criterion, then, most food-sensitive patients do *not* have an allergy.

In addition, clinical ecologists – and practitioners of nutritional medicine (see below) – sometimes use hair analysis to determine whether their patients have a deficiency of certain essential trace minerals, such as zinc, or an excess of a poisonous one, such as lead. Hair analysis is a very new science and a number of problems remained to be ironed out. From the evidence so far available, it appears that this method may be a helpful one provided it's used in conjunction with information obtained from the patient's history and from other tests on, for example, her blood. On its own, though, hair analysis may not be very reliable, and may even lead to entirely the wrong conclusions. For example, an article in the *Journal of the American Medical Association* in 1985 revealed that not only did individual hair analysis laboratories produce widely different results when given *identical* samples of hair, but they were also way off the mark when it came to diagnosis. Thus, one healthy seventeen-year-old girl, according to two reports produced on separate occasions by the same lab, was suffering from fifteen and twenty-seven, respectively, abnormal conditions!

A medically trained ecologist should be aware of these pitfalls and will, in any case, always take a full history and run a battery of tests before arriving at a diagnosis. The trouble is that hair analysis is now available by post and is being used fairly indiscriminately by people who are not qualified to interpret the results, as the *JAMA* report shows. This abuse of what may prove, under some circumstances, a helpful technique, has given hair analysis rather a bad name.

The other aspect of clinical ecology which antagonizes many orthodox medics is the evangelism of some of its practitioners who claim that many, if not all, conditions are due to food or chemical sensitivity.

Healing

At first sight, healing might appear to be the most esoteric of all the alternative therapies discussed in this book. Yet surprisingly enough, according to a survey published in *The Times* in March 1985, it is the most widely practised. And of the 108 GPs (a nationally representative sample) who took part in the survey, 14 per cent said they recommended it to their patients. An earlier study, of 86 GP trainees, published in the *British Medical Journal* in 1983, also revealed healing to be a popular therapy: almost one third of the doctors thought it was useful. Though there is some evidence that the healing process is accompanied by brain-wave changes in both the healers and their patients, and that some healers are able to affect animals, plants and cells grown in the laboratory (thus probably ruling out the placebo effect – see below), we don't really have a clue as to what happens when a person is healed.

Healing usually involves the laying-on of hands, though healers also practise *absent* healing for patients who are unable to visit them in person. Religious faith, they say, is unnecessary, though the patient must have faith in the healer and the healing 'energies', whatever they may be. In some cases the patient actually experiences a sensation which could certainly be likened to the transfer of energy – they may feel a warmth, a tingling or become relaxed and calm. Healers see themselves as the channel through which this energy flows.

Contrary to popular opinion, healing rarely results in

instant 'miracles'. Nor is it a passive process: some healers, notably Matthew Manning, one of the country's best-known, demand that their patients work towards their own health by practising with tapes which help them to relax, to breathe properly and to visualize their bodies healing themselves. They may also be given advice on diet. 'You don't get ill overnight,' Manning is reported to have said, 'so you don't get better that quickly either . . . It may take weeks, it may take as much as two years, seeing someone either every week, every month or every few months.'[1] Manning is also quoted as saying that he believes that anyone can heal, both themselves and other people. 'I'd like to demystify healing. I'm doing some tapes with some very simple ideas, about how ordinary people can change their attitudes and take the first steps in prevention and self-healing for themselves.'

This, as we'll see, is the essence of all alternative treatment and is particularly relevant to cancer therapy (see Chapter 11). Visiting a healer may give your energies a boost, but it's the recuperative powers of your own body that will accomplish the healing process. And this idea, that changes in attitude and lifestyle can both prevent and treat illness is, of course, now being embraced by many orthodox practitioners. Perhaps, then, we should rethink our definition of healing to include not only the laying-on of hands but any other method that results in better health.

Herbal medicine

This is one of the oldest systems of medicine. It's believed that primitive man knew by instinct which herbs had healing properties and which were poisonous. Later, this knowledge was handed down from generation to generation and several centuries before the birth of Christ herbal treatment was already well established. However, it appears that from the sixteenth century onwards, herbal medicine went into a decline. This was later accelerated by the discovery that the ingredients extracted from herbs were even more powerful than the herbs themselves: a number of medical drugs owe their origins to herbs, including digitalis from the foxglove, morphine from the opium poppy, and aspirin from willow bark. Later still, man discovered that he could manufacture the chemical equivalents of some of these drugs synthetically, so that herbs, to some extent, became redundant. Though most herbs haven't yet been exploited in this way by the pharmaceutical industry, there's evidence that many of them do, in fact, contain ingredients which have definite effects on the body. Only a few herbal remedies have been fully researched, however.

So why not abandon herbs altogether and simply use their active ingredients? The reason, say herbalists, is that herb remedies are free from the side effects of drugs. Nor can you become dependent on them. In its *History of Herbal Medicine* the National Institute of Medical Herbalists says: 'In plants the powerful constituents are balanced, potentiated and made more or less accessible by a myriad of other constituents naturally present.' As an example, the Institute cites the herb Ephedra. This yields ephedrine, a chemical belonging to a class known as the alkaloids. Ephedrine will cause a rise in blood pressure if extracted and taken on its own. 'In the plant there are six other alkaloids, the main one of which has the action of preventing a rise in blood pressure and increase in the rate of the heart beat. The isolated drug is dangerous, but the natural herb, with its mixture of constituents in equilibrium, is devoid of danger.' With people becoming increasingly worried about the side effects of drugs – and with most doctors now ready to admit that no drug, despite extensive testing, can be guaranteed absolutely safe, herbal medicine seems an attractive alternative, backed as it is by centuries of experience.

Herbal medicines are usually prescribed in the form of tinctures, prepared by macerating the herb in water and alcohol to produce a concentrated extract and straining it, or infusions, made by pouring boiling water over the herb and leaving it to soak for a certain length of time before straining. Herbs may also be incorporated into lotions, ointments and tablets. The method of preparation and of administration will depend on the type of herb and on the condition to be treated. Most herbal remedies contain a number of constituents and none is ready-made because no two medicines are identical and each patient needs an individual prescription.

Homoeopathy

This is based on the principle of 'like cures like'. Substances which would produce certain symptoms in a healthy person are prescribed in minute quantities to a sick one with the same symptoms. The most potent homoeopathic remedies are considered to be those which are the most dilute – contrary to orthodox medical practice.

Remedies are prepared by *serial* dilutions, usually one in ten or one in a hundred. That is, one drop of the most concentrated preparation is diluted in nine or ninety-nine times its volume of the diluent and the process repeated with each subsequent dilution. Remedies prepared by one-in-ten dilutions are designated X. Thus a remedy which has been diluted twice would be 2X. Similarly, remedies diluted a hundred times at each stage are known as 1C, 2C and so on. Each time a remedy is diluted it is also *succussed*, that is, vigorously shaken, and this shaking seems to be a crucial part of the process: without it, homoeopathic remedies lose their potency.

We tend to regard homoeopathic remedies as perfectly safe, but this isn't necessarily so. At low dilutions, below about 12X, 'there is a possibility of toxic side effects', writes medical homoeopath Dr Hamish Boyd, though higher dilutions are safe.[2] In fact, there comes a point – at about 24X or 12C – when the remedy contains no molecules of the starting substance so, at least from the scientific point of view, it would be expected to have no effect at all. Paradoxically though, it is just these 'high potency' remedies which are considered to be most effective! Not surprisingly, orthodox scientists and medics ridicule this suggestion. But homoeopaths believe that the succussion in some way alters the solution, so making it more potent. Research so far has failed to reveal why this should be so. Although a few research groups have obtained results which, at first, have seemed to lend support to the belief that succussion changes a homoeopathic remedy in some definite way, they have failed to stand up to further investigation.

All the same, homoeopathic remedies do seem to work – even in babies and animals who, one would have thought, should have few, if any, expectations about the outcome of their treatment. It could be argued, therefore, that they should be less susceptible to the placebo effect – though there is no certainty about this. Recent, carefully controlled animal experiments intended as far as is possible to get rid of the placebo effect have suggested that the remedies do produce real results and that these may, in some cases, be mediated *via* endorphins, the body's natural painkillers.[3] Though it's believed that a placebo may also have an effect on endorphin levels, it may be that homoeopathic remedies, like acupuncture, in some way bring about even greater changes than the placebo is able to do on its own.

Hypnosis

In one way, a hypnotic trance is similar to a state of relaxation or meditation (see below). All are altered states of awareness. And research has shown that the brain waves of someone who's hypnotized are similar to those of a person who is awake but relaxed. Dr David Waxman, a medically qualified hypnotist, writes: 'Accordingly, it could be concluded that the deeply hypnotized person . . . is *not asleep* but in a very special state of relaxation.'[4]

What makes this form of relaxation 'special' is that the subject is 'locked in' to the voice of the hypnotist and everything else is blocked out. Moreover, during hypnosis, the right side of our brain, which is associated with the unconscious mind, with dreams, emotions, creativity and so on, becomes dominant over the logical left brain which controls the conscious mind and our purely intellectual activities. It then becomes possible for the therapist to help us get in touch with our unconscious. Thus, as we shall see in Chapter 14, hypnosis may be used in conjunction with psychotherapy. It may also have a role in treating women who are infertile because of some deep-seated fear of pregnancy (Chapter 8).

However hypnosis can work at less profound levels. It can be used simply as a form of relaxation, to allay stress and tension or to alleviate labour pains (see Chapter 7). And you can also be taught to hypnotize yourself so that you're no longer dependent on your therapist.

People often wonder what it's like to be hypnotized. It isn't at all like being asleep – and although it often helps to close your eyes, it's not necessary. In fact, it's possible to be in a light hypnotic trance without realizing it. Experienced hypnotists say that very few people cannot be hypnotized but the success of the technique depends largely on the therapist, his subject and the rapport between them. So though you may fail to 'go under' with one hypnotist, another may be able to put you into a trance with no trouble at all.

Naturopathy

This isn't an individual therapy, but a combination of several, though naturopathy is actually the oldest of the alternative disciplines and is based on the teachings of Hippocrates. The aim is to help the patient preserve or regain her health by paying attention to *all* the factors upon which good health depends. So naturopaths give dietary advice which often includes fasting, practise osteopathic manipulation, and prescribe hydrotherapy (the use of water internally and externally in the form of baths, packs, compresses, sprays and douches), exercises and relaxation. Some naturopaths now prescribe vitamin and mineral supplements as well. Others, though, look askance at this development (for more details, see Chapter 2 on Eating for Health).

Nutritional medicine

Nutritional medicine has much in common with both naturopathy and clinical ecology, based as it is on the belief that many illnesses are due to dietary deficiencies or excesses, food and chemical sensitivities and the toxic effects of poisonous metals (for further details of this approach, see Chapters 5 and 13).

Osteopathy

Osteopathy is very similar to chiropractic although the two techniques began somewhat differently. According to the British Holistic Medical Association: 'Theories and techniques were different but have become more similar over the years, in spite of little contact between the two professions.' The main differences are that chiropractors tend to use diagnostic X-rays more than osteopaths whilst the latter devote more time to massage of soft tissues.

Cranial osteopathy or *craniosacral technique* is a variation of osteopathy though it bears little resemblance to standard osteopathic technique. It is based on the belief that manipulation of the skull and sacral area at the base of the spine can affect the movement of the cerebrospinal fluid (CSF) which bathes the brain and spinal cord. It is said to be able to alleviate all sorts of conditions from migraine to hormonal problems because, or so it's argued, disturbances in the flow of the CSF cause imbalances not only in the head and spine but also elsewhere in the body. The manipulation of the skull is very gentle and causes no discomfort.

Despite enthusiastic reports from practitioners of this technique and their patients, in the UK cranial osteopathy remains very much the poor relation of osteopathy, mainly because most osteopaths don't believe in it. They agree with conventional doctors that the skull is a rigid structure and that, certainly in adulthood, the bones are knit together and impossible to move. Nevertheless it is slowly gaining a following in this country (it's already fairly well established in the US). Two of the three training colleges recognized by the General Council and Register of Osteopaths are now including it in their undergraduate courses.

Reflexology and reflex zone therapy

Both are a form of foot massage but the effects of this massage are said to reach way beyond the feet. Practitioners believe that each foot is divided into ten areas or 'reflex' zones which correspond to different parts of the body. The big toe is related to the head and the second and third toes to the eyes, for example. There is no scientific basis for this belief but it does appear that massage of a particular reflex zone can affect the health of the relevant organ. 'Everyone has reflex zones on their feet,' writes Ann Lett, Principal of the British School of Reflex Zone Therapy of the Feet, 'but they are only painful when there is strain, weakness, damage or disease in the organ to which that reflex zone corresponds. Treatment of the painful reflex zones provokes a healing response throughout the body.'[5] Reflex zone therapy practitioners see themselves as different from reflexologists in that, instead of giving every patient the same standard massage, they concentrate on those zones needing the most attention.

Relaxation techniques

The benefits of relaxation are now well established. Perhaps more to the point is how one goes about becoming relaxed.

SELF-HELP

It's possible to learn the art by listening to tapes or reading books which take you through the steps one by one. There's a bit of controversy, however, about self-help. Dr Malcolm Carruthers, who runs autogenic training (see page 29) courses in London, has warned against relaxation tapes and books. 'When some people release the tension that's on the surface, underlying traumas and anxieties can bubble up,' he reports. This means, Carruthers believes, that when you learn relaxation techniques you need a properly qualified person to help you deal with any unpleasant reactions.

But it seems that not everyone agrees with him. One who doesn't is Dr Robert Sharpe, a behavioural psychologist in private practice. He has, he said, done a lot of research on relaxation tapes and helped to set up a company, Lifeskills, which produces them (see Useful Addresses). 'I know of no reports of [traumatic reactions] where tapes which are educational and training in nature – not hypnotic – have been used,' said Dr Sharpe. He added that Lifeskills tapes have been used in the NHS for ten years and that GPs recommend them to their patients.

LEARNING RELAXATION FROM A THERAPIST

Some people find that they need the more disciplined approach that comes from consulting a relaxation teacher or therapist. But first, there's the problem of what *sort* of therapist to consult: do you go to a hypnotist (see above), attend yoga classes (which will include relaxation and, possibly, meditation) or go on an autogenic training (AT) course? AT is in many respects a Western version of meditation and is also similar to the state you enter when you hypnotize yourself. It begins with instructing yourself that you're feeling heavy and warm, that your heartbeat and breathing are regular and calm.

Yoga teachers help their pupils to relax in the same sort of way – by calm attention to breathing and to relaxing different parts of the body bit by bit. You'll find similar techniques on tapes and in books, too.

Despite its mystical overtones, meditation is not necessarily superior to relaxation, though it is possible that you may have mystical experiences after you've been practising it for some time. Meditation has a number of effects on the body, including lowering of the blood pressure, relaxation of the muscles and slowing of the pulse. 'However,' writes Dr

D. Marcer, senior lecturer in the Department of Psychology at Southampton University, 'it has also been demonstrated that these changes are not unique to meditation. Although this conclusion would be challenged by some researchers, the consensus is that the physiological changes that occur as a result of meditation can also be achieved by other techniques, including controlled muscular relaxation.' He regards meditation and deep relaxation as synonymous.[6]

Biofeedback is simply an aid to relaxation. A subject can learn to control, for example, her brain waves, her blood pressure and her muscle tone, by being wired up to instruments which monitor changes in these characteristics and which, by means of an altered tone or the movement of a needle on a dial, let her know whether she is successful.

Which technique you choose depends on your feelings about it, its availability – and also on your pocket. Yoga is probably the cheapest and most widely available method – and has the added bonus that the postures (asanas) will not only tone up your body but may make it easier for you to relax afterwards. However, not all teachers devote as much time to relaxation, let alone meditation, as others. Many are more concerned with the postures, as their pupils, particularly the female ones, often see yoga merely as a form of body conditioning. Then again, the classes may be too big for you to get the individual attention you may need. There's no doubt, though, that if you do find a good, committed teacher, then you will be helped to some extent.

Autogenic training, while apparently very effective, is expensive – about £150 for an eight-week course. And you may be unable to find a teacher within reasonable distance of your home. There is, though, an organization which may be able to help (see Useful Addresses).

Most of the clinical psychologists who use biofeedback practise in the NHS and so you'll need to be referred by a GP or psychiatrist. At the moment, unfortunately, there's no easy way of finding a *private* biofeedback practitioner. If, however, you already know of one and want to know whether he or she is reputable, you can check his or her credentials with the British Psychological Society (see Useful Addresses).

THE TESTING OF ALTERNATIVE THERAPIES

For a long time, alternative medicine was regarded with deep suspicion by the medical profession. Now more doctors are prepared to try alternative techniques or refer patients to reputable therapists. According to *The Times* survey (see page 21), among younger GPs nearly three-quarters have some faith in alternative medicine and only 3 per cent are 'disbelievers'. (20 per cent either said they didn't know or had no feelings one way or the other.) This gradual acceptance has been encouraged partly by the growing evidence, some of which I discussed in the previous section and some of which you'll read about elsewhere in the book, that a number of the alternative therapies do appear to have a scientific basis.

But none of this convinces the sceptics. Take acupuncture, probably the most thoroughly researched of the alternatives. An article entitled 'Acupuncture and the age of unreason', which was published in the *Lancet* in 1984, argued that the supporters of acupuncture had ignored all the clinical trials which showed it had no effect at all. The author also pointed out that many of the positive results came from Chinese research and implied that because the Chinese had a vested interest in promoting acupuncture, which in China is a cheap, easily available form of medicine, one shouldn't take them too seriously. Similar criticisms – about the quality of the research – have been levelled at homoeopathy. And, as I've already mentioned, we're no nearer knowing whether homoeopathy *really* works and if it does, why.

The placebo effect and controlled trials

It could be – as the sceptics claim – that the placebo effect is at the root of alternative medicine's beneficial effects. That's why the medical establishment would like to see all alternatives tested by *double-blind placebo-controlled trials*. New orthodox treatments have to be tested this way, they argue, so why not alternative medicine?

In such a trial, two or more groups of patients, as alike as possible in terms of age, disease and symptoms are compared. One or more groups are given the active therapy(ies) and one the placebo or dummy treatment. Neither the patients nor their doctors know which treatment is being given until the trial is completed. This means that all the patients are equally likely to believe that their treatment is going to work and so, although this alone may make some of them get better, the effect should be similar in all groups. And because their doctors don't know which treatment they're giving, their *attitude* towards all the patients should be similar. This is important, because a patient's well-being can easily be affected by her doctor's confidence or pessimism.

However, this type of trial isn't – or so alternative practitioners say – the best way of testing their methods. They treat the patient as a whole, not as a collection of symptoms. Two people may well have similar problems but, according to the holistic approach, they may arise from completely different causes. So the treatment must differ. There are additional problems. One is that, for some of the alternatives, it's difficult to design a suitable placebo. With homoeopathy, of course, you can simply substitute for the remedy another pill which looks and tastes the same but which contains nothing but an inert substance. But what about acupuncture and osteopathy – surely there's no way you can 'con' the patient or her practitioner into thinking that she's having active treatment when she isn't!

In fact it is possible to compare acupuncture with a placebo, though not in a double-blind fashion because the practitioner still knows which treatment he's giving. One way is to wire the patient up to a TENS instrument. TENS (which is also discussed in Chapter 7) is a form of electrical stimulation, and normally produces similar effects to accupuncture. But if the instrument is disconnected without the patient's knowledge then, or so it's hoped, she will think she's being treated even though she isn't. (I have my doubts as to whether one can fool patients in this way: as anyone who's tried TENS will tell you, you can actually feel whether the current is on or off. The fact that mock TENS *does* reduce pain (see below) suggests that the doctor's attitude and the sight of impressive machinery may contribute to the placebo effect in at least some cases.) In another form of 'sham' acupuncture, the patient lies face down and the practitioner pinches the skin on her back so that she thinks she's being needled. Both these methods have been used in clinical trials to assess the ability of acupuncture to control pain. The results suggest that, whereas only 30 per cent of patients respond to the placebo, 60 per cent benefit from the acupuncture.

There are two further barriers to alternative research. One is that the practitioners themselves are usually so convinced that their methods work – and are so busy putting them into practice – that they have neither the time nor the inclination to put them to the test. The other is lack of money. Most of the medical research in this country is funded by the drug industry which has little interest in alternative remedies. The industry is as conservative as the medical establishment on which it depends and the last thing it wants to do is to support research which might detract from its existing, thriving, market in allopathic drugs.

In the absence of good clinical trials, how can we tell whether alternative medicine works? One way is simply to study the clinical results. If more than 30 per cent of patients treated with alternative therapies get better – the proportion one would expect if they were simply responding to the placebo effect produced by a new treatment offered by a caring, confident practitioner – then this would suggest that the effects of the therapy are genuine.

In 1985, the *Journal of Alternative Medicine* published the results of one such survey (a shortened version also appeared in the *British Medical Journal*). Dr George Lewith, a medically trained alternative practitioner in Southampton, reported that out of fifty-six patients included in the survey, nearly 60 per cent felt that their condition had improved significantly as a result of treatment. The treatments used were acupuncture, manipulation, herbal medicine, homoeopathy and clinical ecology. Perhaps even more significantly, nearly all of them had previously been treated conventionally without success. They had been ill, on average, for nine years. 'We were able to help many of these patients who had "failed" with conventional medicine,' wrote Dr Lewith, 'thus implying that the philosophies behind alternative medicine may indeed be more powerful at dealing with chronic illness than conventional medicine.'

All the same, this survey is a drop in the ocean. And it doesn't really solve the vexed problem of the placebo effect. The received wisdom is that this never accounts for more than about 30 per cent of the success rate of any therapy. Yet elsewhere in this book I'll be telling you of trials where placebo effects of 40, 50 and even almost 90 per cent have been reported. And as Dr Lewith and his colleagues observed: 'Two-thirds of the patients coming to see us believed that alternative or complementary medicine was very effective and certainly expected a great deal from the treatment . . . Their expectations correlated with treatment outcome, in that if they thought that they were going to get better, they had a much greater chance of doing so. This implies that almost any clinician should, in a responsible manner, reinforce these expectations as they may well be an important part of the therapy.' Dr Lewith seems to be saying, in effect, that practitioners should work to encourage the placebo effect.

But even if it's true that some, if not all, of the benefits of alternative medicine are due to the placebo effect, does that matter? I don't think it does. For the patient, what's important are the results, not the theories. On the other hand, we need to know whether the theories can stand up because, if they can, then alternative medicine will win its way to greater acceptance by the medical profession. Some alternative practitioners are concerned that if they don't prove their case then, by default, alternatives will fall into disrepute. In practice this seems unlikely, given the intense public – and, of course, royal – interest in alternative medicine. However, it wouldn't do any harm to get the big guns of orthodox medicine on its side. That's why research must continue, even if progress is slow. And in the UK an organization – the Research Council for Complementary Medicine – has been set up specifically to foster research and to, in its own words, 'encourage the incorporation of what is best in complementary medicine into the mainstream of modern medical practice'.

THE COSTS OF TREATMENT

Currently only homoeopathy and acupuncture are available on the NHS and, within the health service, their practitioners are thin on the ground. So alternative treatment usually means private treatment. If you have medical insurance, and provided your practitioner is also a hospital consultant, you can claim back the costs of your treatment. In practice, this used to mean that such payments were seldom made, as an article in 1985 in *Here's Health* pointed out:

> As almost no consultants practise any form of complementary medicine, that meant 'pay up yourself' for most patients . . . Only the few people lucky enough to have NHS homoeopathic hospital facilities near them could get their treatment from a consultant – and get its cost repaid. But some persistent patients were already persuading their insurer to make exception to the rules. Backed by firm, even indignant letters from their GP or specialist, some managed to extract ex-gratia payments.

And more changes seem afoot. I understand that a few medically qualified alternative practitioners in general practice have now been given specialist status by insurers so that their patients can now claim back their fees. The doctors apparently managed to convince the insurer that, as they taught their techniques to doctors who *were* consultants, then they should have equivalent status! The rules may be slackened even further. One company is reported to accept claims for some treatment carried out by non-medically qualified staff provided that it was done on the instructions, and under the supervision, of an NHS consultant.

But if your claims aren't accepted, or if you have no medical insurance, then you'll usually have to pay for your treatment, whether or not your practitioner is medically qualified – unless he or she is also your own GP. Fees vary considerably: the lowest I came across was £3 per consultation and the highest (in Harley Street) about £70. The average for a first consultation, which may last between thirty minutes and an hour, seems to be between £15 and £20; subsequent consultations, which tend to be shorter, usually cost quite a bit less. My impression is that doctors tend to charge more than other qualified practitioners. Healers, however, rarely charge, though they may ask for a donation. And some practitioners say they reduce their fees for people who are particularly hard-up.

MEDICAL AND NON-MEDICAL PRACTITIONERS

I believe that we, the public, would get the best deal if alternative practitioners were trained in both alternative *and* conventional medicine. This is mainly because if complementary medicine were practised as widely as the allopathic sort, then eventually it would be cheaper to come by – either because it would be available on the NHS or because our private fees would be *always* reimbursed by our medical insurers.

But there is another argument in favour of choosing a medically qualified practitioner. And that is that he or she is better placed to treat you adequately. In the absence of an extensive medical training, the reasoning goes, a practitioner may misdiagnose your problem and treat you for some minor complaint when, in fact, you have something much more serious. Nor will he be able to treat you properly if your condition is one of those which, though not serious, will respond better to orthodox treatment. I'm not sure I go along with this argument – feelings run high on both sides of the fence and getting at 'the truth', if it exists, is almost impossible. However it's something you need to take into account when you're shopping around. So let's look at it in a bit more detail.

For starters, I'm convinced that you should *never* consult a practitioner who hasn't had some recognized form of training. At the end of the book you'll find a list of the professional non-medical organizations which govern the standards of training in, and practice of, the various therapies. Each has its own register of members which it will supply on request. I've also included some of the medical societies for doctors practising alternative methods. This isn't to say that other types of practitioner are always inferior. But, given the choice, it's always sensible to consult one who's undergone formal training in alternative therapy, whether or not he or she is a doctor. That said, is there any truth in the claim that a trained practitioner who isn't also a doctor is at a disadvantage when it comes to diagnosis and treatment?

I've heard horror stories from both sides: of doctors practising acupuncture after one afternoon's training, and of lay practitioners failing to diagnose cancer and other serious diseases. But I believe that if you consult a practitioner who is a member of a professional organization specifically concerned with the therapy or therapies he practises, then these disasters are unlikely to occur. A doctor who is, for example, a member of the British Medical Acupuncture Association or has a qualification from the Faculty of Homoeopathy, will have completed an adequate additional training. A trained lay practitioner will have undergone several years' study in many of the aspects of conventional medicine, with diagnosis high on the list. He will also have access to hospital tests, if necessary. Moreover, if he feels he's unable to treat you, he will refer you either back to your own doctor or to a specialist. Interestingly, many doctors put not just their patients but themselves in the hands of lay practitioners, as *The Times* survey revealed. And one naturopath and osteopath told me: 'Most of us have good relationships with local GPs and if one of the GP's patients comes along – usually after the GP has been for treatment! – you can send the patient back to their GP. I've got GPs as patients and I've got a consultant orthopaedic surgeon as a patient.' Comparing himself with one doctor he knows well, he said: 'I don't see as many patients as he does but I send more patients for X-rays, more patients for blood tests, than he does. So I hate to say it – it may sound as though I'm blowing my own trumpet – but I think you'll find the average qualified practitioner is more diligent than even the average consultant.'

And one medically qualified acupuncturist, who believes that all alternative therapists should train first as doctors, admitted: 'I've seen some really awful things that pass for medicine . . . and I feel very concerned about what's happening to the average patient going to the average GP. They're getting a bloody awful deal. There are some rubbish doctors around. I suppose we should really put our own house in order, first.' It seems that neither side has the monopoly of good practice. But if you stick to those whom you *know* have had the proper training, you're less likely to go wrong.

2. Eating for Health

You'll be reading a lot about diet in this book – about how, by changing our eating habits, we may become more healthy. But you'll also be hearing about the views of those experts who believe that even the best, most balanced, diet isn't adequate – that we need, in addition, supplements of vitamins and minerals, and that those of us who are ill may often require them in quite large doses. And I'll be explaining how many other specialists, both orthodox and alternative, disagree, claiming that supplements are not only unnecessary but could, in some cases, be risky.

In this chapter I'm going to look at healthy eating and supplements in a little more detail. As you'll see, the question of what constitutes a healthy diet is not nearly as simple as we're often led to believe. There are no easy answers. We need, therefore, to understand why the experts are divided, to know something about the evidence on which they base their opinions. Then we can form our own judgements about the kind of diet that is 'right' for us and whether we need supplements as well, and at what dose.

This is especially important if we take our advice from popular health magazines or books. They all have their own axes to grind and so will tend to dismiss views that don't fit in with their own. The same, unfortunately, goes for many nutrition specialists. The first task of any practitioner is to inspire confidence and so he's unlikely to admit that his advice may be wrong or, at best, based on inconclusive evidence! So you won't find all that much advice in this chapter. Instead I'll be explaining some of the thinking behind some of the more common dietary recommendations and the growing interest in vitamin and mineral supplements. What you make of it is entirely up to you.

WHAT'S WRONG WITH OUR MODERN DIET?

Perhaps a better question would be: 'What's right with it?' Although, in recent years, there have been some encouraging trends – with more of us switching to wholemeal, rather than white, bread, for example – the standard Western diet is not a healthy one. There's no controversy about this. Nearly all authorities are convinced that we're slowly eating our way to ill-health and early death.

But, surely, you'll say, we're living longer than ever before? In one respect, that's true: the *average* life expectancy has increased remarkably since the beginning of the twentieth century. But this is due almost entirely to the marked reduction in infant mortality which, until very recently, owed little to medical technology.

'Doctors are proud that the average life expectancy of a baby born in the UK today is seventy-three years, whereas in 1900, it was only fifty years,' writes Dr Michael Colgan in *Your Personal Vitamin Profile*:[1]

So we now enjoy an additional twenty-three years. What is seldom revealed, however, is that almost all this increase took place before 1950. By then the average life expectancy had already risen by eighteen years to sixty-eight years. This huge improvement occurred without the benefit of mass immunization, antibiotics or the supertechnology of modern hospitals.

Most of the increase in life expectancy came from reducing infant mortality, not from reducing disease in adults. Every baby who dies at birth drastically reduces average life expectancy. For example, if we take one hundred people who live to the age of eighty, then their average life is eighty years. If we take one hundred babies who die at birth (age zero), then their average life is zero years. Taking the two hundred together the total years lived by the combined group is: 100 (babies) × 0 (years old) + 100 (adults) × 80 (years old) = 8000 years. To get the average length of life, we divide the total years lived by the number of persons. That is 8000/200, which equals *40 years*. The babies who died at birth have halved the life expectancy. So, calculating life expectancy from birth on can be deceiving.

In 1900 many babies died in infancy, so the average life expectancy looked very low. Once past childhood, however, people lived nearly as long as they do now. If we ask what our life expectancy as adults is in comparison to our forebears, most of the apparent gains disappear. In 1920, a fifteen-year-old male had a remaining life expectancy of fifty-five years. His father, at the age of forty-five in 1920, had a remaining life expectancy of twenty-seven years, almost the same as the forty-five-year-old today. For an adult aged sixty-five, life expectancy has increased by only four years . . .

And, as Dr Colgan points out, though most of us do reach old age it's at high price.

. . . most hospitalization is now for the chronic degenerate [sic] diseases, against which medical treatment is ineffective. Cardiovascular disease, cancer and mental degeneration now claim more hospital beds than all other illnesses combined. Despite their fine and dedicated service to many individuals, the vastly expensive development of hospitals in recent years is inappropriate and ineffective against the new pestilence.

There are other signs of slippage in the state of Western health . . . In America eight people in every ten over the age of sixty-five have at least one chronic condition. The major degenerative diseases are more than holding their own against medicine . . .

An obvious explanation for this apparent epidemic of degenerative diseases is that, as a greater proportion of us survive to adulthood, then it's inevitable that more bodies should break down. But there's more to it than that. 'In England,' Colgan tells us, 'you are nine times more likely to have heart disease than a Japanese person, and no one would charge that UK medicine is only one-ninth as effective as Japanese medicine. Our environment and nutrition are the culprits, because Japanese people who move to England or the United States quickly change to develop heart disease as frequently as the indigenous population.'

Colgan is 'into' supplementation and we'll be looking at the pros and cons of that a bit later. That apart, though, his concern about the Western diet is being echoed – albeit in less emotive words – by authorities everywhere. And some of the loudest voices are coming from the medical establishment.

Take this 1985 report in the prestigious *New England Journal of Medicine*:

> Physicians and nutritionists are increasingly convinced that dietary habits adopted over the past 100 years make an important etiologic [causal] contribution to coronary heart disease, hypertension [high blood pressure], diabetes and some types of cancer. These conditions have emerged as dominant health problems only in the past century . . . The longer [though not so much longer!] life expectancy of people in industrialized countries is not the only reason that chronic illnesses have assumed new importance. Young people in the Western world commonly have developing asymptomatic forms of these conditions . . . the members of technologically primitive cultures who survive to the age of 60 years or more remain relatively free from these disorders, unlike their 'civilized' counterparts.

Lessons from the stone age

The diet of stone age man, and of certain primitive tribes today, is very different from our own. The authors of the *New England Journal of Medicine* article quoted above have made a detailed analysis, using fossil records, of the prehistoric diet and have compared it with that of present-day cultures whose way of life hasn't yet been influenced by Western ways. Their findings are startling: '. . . the range and content of foods [these tribes] consume are similar (in the sense that they represent wild game and uncultivated vegetable foods) to those that our ancestors ate for up to 4 million years.'

As we've seen, in general, members of primitive societies – even if they live to a ripe old age – do not suffer from the chronic degenerative conditions that begin to afflict us while we're still in our teens and which have disabled many of us by the time we're middle-aged. The authors of this article – and many other authorities – believe that the reason for this is that evolution hasn't yet had time to catch up with modern industrialized eating habits. 'The human genetic constitution has changed relatively little since the appearance of truly modern human beings . . . about 40,000 years ago. Even the development of agriculture 10,000 years ago has apparently had a minimal effect on our genes . . . Such developments as the Industrial Revolution, [modern farming methods], and modern food-processing techniques have occurred too recently to have had evolutionary effect at all.'

The stone age diet, they argue, is therefore the one that we humans were genetically programmed to eat, digest and metabolize. The modern diseases of affluence are simply the result of overburdening our systems with food with which they were never designed to cope. Common food allergies – to the dairy produce and wheat which never crossed our ancestors' lips – can be explained along the same lines.

Lessons from Japan

I've already mentioned that the Japanese are much less prone to heart disease than we in the West but that when they emigrate and adopt the Western lifestyle, they lose this protection. Although the Japanese way of life differs from ours in many ways, most observers believe that it's the dietary changes that are most important.

Indeed, we now have evidence for this from Japan itself. The Japanese diet has altered radically since 1950. According to a 1985 report in the *Lancet*, the Japanese now eat three times more fat, more 'fast' foods such as hamburgers and less of the traditional, highly varied diet of rice, fish and vegetables. And chronic degenerative diseases now account for nearly two-thirds of all deaths, compared with just over a quarter in 1950. Some of this increase is more apparent than real because fewer Japanese are now dying from diseases such as tuberculosis, pneumonia and bronchitis. Nevertheless, there's no doubt that the Western 'killer' diseases are taking a genuinely higher toll: during the same period, mortality from heart disease has *doubled*, deaths from diabetes have *tripled* and cancer is now the main cause of death.

OFFICIAL DIETARY RECOMMENDATIONS: HOW GOOD IS THE ADVICE?

A number of recent reports – from committees set up to advise the UK and US governments – have recommended changes in major aspects of our diet. These recommendations can be stated very simply: we should eat less fat, less sugar, less salt and more fibre. In many respects – though with some important differences which I'll discuss later – this 'new' diet is very similar to that of our stone age forebears.

Elsewhere in the book (Chapter 11) I'll be looking at the link between diet and cancer. Here I want to concentrate on some of the other 'diseases of civilization'.

Fat and heart disease

Studies of population have revealed a strong link between the amount of fat we eat and our risk of heart disease. At first sight the culprit appears to be *cholesterol*: the higher the level of cholesterol in the blood, the greater the chances of a heart attack. There's also evidence that if we cut our total fat intake while increasing the *proportion* of *polyunsaturated* fats in our diet the amount of cholesterol in our blood will fall.

This, of course, has led to the popular notion that we should avoid foods rich in cholesterol, such as eggs. In fact, there's little evidence that this would do much good. Most of the cholesterol in our blood doesn't come from the cho-

lesterol we eat but is made in our bodies from other substances in our diet, including protein, sugar and fats. In fact,
the stone age diet contains almost as much cholesterol as the
modern, much-criticized one! It does, however, have only
half as much fat. And, although stone age man ate quite a bit
of meat, that meat – from game – contained a much bigger
proportion of polyunsaturated' fats than that from our
modern farm-reared animals.

But even a low blood cholesterol may not be all it's cracked
up to be. Though high blood cholesterol increases the risk of
heart disease, it doesn't necessarily follow, unfortunately,
that by lowering the level, the risks are reduced. Many trials
have put the theory to the test but, as several recent articles in
the medical journals have pointed out, no conclusive answers
have been obtained. 'Most of the . . . cases of CHD [coro-
nary heart disease] in the population arise from the large
number of people whose cholesterol values are around the
average,' a 1984 editorial in the *Lancet* points out, 'not from
the few in whom the concentration is conspicuously high.
Unfortunately it is only among the latter that direct evidence
of the benefit of reduction can be obtained [because they're
the only ones who can be identified as being at risk].'

The *Lancet* also discusses the result of a trial where some of
these high-risk people had their blood cholesterol lowered
with a drug – not by diet. The results were fairly encouraging
and the editorial concludes: 'the benefits that emerged for
those at highest risk gave further support to the case for cholesterol reduction in the population as a whole'.

Not all the experts agree, however. Subsequent articles in
the *Lancet* and other medical journals have pointed out that
it's one thing to use a drug to lower very high cholesterol
levels, quite another to try to alter much lower levels through
dietary changes, especially as most people who die from
CHD do *not* have elevated blood cholesterol concentrations.

The most that can be said is that by eating less fat and by
increasing the proportion of polyunsaturated fats in your diet
you *may* lower your risks of heart disease. On the other hand,
you may not.

EPA, FISH OIL, ESKIMOS AND HEART DISEASE

There was something else different about the fats in the stone age diet. The game the hunter-gatherers caught contained appreciable amounts of a polyunsaturated fatty acid known as eicosapentaenoic acid (EPA) which is almost completely absent from modern beef, for instance.

Eskimos eating a traditional fish diet are seldom bothered by heart disease. Yet their diet is very high in fat. Studies have indicated that one of the key ingredients is EPA, which today is found in abundance only in fish and in the meat from cold-water mammals such as seals. Further research has shown that EPA is capable not only of reducing blood cholesterol levels but may also protect against high blood pressure, damage to blood vessel walls and blood clots, all of which increase the risks of heart disease. It could be that the benefits of polyunsaturates are due primarily to the EPA. We can make our own EPA from some of the other polyunsaturates, which are found in plants – and those of us who are vegetarian do seem to be less at risk of heart disease. But a fish diet provides much more EPA than even vegetarians can produce on their own. And, according to a study reported in the *New England Journal of Medicine* in (1985, as little as half a pound of fish a week can *halve* our chances of dying from a heart attack! Interestingly, the study also found that the consumption of fish had no obvious effects on blood cholesterol levels. Other studies have also suggested that the beneficial effects of a small amount of fish have nothing to do with blood cholesterol.

FAT: CAN WE DRAW ANY CONCLUSIONS?

Many observers question that dietary fat has anything to do with heart disease. They point to other evidence which seems to refute the theory. For instance, Dr Barbara Pickard, from the Department of Animal Physiology and Nutrition at Leeds University, wrote in a letter to the *Sunday Times*:

The United States might have seen a fall in heart disease incidence, but they still eat far more meat than we do. France has the highest consumption of animal fat in the EEC, and yet has one of the lowest incidences of heart disease.

Because of these and many other anomalies, many eminent researchers have strongly condemned the view that animal fat causes heart disease.

While there is every reason to advise individuals to eat unrefined cereals, fresh fruit and vegetables, there is no evidence that they should forgo whole milk and butter, meat and eggs to achieve a healthy diet.

Surely we should be pointing the finger of blame for the nation's ill-health on a sedentary existence and on highly-refined, over-processed, additive-laden foods, rather than on simple, traditional wholesome foods.

Similar doubts are being voiced in the US, where the death rate from heart disease, though still high, has fallen by over 30 per cent since the late 1960s. 'Apparently, we have been doing all the "right things" during the past 20 to 25 years,' suggests an 1985 editorial in the *New England Journal*. '. . . But exactly what have we done?' The answer, it concludes, is that we just don't know. Fat consumption is down, as are average blood cholesterol levels. But so is cigarette smoking – another important contributor to heart attacks. At the same time, Americans are taking more exercise and evidence suggests that this, too, helps safeguard our hearts.

Salt and heart disease

High blood pressure increases the risks of heart disease and animal experiments and studies of human populations have suggested that the amount of salt in the diet is directly linked with the incidence of high blood pressure. Does this mean, though, that by cutting our salt intake we, as individuals, can keep our blood pressure at a healthy, low level?

Unfortunately, it doesn't. The salt–blood pressure story remains unproven. In fact, a study of twelve patients with mildly raised blood pressure, reported in the *Lancet* in 1984, found that reducing dietary salt had unpredictable effects: in five patients it *increased* blood pressure! There's other evidence to suggest we may be barking up the wrong tree. Some studies have shown that vegetarians have a lower blood pressure than people who eat meat. 'The effect,' according to the *Lancet*, 'is small but seems to be associated with a diet that is by no means strict since it includes moderate use of eggs and dairy products . . . The reason for the blood-pressure fall is obscure: it was not related to changes in sodium [salt] . . . intake.'

Yet several official reports have proposed that we could all benefit from reducing the amount of salt in the diet. The much-publicized 1983 report from the National Advisory Committee on Nutrition Education (NACNE) was one of them. Yet NACNE actually admitted that many studies had failed to show a link between salt and high blood pressure. Maybe, the report suggested, this was because only *some* people were susceptible to salt in this way. However, the committee felt there was still enough evidence to support the suggestion that we could *all* do with less of it. Other experts, though, are concerned that such blanket recommendations may do more harm than good because of the risk that a lower salt intake may *increase* blood pressure in a sizeable minority of people (see above).

Incidentally, to confuse the picture even further, the stone age diet contained even less salt than the 'anti-salt' lobby now believes we should be eating! On the other hand, it contained far more calcium – and recent evidence suggests that it may be that it is a high intake of calcium, rather than a low intake of salt (sodium), which protects against heart disease. As the *Lancet* stated in 1984: 'We are certainly a long way from being able to give dietary advice.' We're still getting it, though!

Sugar

The dangers of sugar are much more clear-cut: I've yet to see a report which suggests that we shouldn't eat less of it. Apart from rotting our teeth, a high-sugar diet contributes to overweight, and may increase the risk of heart disease, diabetes, and certain forms of cancer (see Chapter 11). We eat far more of the stuff than our prehistoric ancestors: they didn't have refined sugar and though some of them definitely ate honey, fossil records indicate that they didn't go for it in a big way – at any event, not enough to rot their teeth.

The sugar picture is far from complete – the evidence that it contributes to degenerative diseases is merely circumstantial. On the other hand, there appear to be no dangers from switching to a low-sugar diet. Sugar is useful as a quick energy source – nothing else. And we can get all the energy we need from other foods in our diet which, in addition, provide vitamins and minerals. Instead of filling ourselves up with sugar, we should eat a diet high in unrefined carbohydrates – from cereals, fruit and vegetables.

Fibre

Unrefined carbohydrates have another merit – they're high in fibre. Stone age man ate nearly 46 grams of fibre each day, compared with the 20 grams in the standard British diet. A high-fibre diet seems to protect against all sorts of diseases including heart disease, some forms of cancer and diabetes. Interestingly, some studies suggest that the risk of heart disease depends more on fibre intake than on dietary fat.

The temptation, of course, is simply to sprinkle bran – a very concentrated form of fibre – on your food. That's not a good idea, though. If you increase your fibre intake that way you risk depriving yourself of vitamins and minerals. Instead you should up the quantity of unrefined carbohydrate which will supply both the fibre and essential nutrients; for example, eat wholemeal bread and pasta rather than those made from refined flour, have muesli instead of cornflakes for breakfast and replace white rice with brown.

Vitamins and minerals

Any discussion of vitamins and minerals lands us right in the middle of what is possibly nutrition's most controversial area. The official view is that we need only enough of these to protect us against certain well-known deficiency diseases such as scurvy (due to a deficiency of vitamin C or ascorbic acid), pellagra (due to vitamin B_3 deficiency) and beriberi (a vitamin B_1 deficiency). The amounts needed are quite small and the orthodox line is that we can obtain these recommended daily allowances (RDAs) in sufficient quantity from the foods we eat.

The alternative view is that not only doesn't our food provide the RDAs but that the RDAs themselves are inadequate: that they're based on several faulty assumptions. Let's take a closer look at these claims.

CLAIM 1: OUR FOOD DOESN'T SUPPLY EVEN RDA LEVELS OF VITAMINS AND MINERALS

The modern diet, as we've seen, differs considerably from that eaten by stone age man and from that eaten by certain primitive peoples alive today. Not only does it contain different amounts of polyunsaturated fats, and refined carbohydrates, but it may well contain fewer vitamins and minerals as well. Several vitamins, notably vitamin C and some of the B vitamins, are very fragile – they're destroyed by storage, freezing, cooking and food-refining processes. Even the relatively stable *fat-soluble* vitamins such as A and E are somewhat vulnerable to food-processing techniques. Minerals may also be depleted by food-processing. And there's a further complication: the mineral content of the foods we eat depends on the minerals in the soil that food comes from – whether we're eating vegetables which grow directly in the soil or the products from animals fed on the local vegetation. And our ability to *use* those minerals depends to some extent on the vitamins in our diet. So a vitamin deficiency could lead to a mineral one as well.

Of course, the fresher our food – and the less we mess about with it before we eat it – the more minerals and vitamins we get and our bodies absorb. But how fresh is fresh? How many of us eat produce straight from our own gardens or from the local nursery? 'Fresh' food from the supermarket may have been in cold storage for weeks before it's put on the shelves. According to Dr Michael Colgan, a lettuce kept in the fridge loses half its vitamin C in three days; asparagus, broccoli and green beans have lost half theirs by the time they get to the greengrocer. Yet RDA levels are based on the *theoretical* vitamin and mineral contents of fresh foods; they make no allowances for losses due to storage, food-processing or cooking. So even if we eat a wholefood diet – irrespective of its other, obvious merits – unless we get our produce straight from the farm or the market garden and eat it raw, we can't be sure that we're getting our RDAs. Add to that the fact that many of us eat – at least some of the time – 'fast', processed foods and you can see there may be a genuine cause for concern.

Indeed, several US nutrition surveys have revealed that vitamin and mineral deficiencies are widespread. 'The most recent nationwide food consumption surveys of 1977-78,' explains Dr Jeffrey Bland in *Your Personal Health Programme*,[2] 'involving a three-day dietary analysis for 37,785 individuals, show that large percentages of Americans are consuming significantly less than the recommended levels of at least six nutrients, including vitamins A, C, B_6, calcium, iron and magnesium. Intakes of vitamins D and E, folic acid, zinc and iodine were not measured in the study, but judging from the known deficiencies, several of these are also likely to be problem nutrients.'

In the UK, too, there's evidence of deficiencies – at least of some vitamins and minerals (the UK guidelines for RDAs are less comprehensive than those in the US). The NACNE report points out that iron deficiency is still a 'relatively common problem' and adds: 'The principle dietary change which could lead to an improved iron status is the more widespread consumption of fruits and vegetables since vitamin C is proving to be one of the chief promoters of iron absorption . . .' The report goes on to discuss the fact that though most of us *appear* to be getting at least the RDA amount of vitamin C, in practice this may not be the case. 'Although the average amount of vitamin C purchased per capita is considerably in excess of 30 mg [the UK RDA], there are not only losses in cooking but a variability in intake such that perhaps 10% of households have been estimated to consume less than 30 mg vitamin C per head.'

That estimate, too, may be on the conservative side: the vitamin content of 'fresh' foods such as oranges and of commercially prepared 'pure' fruit juices can vary enormously so there's no way of knowing how much of this vitamin you're actually getting.

Even authorities who are, in principle, against wholesale vitamin supplementation, agree that most of us *might* benefit from taking a modest, RDA-level, daily supplement. (Incidentally, there's no convincing evidence that synthetic vitamins are in any way inferior to those prepared from natural products.) For example, Arnold Bender, formerly Professor of Nutrition and Dietetics at London University and the author of a book which sets out to debunk the supplementation movement, writes: 'Using tablets [supplements] as a form of insurance is still fairly uncertain.' But he adds: 'Small amounts will not do any harm and they might possibly do some good.' He also recommends supplements for those largely living off 'junk' foods and for people recovering from an illness.[3]

CLAIM 2: RDA LEVELS, EVEN IF THEY ARE PRESENT IN OUR DIET, ARE NOT ENOUGH TO MEET OUR NEEDS

RDA levels are defined as follows: they are 'the amounts sufficient or more than sufficient for the nutritional needs of practically all healthy persons in a population'. But how healthy is 'healthy'? The evidence I discussed earlier suggests that many of us, though apparently fit, have already started on the downhill course towards furred-up arteries, cancer and several other degenerative diseases.

And what about the people the RDAs *don't* cover? 'Practically all' clearly doesn't include everyone. Moreover there's now evidence that, just as some people eat massive amounts of fattening substances and never get fat or smoke and never get lung cancer, so we have differing vitamin and mineral needs as well. The RDAs assume that, at most, some people need about twice the amount of those essential nutrients required by others. But a number of studies have shown that this assumption could be wide of the mark: for instance some 'normal' people appear to need five or even ten times the RDA![4] Once they get ill their requirement increases yet again. And the stone age diet contained thirteen times the UK RDA level of vitamin C![5]

You can't, of course, know what your requirements are, whether the RDAs are adequate for you or not. But, as I'll be discussing later in the book, there is some evidence that in some cases, ill-health may be due *entirely* to deficiencies of one or more vitamins and minerals.

Unfortunately much of this evidence is scientifically dubious because it generally comes, not from properly controlled trials on human beings but from one of the following: animal studies – and animals differ substantially from people; discoveries of nutrient deficiencies in people with certain conditions – which doesn't prove that the deficiency caused the disease, it could be the other way round; or from 'therapeutic' trials, where the suspected or known deficiency is corrected by supplementation – if the patient recovers then it's assumed that the deficiency was to blame for the disease. This doesn't necessarily follow, though, because the patient could be responding to lots of other things as well, including her practitioner's confidence in his therapy. Or she might have got better, anyway, without treatment.

In general, the results of properly controlled trials of vitamin supplementation have been rather inconclusive: although RDA levels do seem to help some people, there's as yet little good evidence – with a few exceptions, some of which I'll be discussing in subsequent chapters – that much larger doses have any additional benefits. 'Remember,' writes US biochemist Dr Charles W. Marshall in his book

Vitamins or Minerals: Help or Harm?,[6] 'that the number of medical conditions which large dosages might help is quite small and that all such conditions require medical supervision. Remember, too, that you are more likely to have troublesome side effects than to benefit from large amounts of self-prescribed supplements.'

Which brings us to the supplement-supporters' next claim.

CLAIM 3: SUPPLEMENTATION IS SAFE

Even the most fervent critics of supplementation concede that RDA doses are safe enough. The difficulty comes in estimating the risks of much higher ('mega') doses. Those who use them report few side effects. Nevertheless, scattered in the literature are the most appalling tales of what can happen to people who overdo their supplements. Marshall cites a number of them in his book.

For example, the US RDA for vitamin A for women is 2670 IU (International Units) a day. Yet some alternative practitioners recommend 25,000 or even 50,000 IU! If taken for short periods of time (a month at most) these appear to be safe – for *most* people. But if you continue taking them, you'll almost certainly run into problems. 'Chronic vitamin A poisoning is noted in the medical literature at doses of "only" 25,000 IU per day for several months,' Marshall points out. And other reports have suggested that much lower doses (only twice the RDA) may be toxic for a few people. Symptoms of vitamin A poisoning include blurred vision, blinding headaches, nausea and vomiting. Severe poisoning can result in liver failure and death.

Vitamin E may also cause trouble. The RDA is 15–30 IU per day and though doses of up to 1000 IU are sometimes used with no apparent ill effects, many investigators believe that anything above 200 IU a day is potentially hazardous and should only be taken under medical supervision. Overdose symptoms include muscle weakness and fatigue, and have been observed with doses of around 450 IU. And though vitamin E has been reported to make blood less prone to clotting – and therefore to protect the cardiovascular system – doses of 800 or more IU may have the opposite effect!

Vitamin D supplements are even more risky – excess can lead to a whole host of adverse reactions including irreversible damage to muscles and hardening of the arteries. Vitamin A and D supplements may be particularly dangerous if you're pregnant or trying to conceive. For more details, see Chapters 7 and 8.

Even good old vitamin C, megadoses of which are reputed to fight off colds, isn't as safe as is often made out. It can cause diarrhoea and, if you suddenly stop your supplements, you may develop what's known as 'rebound scurvy'. This comes about because your body adapts to the higher vitamin levels and after a time can't manage without them. Fortunately you can avoid this problem by tailing off your supplements gradually.

Vitamin B megadoses may also cause problems. Thiamine and riboflavin seem safe but very high doses of B_6 and B_3 have been associated with side effects (see Chapter 3 for further details on B_6). Folic acid, while not directly toxic, can mask the symptoms of pernicious anaemia. This is a very rare and serious condition which if not treated – with injections of vitamin B_{12} – leads to irreversible degeneration of the nervous system and, ultimately, death.

What about mineral supplements? The RDA for zinc, for example, is 15mg a day. Yet doses of 50mg are often recommended to correct zinc deficiency – often based solely on the results of hair analysis which, as I mentioned in Chapter 1, are often unreliable. At this level side effects are unlikely, fortunately, but doses any higher than this can lead to copper deficiency and anaemia.

It seems that megadoses of practically any supplement may be harmful for some people. This is the other side of the coin: if we all have different nutritional needs then our bodies will also vary in the amount of these nutrients they can tolerate. The only way to be sure that you have a real deficiency and one that's likely to respond to supplementation is to consult a doctor with experience of nutritional methods. He will have access to a number of tests – of which hair analysis is only *one* – which can be used to determine your needs more accurately. In addition, he'll be on the look-out for symptoms of toxicity and so can reduce or stop your supplements at the first hint of side effects. Never use megadoses without this sort of back-up.

The tables on pages 57–61 show some of the most important vitamins and minerals, their richest sources, the RDAs (I've used the US rather than the UK version as this is more complete) and the doses accepted as safe by the majority of alternative nutritional specialists for long-term use in *most* people. However, as you'll see, toxic effects have sometimes been observed at doses lower than this 'safe' maximum and taking a high-dose supplement over weeks or months may increase the risks. My own view is that you should only take large supplements on the advice of a medically qualified practitioner of nutritional medicine. If you're ill enough to need them, then you're ill enough to see a doctor.

Sources

Vitamins	
Water-soluble vitamins	Richest source (but note that some of these are much richer than others: consult a nutrition book for details)
C	rose-hip syrup, black-currants, broccoli, citrus fruits, cabbage, cauliflower.
B_1 (thiamine)	yeast, rice husks, wheatgerm, soya bean flour, liver, pork, poultry, eggs, milk, seafoods, rice, nuts, potatoes, beans, peas, corn.
B_2 (riboflavin)	yeast, wheatgerm, liver, meat, green vegtables, milk, yoghurt, cheese, green vegtables, pulses.
B_3 (niacin, nicotinic acid, nicotinamide)	yeast, liver, meat, chicken, fish, cheese, grains, eggs, pulses.
B_6 (pyridoxine, pyridoxal phosphate and pyridoxamine)	yeast, wheatgerm, oats, liver, fish, nuts, vegtables, fruit, eggs.
B_{12} (cobalamin)	foods of animal origin: liver, meat, fish, eggs, milk.

Biotin	yeast, liver, eggs, oats, wheatgerm, peas, soya beans, rice, milk, cheese, yoghurt.
Pantothenic acid	yeast, liver, nuts, wholewheat, meat, poultry, oats, pulses, brown rice.
Folic acid	yeast, soya flour, wholewheat, nuts, liver, green vegtables, pulses, citrus fruits, eggs, brown rice.

Fat-soluble vitamins

A	animal and fish products: liver, milk, butter, cheese, eggs. Added to margarine.
D	fish liver, fish, eggs – but most adults get most of their requirement from the action of sunlight on the skin.
E	wheatgerm, vegetable oils, cod liver oil, asparagus, spinach, soya beans.

Minerals

Calcium	milk, cheese, cereals, vegetables, pulses.

Copper	liver, oysters, crab, yeast, olives, hazelnuts, pulses.
Iron	veal, liver, blood, fish, soya beans, lettuce, corn, beans, spinach, dried fruit.
Magnesium	soya beans, nuts, yeast, wholewheat, brown rice, dried peas, seafoods, bananas, dried fruits, meat, vegetables.
Selenium	liver, seafoods, meat, cereals, dairy produce – but content in cereals, vegetables and dairy produce can vary, depending on the soil.
Zinc	oysters, liver, yeast, shrimps, crab, beef, cheese, sardines, wholemeal bread.

Doses

Vitamins	RDA	Maximum	Minimum
	for adult, non-non-pregnant non-lactating women[c] as noted.	'safe' dose for long-term use[b] – but larger doses may be used therapeutically (see text)	dose at which toxic symptoms have been reported
C	60 mg	6000 mg	1000–4000 mg[a]
B_1	1.0 mg	100 mg	10,000 mg[a]
B_2	1.2 mg	100 mg	–
B_3	13 mg	1000 mg	500 mg for nicotinic acid;[a] 1000 mg for nicotinamide[b]
B_6	2.0 mg	1000 mg	50 mg[a,d]
B_{12}	0.003 mg	1 mg	–
Biotin	(0.1–0.2 mg)	0.4 mg	–
Pantothenic acid	(4–7 mg)	1000 mg	–
Folic acid	0.4 mg	1.0 mg	–
A	2670 IU	10,000[b] 15,000IU[c]	5000[e] 25,000[a]
D	200IU	1000IU	? but anything over 1000IU considered excessive[b] – prolonged intake above 2000IU 'considerably risky'[a]
E	15–30IU[b]	1000IU	100–400IU[a]

Minerals	RDA	Maximum	Minimum
Calcium	800 mg	1200 mg	10,000 mg[a]
Copper	(–3 mg)	5.0 mg	? but 'excess' toxic[b]
Iron	18 mg	30 mg	30 mg[b]
Magnesium	300 mg	600 mg	600 mg may be toxic for people with poor kidney function[a]
Selenium	(0.05 mg–0.2 mg)	0.2 mg	2.5 mg[a]
Zinc	15 mg	30 mg	50 mg[a]

Values in parentheses indicate that no RDA has been established: these are rough estimates of 'safe and adequate' intakes.[c]

Sources:
a: *Vitamins and Minerals: Help or Harm?* by Charles W. Marshall, George F. Stickly Company, 1983.
b: *Your Personal Health Programme* by Jeffrey Bland, Thorsons, 1983.
c: *Medical Applications of Clinical Nutrition*, edited by Jeffrey Bland, Keats Publishing, 1983.
d: *Lancet 1*, 1985, 1168.
e: *The Dictionary of Vitamins* by Leonard Mervyn, Thorsons, 1984.

3. The Premenstrual Syndrome (PMS or PMT)

There are still doctors who believe that PMS isn't a medical problem. They say that, as nearly all women notice some physical and emotional changes in the days leading up to their periods, these are 'normal' and therefore don't require treatment. For many women this may be true: the changes are fairly mild, brief and pass almost without notice. But what of the rest? Is it normal to have tender breasts, to put on weight and to feel bloated? Is it normal to feel so uncontrollably angry, anxious or depressed that life becomes intolerable? Specialists disagree about how common these symptoms are but it seems that at least 10 per cent and possibly as many as 50 per cent of us experience them – sometimes for up to *two weeks* out of every four.

British specialist Dr Katharina Dalton was one of the first people to produce evidence that turned PMS from a vague 'women's ailment' into a recognized medical condition. She believes that women with PMS don't produce enough progesterone and it is this which is responsible for all those distressing symptoms. Dr Dalton recommends correcting this deficiency by giving extra progesterone, either by injection or in the form of suppositories inserted into the vagina or rectum. In her book *Once a Month*[1] she gives a number of dramatic examples of the success of her therapy.

Unfortunately, progesterone is *not* the answer to PMS. That's not to say that it doesn't work for some women: Dr Dalton's experience shows that it can be enormously helpful. But there are two problems: one is that most women with PMS produce as much progesterone as women who don't have any premenstrual symptoms – so how can they be progesterone-deficient? The other is that when the hormone has been tested under the rigorous conditions of a double-blind placebo-controlled trial, when neither the women nor their doctors knew whether they were getting the real treatment or one that simply looked like it, the placebo turned out to be just as good as the progesterone.[2]

A number of other studies have shown that a dummy treatment is often very successful in PMS. In one trial nearly 90 per cent of the women felt better.[3] This, of course, has raised the old bogey that PMS could be all in the mind. While there is some evidence for this – and I'll be looking at it later – most specialists believe that the picture is much more complicated and though psychological factors do play a part, it's probably only a minor one.

PMS and other hormones

With progesterone out of the way, researchers turned their attention to other hormones. Did some women, they wondered, produce too much oestrogen rather than too little progesterone? But this theory didn't last long, either. Most researchers haven't been able to find any obvious differences in oestrogen levels that holds good for all women with PMS.

Then, for a while, the hormone prolactin (high levels of which make some women infertile) caught everyone's imagination. One intrepid male scientist injected himself with prolactin – and promptly developed symptoms of premenstrual tension![4] But studies of women with PMS have shown that most of them don't have raised prolactin levels.

MEDICAL TREATMENT FOR PMS

Progesterone

This is still used, and as I've explained it does help some women. Possibly this is because they *do* happen to have a genuine progesterone deficiency. Or maybe it's because progesterone sometimes has a tranquillizing effect and so makes them less anxious and tense. But then again it may be that they feel better simply because they *expect* to.

Dr Dalton reports that the progesterone has negligible side effects and is perfectly safe. However, other doctors have found that patients on progesterone therapy may become tired and depressed. Some women even find that pro-gesterone makes their premenstrual symptoms worse. It may also upset their normal menstrual pattern.

Artificial progesterones and the Pill

Dr Dalton claims that only natural progesterone is effective in PMS. Other investigators disagree and say that artificial progesterones – progestogens – do the job just as well.

Similarly with the Pill. Some researchers say it helps PMS, others that it makes it worse. Some have found that it's the oestrogen in the combined Pill that disagrees with women, but others have discovered that the progestogen-only Pill (the 'mini' Pill) is just as bad.

Diuretics and low-salt diets

Diuretics make you produce more urine and so rid your body of excess fluid. And they do seem to help women whose main problem is feeling bloated or putting on weight. However they don't appear to have much effect on mood changes. The other drawback to diuretics is that they may make the body lose minerals such as potassium and magnesium and this can make PMS symptoms worse! Doctors are usually on the look-out for potassium deficiency and may well prescribe potassium supplements to correct it. Most of them are un-likely to think about magnesium deficiency, though, and, as I'll explain, this seems to be one of the main causes of PMS.

Some medical specialists – and some alternative prac-titioners, too – recommend a low-salt diet as a way of pre-venting water retention. And this does help some women. But for others it does nothing at all. A low-salt diet also takes quite a bit of getting used to – and it doesn't cure PMS; it stops some of the symptoms but only while you stick to it.

Bromocriptine

This drug reduces prolactin levels. So it might work for those few women who have increased amounts of this hormone. It's also a useful treatment for the painful breasts that are a common symptom of PMS. But bromocriptine appears to have no effect on general fluid retention problems, nor on any of the other symptoms. Bromocriptine may also cause side effects, including nausea and fainting.

Danazol

Danazol gets rid of PMS symptoms in up to 80 per cent of women – at least according to a few recent reports. However this is an extremely potent drug and affects both your ovaries and the parts of your brain that regulate ovulation. Not surprisingly, one of the most common side effects is that you stop menstruating. This plus the other problems, mentioned in Chapter 12, make it very much a last-ditch treatment for women whose PMS won't respond to anything else.

Drugs which reduce prostaglandin levels

Prostaglandins (PGs) are natural, hormone-like chemicals. They appear to be one of the main causes of period pains (see Chapter 4). And many researchers now believe that excess amounts of prostaglandins could explain some PMS symptoms, too. Drugs such as mefenamic acid (Ponstan) reduce prostaglandin levels and do seem to be an effective treatment for some PMS symptoms such as tension, depression and headaches. But if breast pain and/or fluid retention is your main problem, anti-prostaglandins probably won't help you. The other drawback to this type of drug is that, if you take it more than a couple of days before your period is due, the period may come later than you expected.

Some researchers also think that anti-prostaglandins may actually sometimes make PMS worse. This is because there are two types of prostaglandins: the 'bad' ones that may cause PMS and the 'good' ones which, research suggests, may help to *prevent* it. The drugs, however, can't tell the difference. So if you're not producing adequate amounts of the 'good' prostaglandins to start with, drugs may make things worse.

Can you take these drugs if you're trying to conceive?

The anti-prostaglandins are probably safe enough – mainly because you'll only need to take them for a few days a month and then only around period times when you can't conceive anyway. But, as they haven't been *proven* safe in pregnancy, some authorities think that, if you're sexually active, you should only take them once your menstrual flow has started – as it's only then that you can be more or less certain that you haven't conceived. Which, of course, defeats the whole object of using them to treat *pre*menstrual symptoms.

It is all right to take bromocriptine when you're attempting a pregnancy – after all, it's also used to treat women with some types of infertility. But, if you are planning to conceive, tell your doctor first so that you can be given the appropriate dosage and have your hormone levels monitored.

Dr Dalton is reassuring about progesterone, pointing out that during pregnancy the body produces much more of this hormone than is used for PMS treatment. However other specialists believe it's unwise to take any extra female hormone if you're planning to conceive. This applies particularly to the artificial progesterones (progestogens). We don't know that they do any harm to the foetus, but these days most doctors err on the side of caution. Women on the Pill, for example, are usually advised to stop taking it at least three months before they start trying to conceive and the same goes for those taking progesterones for premenstrual problems.

You should never take danazol if there's the remotest chance that you might be, or become, pregnant while taking it.

HOW MUCH OF PMS IS IN OUR MINDS?

No, I'm not suggesting that women with PMS are merely suffering from an overactive imagination. Their symptoms are obviously genuine. But we can't ignore the evidence that psychology may have something to do with their symptoms. Throughout this book I'll keep returning to the fact that our emotions can, and do, have effects on our body. When we're under stress all sorts of changes go on: extra hormones flood into our bloodstream and there are changes, too, in the chemicals in our brains which affect our mood. Then there's the evidence which suggests that certain types of people are more prone to certain conditions such as cancer or migraine (see Chapters 11 and 13) – and one explanation is that their different personalities are linked with subtle differences in body and brain chemistry.

Many women with PMS find their emotional symptoms – the irritability, the anger and the depression – the hardest to handle. Hormones are obviously only a small part of the explanation because one woman who has severe PMS may have an identical hormone pattern to another who has mild symptoms or none at all. Nevertheless, our hormone levels do change premenstrually – in *all* women progesterone levels drop just before menstruation. Could it be that women with PMS are psychologically more vulnerable to this *relative* progesterone deficiency? There is some evidence for this theory, though the experts are still arguing about how important it is.

1. Women who get psychological symptoms premenstrually tend to have them at other times of the month, too, though in a less severe form.
2. Women who think they're premenstrual – even when they're not – complain of more symptoms than when they believe they're in some other phase of their cycle.
3. Women with PMS tend to lack self-esteem when compared with women who don't have any problems premenstrually.
4. Neurotic women suffer more PMS symptoms.

But which comes first? Is a certain type of woman more prone to PMS or is it the other way round: that if a woman does have PMS she's more likely to feel low, neurotic and unsure of herself than if she sails through each month with few problems? Not surprisingly such questions remain controversial.

Still, there's also some evidence that PMS symptoms can be improved if a woman is taught to relax and to adopt a calmer attitude to her condition. Interestingly, though, some studies have shown that such formal 'desensitization' – as the psychologists call it – may be unnecessary and that a simple chat with someone who understands can work just as well!

Which brings us back to the placebo effect. Can PMS really be a physical problem when it responds so well to therapy aimed at the mind?

Endorphins and PMS

Endorphins are the body's natural painkillers. And a few researchers are now investigating the possibility that changes in endorphin levels may be to blame for many PMS symptoms. They could be onto something. For example, there's evidence from work with female monkeys (which have a menstrual cycle similar to ours) that the level of endorphins increases during the second half of the cycle and then falls steeply just before menstruation. The increase, the researchers believe, could explain why some women tend to get tired and depressed: the subsequent fall would have the opposite effect and give rise to anxiety and irritability.[5]

The theory has, in fact, been put to the test. A drug is available which stops endorphins working. When this is injected into normal people they start feeling 'premenstrual'.[6] These results help explain why almost any treatment will work for many women with PMS. If they believe in it they'll be comforted and reassured: they'll produce more endorphins and so feel better! Some authorities are so impressed by these findings that they believe we need to look no further. 'The conclusion would seem to be that if a treatment relieves symptoms and produces no damaging side effects then that treatment is worth using even if the explanation for its efficiency is not yet known,' suggests Dr Mary Jones in the *British Journal of Sexual Medicine*.

IS PMS A NUTRITIONAL DISEASE?

But maybe we can do better than that. There is now a treatment which is safe, which works – and which is producing even better results than one probably would expect if it were yet another placebo. Even more important, it appears to have a sound scientific basis.

There's now fairly good evidence that it's the foods we eat – or don't eat – that are the real villains of the piece. Not only does this help to explain the symptoms of PMS, but it also goes some way to explaining why some – but not all – PMS sufferers have abnormal hormone levels. And why, too, some women should be particularly sensitive to changes in endorphins. For the first time there's a theory which ties everything together. The other exciting thing about the research on diet is that it has broken down the barriers between orthodox and alternative medicine. Many orthodox researchers, realizing that most of their 'medical' theories seem to have led up a blind alley and that drugs only alleviate PMS in some women, are turning enthusiastically to the nutritional approach.

The evidence

A long time ago now, one of the first researchers to examine PMS seriously noted that the condition appeared to be more common in women who were on a poor diet. Since then a number of other people have noticed the same thing. Women who eat wholefoods, especially if they're also vegetarian, tend to suffer less from PMS than those who eat junk food and/or large quantities of meat.

THE DIFFERENT SORTS OF PMS

One of the problems with PMS research has been the puzzling differences between individual women: symptoms differ and so do hormone levels and so, not surprisingly, do the results of treatment. Now, though, this mystery seems solved: PMS is, in fact, not a single syndrome but a group of them. This discovery was made about fifteen years ago by American gynaecologist Dr Guy Abraham, the leading exponent of the dietary approach. He classifies PMS into four main groups: PMT-A, PMT-H, PMT-C and PMT-D. Women with PMT-A do seem to have abnormal hormone levels, with high oestrogen and low progesterone. And they're the ones that complain most of anxiety, irritability and nervous tension. PMT-H women have water retention problems, get bloating and breast pain. The PMT-C people binge on sweets just before their periods and then feel weak and headachy. Women with PMT-D are in the minority but perhaps the worst off. They get very depressed – sometimes even suicidal – forgetful and confused. Like PMT-A sufferers they too tend to have abnormal hormone levels but in their case it's usually the progesterone that's too high and the oestrogen too low.[7] In practice, many women don't fit exactly into any one of these groups: they have some symptoms right across the board. But, for most, their *main* symptoms fall into one or two of the four groups.

Dr Abraham has found that all women with PMS suffer from a common dietary problem: they aren't getting enough vitamin B_6 or magnesium. In addition, he's discovered, women with PMT-A tend to eat large amounts of dairy produce, those with PMT-H too much refined sugar, and PMT-Cs too much animal fat. PMT-Ds seem especially vulnerable to the effects of environmental lead.

How does all this tie in with PMS? The explanations hinge on our understanding of a whole host of complicated biochemical processes which suggests that vitamin B and magnesium deficiencies can upset female hormone levels and also interfere with the mood-altering chemicals in our brain.

Diets high in dairy produce contain excessive amounts of calcium and this tends to make any magnesium deficiency worse. A magnesium deficiency will also allow more lead to get into our bodies. The high animal fat diet of the PMT-Cs means that they'll produce too much of the 'bad' prostaglandins – the sort that give rise to premenstrual aches and pains – and not enough of the 'good' PGs. These PGs actually reduce inflammation and guard against water retention but our bodies can only make enough of them if we include certain vegetable oils in our diet.

This is just the bare bones of the theory. But it explains why the search for hormonal difference has led to such puzzling results: some women *do* have altered hormone levels but these are just *one* result of a dietary deficiency. This isn't to say that altered levels don't cause problems: they do. But the dietary deficiency is more basic: it can cause symptoms even when the hormone levels are normal.

THE ROLE OF EVENING PRIMROSE OIL (EPO)

I've already mentioned how a diet high in animal fat seems to make some forms of PMS worse; this is because animal fats are the startling products for the 'bad' prostaglandins. Conversely, 'good' prostaglandins come from the kind of fats we find in vegetable oils. The 'bad' PGs – and some other equally nasty related products which our bodies also make from animal fats – are responsible for breast inflammation and water retention, and encourage the uptake of calcium (and so may exacerbate a magnesium deficiency). The 'good' PGs, on the other hand, have largely beneficial effects. They may even make our tissues less sensitive to prolactin which, as we've seen, may sometimes cause PMS symptoms such as painful breasts. There's also a suggestion that the 'good' PGs may offset some of the effects of the other hormones.[8]

Our bodies make the 'good' PGs largely from a substance known as cis-linoleic acid. This is found in reasonably large quantities in safflower, corn, sunflower seed and evening primrose oils. Hence the importance of including these in our diet. But it's not quite that simple. Cis-linoleic acid must first be converted into a compound known as gamma-linolenic acid (GLA) before it can be turned into prostaglandins. The trouble is that the enzyme responsible for this conversion is extremely sensitive. It needs adequate amounts of magnesium if it's to perform properly. And it positively dislikes stress, alcohol and animal fats!

So many researchers believe that our modern way of life with its stress, junk food, etc. won't agree with this enzyme at all. It just can't make enough GLA to produce normal amounts of those 'good' PGs. Other enzymes involved in the production of these PGs need adequate levels of zinc and the vitamins B_6 and C, so they, too, may be affected by a faulty diet. But the same conditions that stop our bodies making enough 'good' PGs may actually encourage the production of the 'bad' ones. Result: more PMS.

Until recently this was no more than an interesting theory. But now researchers have measured the levels of GLA in women with PMS (it's difficult to measure the PGs themselves) and they've discovered that they really do make less GLA than women who don't have PMS. They also make excess amounts of the chemicals that the body uses to produce the bad PGs. This doesn't prove the theory but it makes it much more convincing. It also helps explain why evening primrose oil seems to help so many PMS sufferers: unlike the other vegetable oils, it is rich in GLA.

THE PROOF OF THE PUDDING?

Dr Abraham has had tremendous success in treating PMS by switching the women onto diets that correct their various deficiencies. He advises them to eat wholefoods, cut down their consumption of refined sugar and salt, and to limit their intake of alcohol, coffee and tea (which may make breast problems worse – see Chapter 12). In addition they're told to go easy on meat, animal fat and dairy products, to eat lots of green vegetables and wholegrains, and to try to use more vegetable oils such as safflower. The result is to increase their magnesium and vitamin B_6 levels, to keep the bad PGs in their place and to encourage the production of the good ones. (This diet, incidentally, is the kind that nutritionists now believe we should *all* eat if we're to stay healthy.) He's discovered that the younger you are the more likely your PMS is to respond to diet alone. Women in their thirties may need extra vitamin and mineral supplements as well. Only 10 per cent of women still have PMS problems after following such a regime, he reports.

Other researchers, notably Dr David Horrobin, Director of the Efamol Research Institute (Efamol is one of the leading brands of evening primrose oil) say that up to 95 per cent of women with PMS improve if they take evening primrose oil as well.[9] This is because the oil gives that little extra boost that some of us may need even if we're on a good diet. EPO has also proved successful when other treatments have failed and seems particularly useful for women whose main complaint is painful breasts. However, it's no good taking EPO on its own without changing your diet. You still need that extra magnesium and B_6 plus zinc and vitamin C if it's to do its stuff. And if you're not prepared to change your eating habits, you'll certainly need supplements.

Despite these promising results, we can't say that the problem of PMS is solved. It looks as though the nutritional approach does work better than a placebo but there haven't yet been enough controlled trials to be certain about this. And there are some women – admittedly a very small minority – who don't benefit.

FOOD ALLERGIES AND CANDIDA: OTHER POSSIBLE CAUSES OF PMS?

Some nutritional specialists believe that PMS may be attributable to food allergies, a severe Candida (thrush) infection or, possibly, both (you can have Candida without realizing it – see Chapter 5). There's some evidence for this: a woman's PMS can clear up dramatically when she's given anti-Candida therapy (see page 122). PMS sufferers often have a history of allergies, and their doctors report that a diet that excludes wheat, say, or milk (two foods which commonly cause allergic reactions) can banish PMS in a matter of weeks.

CAN YOU TREAT YOURSELF?

I'd say no. You can certainly change your diet and there's any amount of information available on how to go about it. (For further information, see Useful Addresses.) But if this makes no difference – or if your symptoms get a bit better but don't clear up entirely – you need professional advice.

Though the two main PMS supplements – vitamin B_6 and magnesium – are available over the counter from most health food shops, different people need different amounts. If you take B_6 but don't take enough extra magnesium you could even find that your PMS gets worse! There's also a slight risk of a B_6 overdose. Dr Jeffrey Bland quotes a maximum safe doses of 1000 mg a day (see page 60) but British researchers tend to be far more conservative. Even so, they disagree amongst themselves about dosage: some believe that up to 200 mg a day is all right; others have reported side effects on doses as low as 50 mg a day.[10] Then, depending on your particular symptoms and lifestyle, you may need other vitamins and minerals as well, including zinc, chromium and vitamins C and E. Only a specialist is in a position to advise you about this. Ask your GP to refer you to one.

Alternatively, contact the Premenstrual Tension Advisory Service (see Useful Addresses). This is a postal service which has links with doctors who are members of the British Society for Nutritional Medicine. The PTAS will design a dietary programme geared to your particular symptoms and can also supply supplements containing the correct balance of minerals and vitamins that you may need for the first few months. The service can also refer you, if necessary, to a properly qualified medical specialist.

OTHER ALTERNATIVE APPROACHES TO PMS

All alternative practitioners agree that a wholefood diet is the key to beating PMS and that any other treatment takes second place. This is certainly the essence of the *naturopathic* approach – and some naturopaths prescribe mineral and vitamin supplements as well.

Of course any alternative treatment comes with a large helping of sympathy and reassurance – and this by itself may, as we've seen, work wonders. Specific therapies – such as *acupuncture* or *herbs* – may help to relieve some of the worst symptoms until the dietary changes begin to take effect. Herbs seem able to correct a disturbed hormone balance while acupuncture is known to bring about the release of endorphins. *Exercise*, too, affects our endorphin levels and most specialists, including those at the Premenstrual Tension Advisory Service, believe that regular exercise is a vital part of any PMS programme. *Osteopathic* treatment may help relieve bloating.

CONCLUSIONS

Although the alternative treatment of PMS is still in its infancy, as far as scientific research is concerned, preliminary results are very encouraging and suggest that the syndrome can be cured or at least made more bearable in the vast majority of cases. And once you change to a healthier diet and start taking more exercise, you'll become fitter the rest of the month too.

As one former PMS victim reports: 'I had bad periods and PMT, dry skin and hair; I was edgy, smoked and generally up and down . . . over the years I had seen gynaecologists who never found anything wrong . . . I had periodic doses of antidepressants, tranquillizers and sleeping tablets.' Now after several years of psychotherapy and changing to a wholefood diet with extra vitamins and minerals, she says her PMS has 'almost vanished . . . and my skin and general physical appearance have improved enormously . . . I am extremely healthy generally.'

4. Menstruation and Problem Periods

WHAT'S NORMAL?

When you stop to think about it, what could be more *abnormal* than a regular monthly bleed? It serves no useful purpose, other than to tell us we're not pregnant (and even then it's not foolproof – pregnant women can, and do, occasionally menstruate). It's not even a totally reliable indicator of fertility: a woman who's not ovulating may still have regular periods and conversely you can conceive (though it's unlikely) without having periods. And menstruation certainly isn't necessary for good health: you can go for months – even years – without it, and be perfectly fit.

Yet most of us take our periods for granted. We put up with them month after month, year in, year out, without complaint. We accept the inconvenience – and the occasional embarrassment when our period catches us unawares – and the hassle (and expense) of sanitary protection. And all because we've come to regard menstruation as a normal part of life. But is it really?

Drs Anne Anderson and Ann McPherson write:

> In primitive communities menstruation was probably a very infrequent event since a late menarche, lactational amenorrhoea (absence of periods due to breastfeeding), and poor nutrition, as well as pregnancies, left the woman little time for menstrual cycles. Today's woman is faced with a much earlier menarche – around the age of 12 years – probably brought about by improved nutrition in childhood – but now occurring several years before she will be ready in most instances to contemplate a pregnancy. Furthermore, the menopause may not come for 40 years beyond the menarche, and women in this time will on average have only two full-term pregnancies and perhaps breastfeed with

lactational amenorrhoea for two years at most. Thus, modern-day woman in our society will probably experience 400–500 menstrual cycles in her reproductive life. It may not therefore be surprising that women today have so many problems with their menstrual cycles, given that they occupy so large a part of their lives. The excesses of childbearing in the past have been exchanged for the excesses of menstruation in the present.[1]

But though period problems are so common – they are in the 'top ten' of complaints treated by general practitioners – no one has been able accurately to define just what is a 'normal' cycle and what's an abnormal one. Many women, for instance, have cycles that are shorter or longer than the textbook 28-day one, which is only an *average*. Some women bleed only for a couple of days; others for as long as a week. Some women are *always* regular; others never know when to expect their period. Teenagers and women approaching the menopause may miss several consecutive periods. And women in both age-groups may experience a heavier blood loss than those in their twenties or thirties.

Then there are the women who have some abdominal pain or discomfort in the middle of their cycles. This seems to coincide with ovulation and is thought to be due to the rupture of the follicle – the pocket containing the egg. Some women may have a slight bleed at this time – often only a few spots – probably due to changes in hormone levels.

Even if you are lucky enough to have regular, trouble-free periods most of the time, you may still get the occasional 'odd' one that comes too late, too early or is missed entirely for no obvious reason (I'm assuming that you are not pregnant). Or your period may be heavier or lighter than is usual for you. Finally, of course, there's period pain (dysmenorrhoea). It's estimated that this affects up to 60 per cent of us to some extent at some time. And some of us are literally disabled by it for one or two days a month.

All these variations are common: they affect a few of us all the time, some of us some of the time and nearly all of us occasionally. No wonder that many specialists have come to the conclusion that when it comes to menstruation it's impossible to lay down hard and fast rules about what's normal and what isn't. Especially, one might add, as most of them are men and so have never had a period in their lives.

CHANGING PATTERNS: WHEN TO SEEK ADVICE

The early years

When you first start menstruating your periods may well be irregular and the amount of blood lost each time may vary. This is annoying but not something you need to worry about: menstrual cycles often do take several years to settle down. You may also find that at first your periods are pain-free but that, after a time, you start getting dysmenorrhoea. Again, this is hardly ever a sign that something's *wrong*: research has shown that it's only when you're ovulating that your periods may be painful and most young girls' ovaries don't start releasing eggs until some time after their periods start.

Until recently, teenagers with irregular and/or painful periods were often prescribed the Pill, a very effective treatment for both these conditions. Now, though, most specialists consider it unwise to put young girls on the Pill (unless, of course, they need contraception and feel none of the other methods is reliable enough). This is because the centres in our brains which control ovulation take time to 'learn' their job and may be particularly sensitive in those first few years to interference by the hormones in the Pill. Switching them off – which is what the Pill does – so soon after they've been switched on may be asking for trouble. There's some evidence that a few women who have irregular periods *before* they go on the Pill may find it particularly difficult to conceive when they come off it. Though the results from research are fairly reassuring and suggest that eventually most ex-Pill-users do have the babies they want, it may take them longer than if they hadn't used this form of contraception. A very small minority may even need fertility drugs to get ovulation started again.

As a teenager, having a family may be the last thing on your mind and you'd do *anything* to have regular, painless periods. But will you feel the same when you're thirty or thirty-five and trying desperately for a baby? Can you afford to take even that remote chance that the Pill may affect your future fertility?

When your menstrual cycle is established

Eventually your periods will settle down into some sort of pattern, though it may not be the one you'd have chosen! Many women have irregular periods for most of their reproductive lives and that's normal for them. Irregular periods, provided you have no other symptoms, seldom indicate that anything is wrong and, apart from the Pill, conventional medicine has very little to offer in the way of treatment.

Similarly, if you're usually regular but then have the odd early, delayed or missed period, this is nothing to worry about. The control of our menstrual cycles is incredibly finely balanced and the slightest thing can throw it off: stress is a common culprit as are emotional disturbances such as anxiety and depression. However, it's also worth remembering that pregnancy is the commonest cause of missed periods so, when in doubt, have a pregnancy test.

The time to seek help is when you notice a permanent change in your menstrual pattern. Suppose your periods are usually regular, relatively painless and your blood loss doesn't vary much from month to month. If you then start to bleed unpredictably, heavily or painfully you should see a doctor. The younger you are, the less likely it is that there's anything seriously wrong – and even in older women these symptoms aren't necessarily a sign of trouble – but they need investigating just in case.

If your periods stop altogether, again you need professional advice. Usually, this *amenorrhoea* is only temporary and will right itself in time. Possibly you're recovering from a severe emotional shock or maybe you've just come off the Pill. In both cases your normal cycle may take several months to re-establish itself. Or are you an avid amateur athlete? Regular vigorous exercise can cause amenorrhoea. The cure here is to cut down on your exercise.

Generally, specialists advise waiting for at least six months before doing any tests. Even then they may discover nothing much amiss. Whether they suggest treatment with hormones or other fertility drugs (see Chapter 8) depends on whether you want to conceive and, if so, how soon. If you don't plan to have a family immediately, they may well suggest leaving things as they are for the time being.

Having said that, they'll also warn you that ovulation may start up again at any time and therefore you'll need some form of contraception if you *don't* want to become pregnant. It's probably not a good idea to take the combined Pill (or to go back on it) for the reasons mentioned above. Some authorities, though, believe the progestogen-only Pill is a suitable contraceptive for women with amenorrhoea. But if you're against the whole idea of hormones you may prefer to use barrier methods instead. These can be very effective (see Chapter 6 for further details).

I'll be discussing period problems and their conventional and alternative remedies in more detail a bit later on. For the moment though I want to look at something else which is part and parcel of *every* period, normal or not.

COPING WITH PERIODS: SANITARY PROTECTION AND VAGINAL HYGIENE

We've *all* had to find some way of dealing with our menstrual flow. Many of us have found that tampons are the best solution. If you use tampons – and provided your loss isn't exceptionally heavy – you can almost forget, most of the time, that you're having a period.

But, in the past few years, we've heard a lot about toxic shock syndrome (TSS), a condition caused by a bacterial infection. It's potentially fatal and has been linked with the use of tampons. Other reports suggest that tampons may cause vaginal ulcers. And homoeopath Dr Trevor Smith claims in his book *A Woman's Guide to Homoeopathic Medicine*,[2] that tampons may also be to blame for some cases of endometriosis and dysmenorrhoea. Because of this, some experts believe that women shouldn't use tampons at all. 'The various harmful effects of tampons means that their use should be discouraged,' writes Leon Chaitow, a well-known naturopath, in the *Journal of Alternative Medicine*.

But I don't think we need to take this advice too seriously. For a start, TSS is extremely rare and in the US at least has been associated with one particular super-absorbent type of tampon. (It appears that tampons made from cotton and rayon – the majority – don't increase the risk of TSS. But those containing an artificial form of cellulose – to make them more absorbent – may, because some women will be inclined to change them less frequently, so allowing any bacteria to multiply.) In addition, TSS isn't confined to tampon users – even men and children can get it! Ulcers, too, are rare. To put these problems in perspective, millions of women use tampons and the vast majority have no problems at all. So, if there is a risk, it's a tiny one. And you have to weigh that against the fact that many of us would find our periods pretty intolerable if we had to abandon tampons in favour of pads. So I wouldn't pay too much attention to the warnings of male experts like Mr Chaitow. I agree with the more realistic advice of Dr Ann McPherson: 'If you get no problems with tampons,' she says, 'there seems no particular reason not to use them.'

However, it's probably a sensible idea to keep your super-absorbent tampons for the days when your flow is at its heaviest: at other times these tampons can make your vagina too dry, and ulcers – and possibly TSS – slightly more likely.

So use the less absorbent types instead. Some studies have also suggested that applicator types of tampon may be more likely to cause ulcers than the ones you insert with a finger. And for the very light days – usually right at the end of your period – you may find that just a pad or even a panty-liner is all that's required.

There may be the odd occasion in your life when you'd be well advised not to use a tampon at all: just after having a baby, for example, when there's a greater risk of infection. And if you're suffering from a recurrent vaginal infection such as thrush (see Chapter 5), taking a break from tampons for a few months may help. You should *never* use a tampon to absorb your vaginal secretions between periods. Some feeling of wetness is normal for nearly every woman (see Chapter 8 on infertility) and healthy vaginal mucus doesn't smell unpleasant provided you wash and change your underwear regularly. Moreover, those secretions actually help to keep your vagina clean and guard against infective organisms; so the last thing you want to do is dry them up. An excessive or smelly discharge is a sign of an infection which needs treatment (Chapter 5), and tampons will only make it worse.

For the same reason, never use vaginal deodorant sprays or tampons that contain deodorant. If your vagina is healthy you don't need them and the chemicals they contain may irritate the delicate tissues and increase the chances of infection.

PERIOD PROBLEMS

No periods or infrequent ones

The medical terms for these conditions are, respectively, amenorrhoea and oligomenorrhoea. They are usually considered together because in most cases the causes and treatment – both conventional and alternative – are the same.

As explained above, women who've just come off the Pill may fail to menstruate normally. So may those who've lost a large amount of weight: women with anorexia nervosa nearly always lose their periods. In rare cases, a tumour or some chromosomal abnormality is responsible (though in the latter case a woman will probably never have had normal periods). Of course, it may be that you're simply approaching the menopause and your reproductive system is winding down. Unfortunately this can also happen to young women whom, one would think, should be years away from the menopause.

Irregular periods

Most medical textbooks include irregular menstruation in the same category as amenorrhoea and oligomenorrhoea, probably because it, too, can be a bar to conception. But we have a bit of a language problem here: some books take 'irregular' to mean 'infrequent' as well, whereas this may not always be the case. Your periods may well occur reasonably often – even though you're never sure when they're going to turn up. So do you have a medical problem or not?

You may have. The evidence suggests that many women with irregular periods are not ovulating – though a temperature chart (see Chapter 8) will help you find out whether this applies to you. But even if you are producing eggs – some of the time at least – you'll have no idea, from month to month, when an egg is going to be released. If you're trying to conceive, intercourse then becomes somewhat like a game of Russian Roulette.

CONVENTIONAL TREATMENT

If your problems go on for more than about six months your doctor may refer you to a specialist who will order tests to check your hormone levels, which will show, among other things, whether you've reached the menopause, albeit prematurely. He's also likely to suggest a skull X-ray to rule out the – very remote – possibility of a tumour. Commonly nothing serious is found: there's no tumour, and hormone levels are more or less normal. About a quarter of all women with amenorrhoea, though, do have high levels of prolactin which are enough to stop ovulation.

Sadly there's not too much that can be done for a woman who has reached the menopause, no matter what her age. If anorexia is your problem, the best treatment is to put on weight, though this may be easier said than done: anorexia is a complicated psychological condition and often needs specialist hospital treatment. And the latest evidence suggests that a few women, even when they've recovered from their anorexia, are permanently sterile.[3]

The other conditions respond very well to one or more of the fertility drugs (see Chapter 8). However, many specialists believe there's little point in getting regular ovulation and periods going again unless a woman wishes to conceive immediately. You may disagree. Even if you don't want a baby now – or ever – you may feel 'less of a woman' if you're not menstruating regularly. Some sympathetic doctors acknowledge this and may be willing to treat you. Still, you need to bear in mind the fact that the drugs seldom cure your problems and you'll probably need to stay on them indefinitely if you want to keep your periods. There's also the risk that when you finally *do* want to conceive, your body may be so used to the drugs that it won't respond as well as if you hadn't taken them for all that time.

Fertility drugs will also help women with frequent but irregular periods. But, again, you may not be offered them – or want to take them – unless you wish to conceive. If you simply want regular periods but don't want a baby you may be prescribed the Pill. But, as I've explained, this may not be the best way to deal with your problem.

ALTERNATIVE TREATMENT

Many of the alternative therapies used for infertility (Chapter 8) apply. And most of the alternative practitioners I spoke to claimed reasonable success in treating these sorts of period problems. Some of it, I'm sure, can be explained by one word: reassurance. If a practitioner you trust tells you he can sort you out, this alone may be enough to cure you! And don't forget that menstrual problems disappear often without any treatment at all.

Acupuncture

Some of the success stories I have heard concern women with long-standing and deep-seated emotional problems. They usually had other period symptoms as well, such as pain and heavy bleeding, which hadn't responded to drugs. As I'll explain later, this all suggests that at least part of their problem was psychological and therefore they were prime candidates for the sort of informal psychotherapy alternative practitioners excel in: that is, sympathy, caring and a willing ear. Acupuncture also helps to relax you – yet another reason why it might help. Perhaps it doesn't matter that the acupuncture was almost an incidental part of their treatment. The important thing is that it worked.

'A friend of mine had very irregular periods,' reports a medically qualified acupuncturist. Oddly enough she didn't seek treatment for that. But she was troubled by pre-menstrual symptoms, in particular, painful breasts. 'I treated her once a fortnight. And within a matter of hours after every other treatment, she would have a period. So once a month she would have a period whereas before she was having one once every three or six months. She said the first time she thought it was just coincidence; the second time she thought it was peculiar and the third time she was convinced.' Even when she stopped having acupuncture the periods stayed regular – at least for a while. The acupuncturist hasn't seen her for some time and so doesn't know whether his treatment had any lasting effect.

Herbs and homoeopathy

Herbalists and homoeopaths say that irregular periods

respond well to their remedies though quick results aren't guaranteed. It can take up to six months or more to get a regular menstrual cycle established and if one was being sceptical one could argue that the cure had nothing to do with the treatment. Usually, though, some improvement is noticed in the first few cycles, which suggests that something about the treatment – whether the medicines themselves or the practitioners' powers of persuasion – is responsible. However, several practitioners told me that amenorrhoea following the Pill was more difficult to treat.

As far as herbs are concerned, I would expect them to have some effect. Several are known for their ability to bring on periods (and may, in big enough doses, cause an abortion). Others contain hormones and so may help to correct a hormone imbalance. Needless to say, these are powerful medicines and should only be taken on the advice of a qualified medical herbalist.

Diet

As with so much of holistic medicine, dietary advice forms an integral part of any treatment. Gross malnutrition can cause amenorrhoea: there's plenty of evidence for this both from studies of populations living at starvation level and of women with anorexia. Whether an apparently well-nourished woman can nevertheless be suffering from dietary deficiencies is open to question. But alternative nutritionists say they get good results from advising women on ways of changing their diet. We've seen that magnesium, vitamin B_6 and evening primrose oil are often useful treatments for PMS and there's a little evidence that they may help to correct menstrual irregularities, too. Extra zinc may also be required, particularly if you've been on the Pill. Extra vitamin E and C is sometimes recommended, as are the extracts of animal glands but, as far as I know, there's not much evidence that they do anything for irregular periods. (For more information on diet and supplements, see Chapter 8 on Infertility and Chapter 2 on Eating for Health.)

The trouble with so many of these claims is that there have been no proper scientific trials to test them. Good results could simply be the consequence of the placebo effect.

OTHER ALTERNATIVE THERAPIES

Since relaxation may help get your periods back to normal, any relaxation training may be beneficial. Yoga is probably the first one to try as it combines relaxation with other techniques designed to stimulate a sluggish system. Cranial osteopathy has helped some people.

One novel treatment – and one seldom mentioned – is *lunaception*. This was designed primarily as a form of contraception because – or so it's claimed – it induces regular ovulation. But obviously, if it works, it should be equally good at regularizing periods. The technique is based on the belief that ovulation can be triggered by sleeping with the light on for several days around the expected time of ovulation, usually the 14th, 15th and 16th days of the month. The theory is that in bygone days the light of the moon was the only bright light at night and that this stimulated ovulation – hence the 28-day cycle approximates to the lunar month. Of course this doesn't explain why some women have *regular* cycles which are much shorter or longer than this. And I'm not convinced that it would work if you have very infrequent periods. However it might be worth trying if you menstruate the usual number of times a year and simply want to be able to predict accurately when your period is due. Be warned, though, it may take several months before this method works, if at all.

Painful periods (dysmenorrhoea)

In this section I'll be talking about *primary* dysmenorrhoea, that is, the kind that starts with, or shortly after, the menarche and is so common, unfortunately, as to be considered almost normal. This form of dysmenorrhoea seldom indicates that you have anything wrong with you. *Secondary* dysmenorrhoea – the sort that starts later, maybe when you're in your twenties or thirties – is a different matter altogether and *always* needs medical investigation because of the possibility that you may have a serious condition requiring urgent treatment – for example, a pelvic infection or endometriosis. I'll be discussing endometriosis later. As for an acute pelvic infection: neither painkillers nor alternative medicine are suitable treatments – antibiotics are the only answer.

WHAT CAUSES PRIMARY DYSMENORRHOEA?

It's now believed that period pains – and the other symptoms such as dizziness, nausea, vomiting and diarrhoea that often complete the package – are due to excess amounts of those chemicals called prostaglandins. There is a lot of evidence to back this theory – not least that drugs which reduce the levels of prostaglandins abolish or significantly reduce period pains for many of the women who take them (see below).

But though prostaglandins may be the chief villains, other factors may be involved as well. Osteopaths, for instance, believe that poor circulation in the pelvic area may be partly to blame and many conventional doctors would probably agree with them. After all, exercise, which improves the circulation, is often recommended as a treatment for dysmenorrhoea and it does work to some extent. As does alcohol, which dilates blood vessels and so encourages blood flow. Perhaps, too, a more effective circulation helps flush away those 'bad' PGs. And don't forget, it also encourages the release of endorphins, the body's natural painkillers: when you exercise you're giving yourself a minute dose of morphine-like chemicals, and if your dysmenorrhoea isn't too bad, this may be enough to ease the pain.

There's also evidence that psychological factors may make period pains worse. Alternative practitioners, with their strong belief in links between mind and body, consider this a very likely possibility. Orthodox researchers, too, have found evidence for this theory: several studies have shown that women who treat menstruation as an illness are more likely to suffer pain than those who regard it as a normal part of life and carry on as usual when they have their periods. Then there's the evidence that psychotherapy and counselling, autogenic training and biofeedback (all therapies aimed at treating the body *via* the mind) can reduce the amount of menstrual pain.

I'm afraid there's no getting away from it: our minds can make dysmenorrhoea worse. This is a far cry from saying that period pains are *all* in the mind. Quite clearly they aren't. But if you're a bit ambivalent about menstruation – perhaps you were brought up to believe that period times would always be troublesome, or maybe you feel resentful that you should have periods at all – then you're bound to feel a bit tense about the whole business. Result: what should only be a minor discomfort turns into crippling pain.

MEDICAL TREATMENT

Doctors always used to say that having a baby was the best treatment. The argument was that menstrual pain was due to a tight cervix and that the process of birth did away with the problem at one fell swoop. Extending the theory a bit more, some specialists believed that if a woman with severe dysmenorrhoea wasn't ready to start a family, her cervix could be stretched artificially with similar beneficial results.

But although menstrual cramps do tend to get less severe as you get older, childbirth doesn't necessarily bring quick relief. Dilatation of the cervix is now seldom used as a treatment for dysmenorrhoea – partly because it doesn't always work but also because it may damage the cervix so that, when a woman does become pregnant, she's more likely to miscarry or have a premature baby.

The Pill is still a popular treatment – which I find rather alarming as teenagers (the last people who should go on the Pill) are the ones who suffer most from dysmenorrhoea. But things are changing: the more progressive doctors now prescribe anti-prostaglandins and one of these drugs, ibuprofen, has recently become available over the counter from chemists.

Ibuprofen (brand names Seclodin, Nurofen and Librofem) has a good safety track record – it's been used for years to treat both arthritis and period pains. In fact, the anti-prostaglandins as a whole seem free from side effects and – an even bigger point in their favour – you only need to take them for those few days a month when you're in pain. This seems a far more sensible idea than taking the Pill: what's the point of dosing yourself with hormones for an entire month when you only need pain relief for one or two days? The drugs work very rapidly, too – usually you'll get relief within half an hour of taking them.

Perhaps the only drawback to anti-prostaglandins is that we don't know whether they have any harmful effects on the unborn child. So you should use them only when bleeding has actually started, then you can be fairly certain you haven't conceived – assuming you're sexually active, of course. The trouble with this regime is that you may not get such good pain relief: the best results are reported for women who take the drugs *before* the pain (and therefore, usually, the bleeding) begins.

But, even so, many women do find that anti-prostaglandins work well for them. One told me: 'Speaking as someone who's suffered violently from the age of thirteen, I've gone through the whole gamut of drugs. I used to have to take large doses of Distalgesic [a strong painkiller] because aspirin and paracetamol didn't touch it. Ibuprofen really works. I take it when the pain starts and it works in twenty minutes.' It is estimated that these drugs help up to 90 per cent of all women with period pain.

ALTERNATIVE TREATMENT

Anti-prostaglandins, effective though they are, don't help everyone. And many people who could benefit may have reservations about taking any drug for years on end, even though it's only for a couple of days each month. So let's look at what else might help.

I've already mentioned exercise. Yoga is said to be particularly helpful and teachers of it claim that regular practice can banish period pains. Some women say that masturbation to orgasm also relieves cramps, though if you're in intense pain this method may not appeal to you.

Then there are techniques such as biofeedback, hypnotherapy and relaxation. Studies have shown that all work to some extent but that none of these techniques gives better results than the others. One suggestion is that they all have two crucial things in common: they teach a woman to relax and they improve her ability to *cope* with the pain. Pain is, after all, a subjective experience, and anxiety and lack of confidence in one's ability to cope can make it seem worse that it really is.

Acupuncture

Acupuncture is often a very effective form of immediate pain relief – maybe because it releases endorphins, maybe because it helps you to relax. But this doesn't explain its long-term benefits: endorphins are very short-lived substances and the effects of relaxation don't last that long either. Yet a short course of acupuncture, say three sessions, can keep you pain-free for up to six months. No one knows quite why this should be so. Does acupuncture have some effect on pro-staglandin levels, perhaps?

Osteopathy

This, too, appears to be a very effective treatment. The aim of osteopathic manipulation – and the exercises which your osteopath will advise you to practise between treatments – is to improve the blood flow in the pelvis. They work mainly on the spine: if your back isn't flexible enough it may interfere with the flow of blood away from the uterus. Many of us do have slightly stiff backs, often due to years of poor posture.

If I grab hold of your finger [one practitioner explained] and I cut off the venous blood going out but leave the arterial blood going in, the finger's really going to hurt; it's going to throb and it's going to get really red. That, applied to the uterus, is what I think is happening. We've got a restriction in the outflow, in blood flowing away from the uterus.

As an osteopath, I look at the mechanical ways the blood is draining out of the pelvis. Blood drains out of the pelvis through the major veins. But there is also a very important secondary plexus (network of blood vessels) in and around the spinal cord. This is a great river of tiny, tiny blood vessels which are draining away from the abdominal and pelvic organs. It's useful because it's the main storm drain channel, if you like. It's in the lumbar spine, so reduced spinal mobility means you have a reduced efficiency in this pumping system.

Sharon, another osteopath, reports that she used to suffer from very bad period pains but, following osteopathic treatment, is now more or less cured. She had, in fact, tried anti-prostaglandins but they didn't work. Nor did hormones. 'Prostaglandins,' she believes, 'can be part of the problem, but if there are other problems, with the circulation or the posture, then anti-prostaglandins aren't going to help.' Hers was a postural problem, she discovered. And after a lot of work, that was corrected. 'It helped enormously. My period problems have reduced to nothing. Occasionally – perhaps once a year – they return but I know it's usually because my lower back has seized up and I need another treatment.'

Obviously, osteopathy isn't going to help you overnight. But osteopaths have another trick up their sleeves which you can use until your treatment begins to have an effect. In fact *anyone* with period pain, whether they're having treatment or not, will find it useful.

Simply lie down with a book under the base of your spine. Then draw two imaginary lines between your hip bones and your vagina. About half-way down each line find a small hollow and press into it for about ten seconds with your thumbs.

Repeat as often as necessary to get rid of the pain. 'These are very good pressure points,' says Sharon. 'They really do help relieve the pain.'

Herbs

Herbalists, too, say that primary dysmenorrhoea is a particularly easy condition to treat. Many herbs act directly on the uterus and can correct muscle spasm. However these alone won't put you right in the long term: as with drugs, you'll need to continue taking them if you're to keep the pain away. So, in addition, a herbalist will try to put right the underlying problem, often by working at relaxing the whole person, so that eventually you may be able to manage without their remedies.

Diet

It is said that menstrual cramps may sometimes be due to a deficiency of calcium and/or magnesium, zinc and B vitamins. A diet low in animal fats will discourage excessive levels of the 'bad' prostaglandins (see also Chapter 3 on PMS) which seem to be at the root of dysmenorrhoea. The eicosapentaenoic acid (EPA) found in fish oil and evening primrose oil (see also Chapters 2 and 3 respectively) is also said to be helpful, possibly because it leads to increased production of the 'good' PGs while preventing the build-up of the 'bad' ones.

Some alternative practitioners claim that painful and/or irregular periods are sometimes due to a severe Candida infection and so may suggest some of the anti-Candida remedies mentioned in Chapter 5.

Heavy periods (menorrhagia)

THE CAUSES

At the back of everyone's mind is cancer. Happily, though, this is rarely a cause of heavy bleeding, particularly if the periods remain regular. Bleeding *between* periods is a more worrying symptom, unless it's slight and always appears to coincide with ovulation. Then it's usually regarded as just another variation of the normal menstrual cycle.

Heavy bleeding may also be a symptom of fibroids, endometriosis and pelvic infection. These conditions, particularly endometriosis and pelvic infection, may also give you pain as well.

Fibroids

These are benign growths. They are very common – it's estimated that one in five women will get them. They may give rise to heavy and, possibly, painful periods but more often they cause no symptoms at all. Fibroids are usually only a problem in women who are still menstruating: generally after the menopause they shrivel up.

Endometriosis

(see page 101) may also cause menorrhagia.

Dysfunctional uterine bleeding

If you suffer from menorrhagia there's a 50/50 chance that no doctor will be able to find anything wrong with you. You'll be told you have 'dysfunctional uterine bleeding' – which sounds impressive but doesn't mean very much. Possibly you may not be ovulating regularly – this may apply if you've just started your periods or are coming up to the menopause. If you don't ovulate, then you don't produce enough progesterone and this can lead to excessive blood loss. But most women with dysfunctional bleeding are ovulating and are not progesterone-deficient.

Another theory is that dysfunctional bleeding is simply the way some of our uteri respond to our monthly cycles. Remember the suggestion that regular menstruation is itself abnormal? Some specialists believe that the hormonal control which governs ovulation and the build-up of the uterine lining is geared primarily to pregnancy: it wasn't meant to cope with years of moderate, monthly bleeding.

There could also be emotional causes for heavy bleeding. It sometimes afflicts women with depression, for example. Women who've been sterilized also sometimes complain of menorrhagia. There could be several reasons for this. One suggestion is that if you were using the Pill before your operation, then your periods will be heavier afterwards. Another is that sterilization interferes with the production of ovarian hormones. But the third possibility is that, because sterilization marks the end of childbearing, the woman may, deep down, have doubts about her role in life. Excessive blood loss may be the physical expression of these doubts. Nearly all the practitioners I spoke to – both holistic and orthodox – were convinced that emotional factors were quite possibly involved in menorrhagia of the dysfunctional type.

MEDICAL TREATMENT

Cancer

This is discussed in Chapter 11.

Fibroids

Sometimes fibroids can be treated successfully with drugs such as the progestogens or danazol. Progestogens are considered safe and relatively free from side effects though they don't agree with all women. Danazol is more of a problem: it suppresses ovulation and sometimes menstruation too.

Though this will certainly cure heavy bleeding, you may not like the thought of interfering with your reproductive system in this way. Danazol is also notorious for its side effects (see pages 65 and 309). Nor does it cure fibroids. In fact, the aim of all drug therapy is to keep the fibroids under control until the menopause, when they'll probably cease to be a problem anyway.

Hysterectomy (see below) is sometimes recommended when drug treatments have failed. But there are alternatives. One is myomectomy – a procedure which removes the fibroids but leaves the uterus intact. And recently doctors in Edinburgh have reported that they can treat these 'difficult' fibroids successfully with an artificial hormone similar to luteinizing hormone releasing hormone.[4]

Endometriosis

See page 102.

Dysfunctional uterine bleeding

Your doctor may prescribe different sorts of hormones: natural progesterones may be given if a woman wants to conceive or artificial progesterones (progestogens) if she doesn't (see also Chapter 3). Though these hormones are popular, no one knows whether they do much good, particularly in women who are ovulating regularly (see above). The combined Pill is said to be very effective but as many women with menorrhagia are in their thirties when the risk of Pill-use begins to rise (see Chapter 6), there's considerable controversy about whether this is the most appropriate treatment. Even more so because it's the higher dose Pills – the ones that are thought to carry the greatest risks – that give the best control of menorrhagia.

Danazol is also sometimes prescribed – though at lower doses than are used to treat endometriosis (see page 102). This means that you'll still have periods though the blood loss should be much less. However, you probably won't ovulate and you may still get side effects.

None of these drugs cures menorrhagia. Some – though not all – authorities say that once you stop taking them your problems will probably be as bad as ever. If you're older than forty or so and have completed your family this may not matter too much – it's just a question of hanging on until you get to the menopause. But if you're younger than this, and especially if you want children, you may be unhappy with the prospect of years of drug treatment.

Anti-prostaglandins are now sometimes used to treat menorrhagia, as are drugs which encourage clotting. Anti-prostaglandins work for about half of the women who take them but unfortunately the effect seems to begin to wear off after several cycles. The other drugs haven't been studied all that much so it's not certain yet how effective they are. The main advantage of both types of drug is that they don't interfere with ovulation, produce very few side effects and need only be taken during menstruation. But again, any benefit will go once you come off the drugs.

Is dilatation and curettage (D and C) a useful treatment for heavy periods?

Most specialists now agree that it isn't. Occasionally it may improve matters for a few cycles but that's all. Although a D and C may reveal an infection, the only real point of doing it is to rule out cancer – an extremely rare cause of menorrhagia in women under thirty-five or even forty. Many authorities believe that D and Cs are therefore unnecessary in younger women.

Aspiration is sometimes used instead of a D and C. The uterine lining is sucked rather than scraped out. This is said to be a gentler and less painful procedure and is usually done under local anaesthetic in Outpatients. However, it can still be painful and many gynaecologists think that a D and C – even though it requires a general anaesthetic and a short stay in hospital – is less traumatic.

Hysterectomy as a treatment for heavy periods

Beware the doctor who tells you that a hysterectomy is the best treatment for you. Provided you haven't got cancer, it isn't. All the other conditions I've mentioned may well respond to drugs. Alternative medicine, as I'll explain in the next section, also has quite a good record in the treatment of menorrhagia. A hysterectomy is the last thing to consider, not the first. Of course, if you don't want any more children you may see hysterectomy as the ideal solution. Why bother with drugs – or any other form of treatment – when one operation will cure your problems in one go? It's an attractive thought.

Sadly, though, hysterectomy may bring its own difficulties. First of all you may come up against a surgeon who wants to remove your ovaries as well – particularly if you're very near the menopause or going through it. If he tells you you don't need your ovaries any more, don't listen to him. Find another surgeon. The evidence is that, in normal women, the ovaries continue to produce some hormones even *after* the menopause (see Chapter 9). And some of these hormones may be important in our sex drive. So hang on to your ovaries! Otherwise you may find yourself with sudden and dramatic menopausal symptoms and with your sex life in tatters.

Unfortunately there's also evidence that a simple hysterectomy may have much more profound effects than used to be believed. Though much is made of the fact that once you know you can't conceive you'll enjoy sex more rather than less, this may not be so. Some women find that, without their uterus and cervix, orgasm becomes less pleasurable, probably because they're missing the uterine contractions that normally occur during orgasm.

Many studies have found that women are more likely to become depressed after the operation. Though not all researchers accept these results, they certainly give pause for thought.

Fibroids

Alternative practitioners say they can't actually get rid of fibroids though they can reduce the bleeding. One acupuncturist told me he's been able to break up fibroids to some extent but another said he didn't believe that acupuncture had any effect on the size of the growth.

A medically qualified homoeopath reported: 'I've had about half a dozen patients who were threatened with a hysterectomy who did not need it in the end. So if you're waiting for surgery it's worth trying.' And if you've had a myomectomy rather than a hysterectomy, homoeopathic remedies may stop the fibroids returning.

Herbs seem to be useful too. 'Fibroids can be kept under control in their early stages,' said a herbalist. But she warned: 'I do not know of any cases where a regression of fibroids has been brought about by herbal treatment.'

It seems then that if you have fibroids, alternative treatment won't remove them. But, by reducing the bleeding, it may well keep you out of the surgeon's hands.

Dysfunctional uterine bleeding

This seems to respond very well to alternative treatment. One of the first things you might like to try is vitamin A supplements because there's some evidence that menorrhagia is often caused by a deficiency of this vitamin. In one study, 44 per cent of patients had a vitamin A deficiency. When they were given supplements nearly 60 per cent of them found their periods returned to normal, and a further 35 per cent reported some improvement.[5] However, because vitamin A can be toxic and different people need different amounts, don't take supplements without professional advice.

Though many osteopaths would say manipulation probably hasn't much to offer, patients receiving treatment for bad backs, for example, return later to say that their periods have improved. And Sharon, who used osteopathy to relieve her dysmenorrhoea, found that her periods became lighter, too. Herbs, acupuncture and homoeopathy are all said to be very successful – as you might expect if you've read the section on fibroids. Reflexology or reflex zone therapy may help, too.

Part of this success may be due to psychological factors: good alternative practitioners are caring people and will spend more time with you than the average doctor is able to manage. I suspect this plays a large part in successful treatment. Otherwise, why should menorrhagia respond to several very different techniques? And even doctors admit that many women with menorrhagia cope without treatment provided they're given bags of reassurance. The other odd thing about the condition is that it can get better on its own.

Endometriosis

Endometriosis can cause all sorts of symptoms including painful and heavy periods, and pain during intercourse. Some women are in pain all the time.

In this condition, fragments of the endometrium or uterine lining get displaced and 'seed' themselves elsewhere in the body, often on the ovaries or on the outside surface of the uterus. No one knows why this should happen though many specialists believe that the menstrual flow may somehow go the 'wrong way', up the fallopian tubes and out into the pelvic cavity.

This displaced tissue responds in exactly the same way as it would if it were still inside the uterus. Every month it grows and proliferates and, with the onset of menstruation, bleeds. This continues until the menopause. Over the years this can lead to scarring of the surrounding tissue and quite often infertility though, ironically, if a woman does succeed in getting pregnant, her endometriosis will improve spontaneously – until menstruation starts again after the baby's birth.

MEDICAL TREATMENT OF ENDOMETRIOSIS

Every practitioner I talked to admitted that endometriosis is an exceptionally difficult condition to treat. Hormones, including those in the Pill, may give some relief but they don't cure endometriosis. The favourite drug now is danazol but very high doses are needed to suppress both ovulation *and* menstruation. Such doses nearly always cause side effects. 'Very few of my patients have stayed on it,' one gynaecologist told me. 'The only reason they remained on it was that it did relieve their pain and as long as it did that they were often willing to put up with the side effects.' Not much of a recommendation.

A new artificial hormone – the same one that's been tested for fibroids – is now undergoing trials. It seems as effective as danazol but causes fewer side effects, so more women may be prepared to try it.

Unfortunately the only lasting cure for many women with severe endometriosis is hysterectomy and oophorectomy (removal of the ovaries). This will mean that a woman will experience an immediate and dramatic menopause. And she has an added problem: even if she were willing to contemplate hormone replacement therapy, she'd be well advised not to have it because the hormones may reactivate the disease.

ALTERNATIVE TREATMENTS

The Endometriosis Society (see Useful Addresses) reports that a whole variety of alternative remedies may help. And, as conventional medicine is still far from licking the problem, you have nothing to lose by turning to alternative medicine. Even so, some alternative practitioners believe that endometriosis is beyond them and will refer patients back to sympathetic gynaecologists for further treatment.

In general any technique which alleviates menstrual pain may make your endometriosis more bearable so you may like to read the section on dysmenorrhoea again. But endometriosis is more than just pain, of course, and requires more far-reaching and intensive treatment than simple dysmenorrhoea.

Diet

Deciding which alternative treatment to try is difficult. Perhaps the first thing to do is to get some dietary advice. A wholefood diet is nearly always recommended and you may need supplements as well. The B vitamins, vitamin E, magnesium, calcium and selenium, and evening primrose oil all appear to have helped some people. But we're now in uncharted territory. It's not clear why any of these should be beneficial in endometriosis. It's thought that the B vitamins may improve oestrogen metabolism; vitamin E may reduce scarring; magnesium and calcium may help to relieve menstrual cramps (one of the main symptoms of endometriosis), while evening primrose oil, by encouraging the formation of 'good' prostaglandins, may reduce inflammation. There *is* some evidence that these PGs may have this effect.

Not everyone needs supplements, however. And if you take them, getting the balance right is well-nigh impossible unless you're an expert. I feel the only course is to consult a doctor who's also a member of the British Society for Nutritional Medicine. He or she may also be able to tell if you're suffering from a systemic Candida infection which, some recent US evidence suggests, may be one of the causes of endometriosis. However, most of the evidence for the success of dietary regimes is completely unproven. Don't pin your hopes on it.

Herbs

Herbal treatment can be amazingly effective and can work where drugs have failed. A report in the *New Herbal Practitioner* in 1983 gave details of three patients, all of whom had been on danazol with no improvement. After herbal remedies they made steady progress; their pain became less and one who'd been infertile managed to conceive. But sometimes, even with herbs, surgery may still be needed for long-lasting relief.

Acupuncture will give some pain relief and one practitioner, who's treated two women with endometriosis, reports that they're both now better. *Homoeopathic* remedies may also help in some cases.

Reflex zone therapy

I spoke to Pam. When endometriosis was diagnosed she had one child, aged ten, but wanted to add to her family. 'They told me they could put me on hormone treatment but that it would be best to have a baby before I started it. But because of the endometriosis the chances of my getting pregnant were less anyway.' So she was given drugs just to ease the symptoms.

She knew someone who practised reflex zone therapy. 'And she offered to treat me. I was very sceptical. I did not believe in it at all. But I thought it could do no harm. Within six weeks I was off any medical treatment at all. My period pains were less and some months I didn't have any pain at all.' And after about six months she conceived. However once the baby was born and menstruation started again, Pam began to experience pain once more and has gone back to the therapist for further treatment.

Does alternative medicine ever cure endometriosis?

We don't know. The trouble is that the condition may go into spontaneous remission only to flare up years later. If you've once had it – even though you're currently free of symptoms – there's always the chance that it'll return. However, it seems to me that alternative medicine may be at least as good as conventional drugs in keeping endometriosis under control. And, of course, it has few, if any, side effects, which is more than can be said of drugs.

CONCLUSION

As we've seen, alternative treatment often seems able to alleviate practically any period problem. We may not know why but, in the end, if you and your uterus are still happily together, does it really matter?

5. Vaginal Infections and Cystitis

HOW PROBLEMS START

Sex

Our genitals are designed for one thing: reproduction. Our vaginas are warm and moist so – especially when we're sexually aroused, when they produce even more lubrication – a penis can slip in without too much trouble. When we give birth, those same vaginal secretions smooth the way for the baby. Our urethras, which carry urine from the bladder to the outside, are very short compared with the male version which opens at the end of the penis. The man needs the extra length because, unlike ours, his urethra has two jobs: as well as being used to pass urine, it delivers semen; and the higher up the vagina it can reach, the better the chances of conception.

This is putting it rather baldly of course. It ignores the fact that sex is such fun that most of us have intercourse many, many more times than is necessary for the survival of the species! But we're the only mammals that do: other species confine their sexual activity to the times when the female is most likely to conceive. Yet the basic anatomy is the same. So it could be argued that our reproductive equipment wasn't meant to take the kind of hammering that we humans tend to give it.

During intercourse, our urethras and bladders also come in for a fair amount of pummelling as they lie so close to the vagina. So sometimes sex, particularly an energetic session, can result in bruising and inflammation. Even if this isn't

enough to cause problems on its own – and for some women it
is – it certainly leaves both our vaginas and urethras vulnerable to invasion by infective organisms.

These bacteria are already lying in wait for just such an opportunity. Our large bowel is packed with them. Provided
they stay there they don't do any harm. But let them get into
our vaginas or urethras and they can wreak havoc. Our
vaginal opening is perilously close to our anus and it's all too
easy for bacteria to get from one to the other – especially
during sex, when they may hitch a ride on a finger or the
man's penis. The vagina is an ideal breeding ground for them
because of its warm, damp conditions. Some of them may get
as far as the urethral opening. And because our urethras
are so short, it doesn't take them too long to get up to our
bladders as well.

Then, of course, there's the fact that our partner may have
an infection. Bacteria can't survive long outside the body.
But put two sets of genitals together (and this applies whether
you're heterosexual or homosexual) and they simply
exchange one warm wet environment for the other.

Other causes of infection

Sex is by no means the only way you can become infected.
Gonorrhoea and syphilis and some other genital infections
including herpes are nearly always sexually transmitted. But
thrush and cystitis can afflict virgins and celibate women of
all ages – elderly spinsters, young girls and nuns get them.
And women who are sexually active can become infected for
reasons that have nothing to do with sex (though regular
intercourse – the more so if you have several partners –
increases the risks of infection).

Tampons and sanitary towels may be the culprit in some
cases. Once they've become stained with menstrual blood
they provide a temporary breeding ground for bugs. The
string of the tampon may get contaminated during a bowel
movement and the bacteria can then get up the string and

into the vagina. A badly fitting sanitary towel can carry fecal organisms from the anus into the vagina and urethral openings.

Even if you're too young or too old to menstruate, or are between periods, your pants can spread contaminated fecal matter from one area to the other. This is probably most likely to happen in children who haven't yet learnt to wipe their bottoms properly. And while on the subject of bottom-wiping, we should always wipe from front to back – and teach our daughters to do the same. If we do it the other way there's a very real risk that fecal microbes will be carried onto the perineum or the vulva.

During our fertile years our vaginas produce lots of mucus. The mucus is a protective barrier; it helps prevent our tissues becoming irritated and sore and so open to infection. The secretions are also usually slightly acid – except when we're menstruating when the blood makes the vagina more alkaline – and bacteria don't like an acid environment. But before puberty and after the menopause these secretions are less in quantity; they're also less acid. Therefore infection is more likely. (A dry vagina is not, however, an inevitable consequence of the menopause. For further details, see Chapter 9.) Other possible infection 'triggers' are soap, vaginal deodorants and bubble baths. These may irritate the vagina or alter the acid balance allowing infection to take a hold. Most organisms which thrive in the vagina can also flourish in the urethra, as I've explained, so an infection which starts in one can spread to the other.

Stress can also make us more vulnerable to infection. There's now plenty of evidence to show that stress depletes our immune system and so makes it less able to fight invaders. Diet may also be to blame in some cases.

I'll be explaining more about the common infections and their triggers later in the chapter. My purpose in mentioning them here is to show just how easy it is for us to become infected. You may by now be beginning to suspect that since many of our infections are 'self-inflicted', in the sense that the microbes responsible come from elsewhere in our bodies, medical treatment may not be the ideal solution. This, of course, is what most of the rest of the chapter is about.

VAGINAL INFECTIONS

How to tell if you have an abnormal discharge

As explained elsewhere, a certain amount of vaginal 'discharge' is normal and doesn't indicate that you have an infection. The secretions of a healthy vagina are generally colourless or milky-white and tend to stain your pants slightly – either white or pale yellow. They also vary, in both consistency and colour, with your menstrual cycle. You'll probably notice a scant, sticky, opaque, white discharge just after menstruation while the 'fertile' mucus – produced around ovulation – is often quite copious, watery, stretchy and transparent. Then, in the second half of your cycle, the mucus decreases in amount and often becomes white and sticky again. When you're pregnant it's also normal for vaginal secretions to increase.

Healthy mucus doesn't irritate your vagina: the only sensation you should notice is one of wetness. Nor does it smell strong – it may have a slight odour but it's not at all unpleasant. It's important for you to get to know your own particular pattern of mucus secretion: then any change will alert you to the possibility of infection. An infected vagina doesn't always hurt or itch. Nor does it necessarily produce an offensive discharge. But it often does.

Diagnosis: why you need to see a doctor

If you do have an abnormal discharge, you should see your doctor. This is no time for self-diagnosis. If you've had one attack of thrush, for example, you may think you recognise the symptoms. But you could be wrong. So the first thing to do is get yourself examined. Too many GPs still don't bother to do an examination and prescribe drugs purely on your description of your symptoms. This is a mistake because while your discharge may sound typical of a thrush infection, it may have another cause.

Even if you do have thrush, you may have other infections as well. These will need to be treated separately. But accurate diagnosis is only possible if a sample of your discharge is taken for examination in a laboratory. So when he's seen what your discharge looks like, a good GP will either look at a sample under the microscope or send it for testing.

This is just as necessary if you plan to use alternative treatment. *You need to know what's wrong with you first*. If it turns out that you have a sexually transmitted disease (STD) such as gonorrhoea or syphilis, chlamydia or trichomonas, you need antibiotics. In any case a lay alternative practitioner is not allowed to treat STDs. A registered medical practitioner – even if he uses alternative methods – is. But he'll use antibiotics, just as any ordinary doctor would.

Lay practitioners are not supposed to treat herpes – another STD – either. If they confine themselves to general dietary advice so that they're treating the whole person rather than the disease, then they're in the clear. But if they use specific anti-herpes remedies, they're breaking the law. (Not all lay practitioners are aware of this: some believe that only gonorrhoea and syphilis are 'outside the law'. But, according to the Department of Health, all STDs fall into the same legal category.)

This usually isn't a problem. Because even for infections such as gonorrhoea, syphilis, chlamydia and trichomonas, for which the first-line treatment is antibiotics, alternative medicine can have an important, supportive role, to increase a person's general health so that recovery is as rapid as possible.

But it is in the treatment of thrush and herpes that alternative medicine may have most to offer. This is because these tend to be chronic infections and to recur from time to time – the organisms which cause them linger on in the body and may, if conditions are favourable, start multiplying again. Alternative therapies may make a big difference by ensuring that your body stays healthy and so doesn't give these bacteria the chance they're looking for. There are also some specific alternative anti-herpes remedies, which I'll be mentioning later on but, because herpes is an STD, you'll need to consult a medically qualified alternative practitioner for them.

In the section which follows, I'll describe the typical symptoms of thrush, but – and this can't be said too often – even if you think you have thrush you'll still need a medical diagnosis before trying alternative treatment. In fact, a properly qualified lay practitioner should also insist on it before recommending a course of therapy.

Thrush

Thrush is probably the most common cause of vaginal discharge. Surveys suggest that up to 40 per cent of us have it – or have had it – at some time. It's caused by *Candida albicans* – a yeast-like fungus. You may also hear some doctors refer to Candida as Monilia.

Most of us have some Candida somewhere in our bodies though usually we're not aware of it because it doesn't give us any symptoms. Candida is a natural inhabitant of our large bowel and quite a number of us – even when healthy – have some Candida in our vaginas, too. Our bodies can accommodate a small number of these organisms without problems.

In the vagina, under normal circumstances, bacteria called lactobacilli – which produce acid from glycogen, a form of starch, secreted by the vaginal walls – prevent Candida overgrowth. But the balance is a very fine one. If it's upset – for example during a period, when the vagina becomes more alkaline, and we use tampons which absorb vaginal secretions – then the Candida can multiply. Dietary factors, as I'll explain later, may be to blame as well. And sometimes, all it takes is for some extra Candida to find its way from the anus to the vagina.

Some people think that thrush is more common than it used to be. Whether there's really more of it about or whether women are now more willing to consult their doctors about it is a matter for debate. However it's true that modern life-styles could well encourage the growth of Candida. Sexual mores and dress have changed drastically since our grandmothers were young. Many women are now on the Pill and this contraceptive makes some of them more susceptible to thrush. The Pill has also brought a greater sexual freedom and, for some of us, sex is often followed by a Candida attack. As for clothes: Candida likes nothing better than a warm, humid crotch. And modern, man-made fibres which hinder the evaporation of perspiration, and tights and figure-hugging jeans, all contribute to that.

Then there are the antibiotics. They've revolutionized the treatment of many severe infections. Unfortunately, they're pretty non-specific and kill all sorts of bacteria, not just the harmful ones. But the antiobiotics used to treat bacterial infections don't kill Candida. So they can upset the delicate balance in the vagina by polishing off the friendly lactobacilli that help to keep the Candida in its place. Ironically, anti-biotic treatment for other vaginal infections and for cystitis (see page 132) may precipitate an attack of thrush!

SYMPTOMS

The typical thrush discharge is thick and white: many people think it looks more than a bit like cottage cheese. It often has a yeasty smell – as you might expect. Many women find the discharge is intensely irritating – their vaginas, vulvas and sometimes their perinea, too, itch and become swollen, inflamed and tender. But it's quite possible for the discharge to cause no discomfort at all. Or a woman may have only a slight discharge but still be in intense pain.

Because symptoms can vary such a lot, diagnosis isn't al-ways easy. Even an obvious curdy white discharge doesn't mean that you definitely have thrush, though lots of GPs think it does. But specialists in *genito-urinary* medicine – who earn their living looking at people's sexual and urinary ap-paratus – assert that the only way to be sure is to take a sample and look at it under the microscope. Even if you do have thrush, there's nearly a one in three chance that you have some other infection as well, according to some authorities. So never jump to conclusions – and don't allow your GP to, either. Insist that he or she does a vaginal examination and takes a sample for testing.

Herpes

Unlike thrush, herpes, a virus, is nearly always transmitted by sexual contact (it's thought that it may, very rarely, be spread by other means such as sharing a towel with someone who has the infection).

SYMPTOMS

The main symptoms are little blisters – rather like cold sores, which are also caused by a herpes virus. In fact, someone with cold sores can give his or her partner genital herpes if oral sex forms part of lovemaking.

The blisters usually appear on the labia or around the entrance to the vagina. But the signs of trouble may start before this with itching, pain or a burning sensation. Then come the blisters, which eventually burst, leaving red, raw ulcers. These then crust over and heal – a process which can take two weeks or even longer.

WHY ARE PEOPLE SO SCARED OF HERPES?

There are several things about herpes which make it, some specialists believe – and many sufferers agree – an even more harrowing disease than either gonorrhoea or syphilis.

1. The pain can be excruciating, especially during urination, when the urine flows over those open sores.

2. Attacks are recurrent, the second and subsequent ones starting sometimes only a week after the previous one has

ended. The only good thing you can say about them is that the first attack is usually the worst.

3. Medical treatment leaves a lot to be desired. It's better than it used to be but recurrent attacks remain a problem.

4. If a women is pregnant when she gets her first attack of herpes there's a risk of miscarriage. More serious is the risk to the baby when it's actually being born: if a woman has an attack then – either her first or a recurrent one – there's at least a 40 per cent chance that her baby will be infected as it passes down the birth canal and through the vaginal opening. If it does get herpes there's about a 40 per cent chance that it will be so seriously affected that it dies.

5. In Chapter 11, I mention the relationship between sex and cancer of the cervix and, as I explain there, some viruses can cause cancer. There is evidence that the herpes virus is one – though not the only one – of these. It doesn't mean that if you have herpes you're also going to develop cervical cancer. Most women with genital herpes don't. But herpes does seem to increase the risks and some authorities believe that all women with herpes should have a yearly cervical smear so that any abnormality is spotted as soon as possible.

6. Though doctors have been advising sufferers that between attacks they can't infect another person, new evidence suggests that the virus can be transmitted even when it's not causing any obvious symptoms.[1] The question in people's minds, of course is: is it *ever* safe to have sex with someone who has herpes?

The medical treatment of thrush

Most attacks of thrush are treated with vaginal pessaries and creams containing *antifungals* which kill Candida. These include nystatin (Nystan) which, though one of the oldest drugs, is still one of the most effective. Cost-conscious GPs will tend to prescribe it in preference to the more modern preparations because of its cheapness. Other antifungals include clotrimazole (Canesten), econazole (Ecostatin, Gyno-Pevaryl) and miconazole (Gyno-Daktarin, Monistat).

To tackle your thrush successfully you need both pessaries and cream – there's not much use in launching an attack on your vagina if you leave the Candida to multiply on your vulva and perineum. A new formulation of Canesten cream, though, is now available in a special applicator and this can be used instead of pessaries. Usually a course of nystatin pessaries lasts fourteen days. With the other drugs, treatment is usually shorter – between one (one dose of the new Canesten cream clears thrush in the majority of cases) and six days. There's some difference of opinion as to how long you need to continue using the other creams on your vulva: some doctors will tell you to apply them only when it itches. Others believe that several weeks' continuous application is necessary to eradicate the infection. Your sexual partner should also be treated because he or she may well be harbouring the Candida even though, if male, he may not have any symptoms.

Sometimes, for really stubborn thrush, you may be given tablets of nystatin. These will deal with any Candida overgrowth in the bowel and so may help prevent reinfection from that particular source. However, specialists aren't sure about how effective oral nystatin is. 'Such evidence as exists shows little difference in overall cure or relapse rates when oral treatment is used,' writes Dr David Barlow, consultant physician in genito-urinary medicine at St Thomas's Hospital, London, in *Women's Problems in General Practice*.[2]

Another oral drug – ketoconazole (Nizoral) – has also been used to treat difficult cases of thrush. But in 1985 it emerged that this drug was associated with very serious – and, in a few cases, fatal – side effects. It hasn't been banned because it is useful in some infections which themselves may threaten a patient's life. Vaginal thrush obviously isn't one of them so, hopefully, doctors shouldn't now be prescribing it for this condition. It may be effective but so are other, gentler remedies – the alternatives I'll be discussing later.

OTHER PROBLEMS

Ketoconazole is in a category all of its own. Oral nystatin doesn't carry the same dangers because it's not absorbed into the blood: its action is confined to the digestive system. But it sometimes causes diarrhoea.

The *topical* preparations (the ones that are applied direct into the vagina or onto the skin) seem safe enough – even during pregnancy (though you may, of course, prefer to try some alternative treatment if the idea of using any drug in pregnancy worries you). But they're not problem-free. Creams and pessaries – particularly pessaries – are messy and some can stain your underwear. Some of the products may irritate the skin so, at first, your vagina may feel more rather than less tender.

If they always worked, this wouldn't matter so much. But they don't. Both pessaries and tablets can deal with the current infection but they can't prevent it recurring – which it often does. Some women find they have to use pessaries, on and off, for months at a time to keep the Candida down. This has the obvious disadvantage that your vagina will be regularly leaking fluid from the dissolved pessary (hardly the ideal treatment if you're trying to get rid of a discharge). It also shows that they're doing nothing to treat the underlying cause of the infection – whatever it was that allowed the Candida to multiply in the first place.

This, of course, is where alternative medicine comes in. But let's leave that for now and look at how good doctors are at treating herpes.

The medical treatment of herpes

Until quite recently there was no way of treating herpes: the attack had to run its natural course though doctors could suggest ways of relieving the pain. Sitting in a warm saline bath (add three tablespoons of salt to the bathwater) is said to soothe and to make urination less painful if you pass water while the relevant bits are being bathed by the salt solution. A local anaesthetic ointment – which numbs the whole area – also helps quite a bit.

Recently, two new drugs have become available which can actually cut short an attack. One is acyclovir (Zovirax) which prevents the herpes virus from multiplying. Acyclovir, when taken regularly, also appears to reduce the number of recurrent attacks. But some authorities believe that it shouldn't be used in this way. There are three problems: one is that treatment is very expensive – a report published in the *Lancet* in July 1984 estimated that the yearly cost per patient was nearly £1500. The second is that no one knows what the long-term side effects might be. Yet many patients might need it for years, if not for life, because once you have the virus it stays in your body even though, between attacks, you feel perfectly all right. The third, and perhaps the most serious, drawback is that the virus may become resistant to acyclovir if it's used too often.

Some specialists think that the other drug, inosine pranobex (Imunovir) is more promising. It's cheaper than acyclovir, and works in a different way, by stimulating the immune system rather than attacking the virus directly. This means that the virus won't become resistant. However, at the moment there appears to be some doubt about whether it can prevent recurrent herpes attacks. Initial reports suggested it couldn't, but more recent ones have been more encouraging. All the same, as with acyclovir, we can't yet be sure that long-term treatment doesn't carry any risks.

The alternative approach to recurrent thrush

If your thrush was just a one-off attack that went away with conventional treatment and never came back, fine. You don't need alternative medicine. But if you're bothered by repeated attacks you must be prepared to put in quite a bit of hard work. To combat recurrent thrush the alternative way requires constant vigilance and, nearly always, some change in your lifestyle. You need to be fairly dedicated to carry it off!

As I've already explained, Candida lives in all of us – most of us have picked it up by the time we're six months old. I've also told you that under normal circumstances our bodies see to it that its growth is kept under control. When that control breaks down, the Candida proliferates and the problems begin.

The alternative approach is aimed at reinforcing the body's natural defence mechanisms by ensuring that the vagina stays reasonably hostile to thrush, and by boosting our general health so that we resist infections – of all sorts – much better. The therapies I'll be discussing aren't intended to attack the thrush *directly*. This would be a pretty hopeless task anyway as there's no remedy which will eliminate the organism completely. And that's why, of course, medical drugs often don't solve the problem. They kill off enough of the Candida to get rid of your symptoms for a time. But unless your body's defences are strengthened as well, the remaining Candida will simply grow and multiply and wham! you've got another attack.

But before going into the details of alternative anti-thrush therapies, for which you may need professional advice, let's look at some of the self-help remedies.

I've mentioned the importance of personal hygiene and that repeated attacks of thrush may be more likely if you wear tight-fitting trousers and man-made fibres. It's also a sensible precaution to wash your pants in non-biological washing powder or, better still, just water alone. This is because washing powders, especially the biological type, tend to irritate sensitive skins and so make them more prone to infection. To be really sure you've removed all traces of Candida – which is an exceptionally hardy organism – you may need to boil your underwear (but use plain water – don't add detergent). Since tampons may be a source of infection you may also like to try using pads instead to absorb your menstrual flow – for a few months at least.

Be prepared to adapt your sex-life. Doctors give conflicting advice to women with thrush. Some believe that you shouldn't have intercourse when you have an attack. Others believe that sex isn't going to make things worse, provided your partner is also receiving treatment. In practice, many women find the whole idea of sex is a big turn off – it's the last thing they want when their genitals are giving them such hell. But even if your symptoms are mild, it's probably sensible to abstain until they've gone altogether. Sex can bruise the vagina and vulva and cause the thrush to flare up again.

While you're free of thrush, you don't need to restrict your sexual activity. But never have sex unless you feel like it. If you're not aroused, your vagina won't be sufficiently lubricated and the friction may trigger off an attack. For more information on managing your sex-life (and for masses of other useful advice on thrush) read *Thrush* by Caroline Clayton.[3]

Avoid antibiotics whenever possible. Thrush often goes hand-in-hand with cystitis, for which doctors usually prescribe antibiotics. But, as I've explained, these kill the 'good' vaginal bacteria, allowing the growth of the Candida to take off. Some of the self-help treatments for cystitis (see page 127) may be better for thrush victims.

Whenever you think your thrush is coming back – at the first itch – apply natural, unpasteurized yoghurt straight from the fridge. This form of yoghurt contains lactobacilli – the bacteria that help keep Candida under control. Many women have found yoghurt works a treat – even better than antifungal pessaries in some cases. 'After having thrush on and off for two years I solved my problem by changing from the Pill to the cap, and using yoghurt to treat the residual infection, having had no joy with Nystan pessaries. This I applied either in my cap or with tampons for about ten days . . . I've finally got rid of thrush,' said one woman quoted in Caroline Clayton's book.

Jean Robinson, better known as former Chairman of the Patients' Association and now as a member of the General

Medical Council, also found yoghurt an effective remedy. She reports in the *General Practitioner* that her thrush was as 'bad as ever' after a course of pessaries. She used yoghurt and: 'instant, blissful, total relief! Three nights' application and the problem was solved.'

Some alternative practitioners suggest that you eat yoghurt as well. Though this won't, of course, treat your vagina directly, it will help prevent Candida overgrowth in the intestine. As thrush sometimes arises from infection *via* the anus, this may reduce the chances of an attack.

Garlic is also sometimes recommended. It contains natural antibiotics which kill Candida, as well as a number of other micro-organisms (unlike medical anti-bacterial drugs, which don't affect the Candida). You can eat it raw if you don't mind the taste – and your family and friends don't object to the way you smell! – or you can try the odourless garlic capsules available from health food shops. Garlic may also be applied direct to the vagina. But – forget what all those self-help leaflets and books say – don't ever put a garlic clove in your vagina, even if you do wrap it in gauze first. A naturopath told me: 'It would sting like mad because you're dealing with a tissue that's inflamed, sore, red raw and you're putting something which is even more hostile in there. Now it may do a wonderful job of sorting out the Candida . . . but it doesn't hold out much hope for the mucus lining . . . I wouldn't *ever* dream of recommending a clove of garlic.' Instead this practitioner suggests you buy a proprietary garlic solution such as Garlisol or make your own solution by squeezing a clove in a garlic press and leaving it in boiled water overnight. But remember even a garlic solution can irritate, especially if you use it regularly.

Can't anything else be done?

The big drawback with all these measures – not just the garlic – is that even if they work they're really only scratching the surface (not literally, one hopes!). While you stick to them they make your vagina less cosy for the Candida, but relax your vigilance and it may start multiplying again. And who wants regularly to have to spoon on yoghurt or garlic solution (or diluted vinegar – another popular self-help remedy), not wear trousers or tampons, boil her pants and be 'careful' about sex? Nor do these solutions work for everyone: it seems that Candida finds some women's vaginas so comfortable that none of these remedies does much lasting good.

Nutrition: the main plank in the alternative approach

These self-help remedies may nevertheless be useful because they often do *something* to keep the Candida under control – albeit temporarily. So if you consult an alternative practitioner, he's quite likely to mention them. For the same reason some practitioners believe that medical drugs your doctor may have prescribed for you – including oral nystatin – have a definite place in treatment. They argue that when you're tackling stubborn, recurrent Candida, you need everything you can lay your hands on, provided, of course, that it's safe. Remedies applied to the vagina, and oral nystatin, can keep the Candida down long enough for the body to marshal its defences.

A severe infection, on the other hand, may overwhelm those defences – they may need extra help. Nutrition, say alternative practitioners, is the key. They advise changes in diet – and possibly vitamin and mineral supplements as well – to make the vagina permanently more hostile to Candida and also to boost the immune system so that it can fight it off.

PREGNANCY AND THE PILL: WHAT THESE TELL US ABOUT THE CAUSES OF THRUSH

Why are pregnant women and those on the Pill more suceptible to thrush? There are two reasons. One is that both pregnancy and the Pill suppress the immune system, so thrush may gain a hold. The other is that the environment inside our vaginas changes: it becomes more alkaline – and thrush grows best in an alkaline environment. Our vaginal mucus also secretes more glycogen, and if there aren't enough of the lactobacilli around to break it down, the Candida will use it to grow.

It seems that women who get thrush even though they aren't pregnant or taking the Pill often also have vaginal secretions which are high in glycogen. Alternative practitioners believe that a diet high in sugars and refined carbohydrates is the main cause. They've found that many of their thrush patients are women who eat a lot of sugary and starchy foods.

THE ANTI-THRUSH DIET

The first thing to do is to cut down on sugar and starch. For severe cases, some practitioners advise avoiding fruit for the first few weeks as this contains quite a bit of sugar. Many also believe that foods containing yeasts and other moulds are best avoided: this means no bread, cheese, or alcoholic drinks. There are a number of other prohibitions, including malted products, foods containing the additive monosodium glutamate, vinegars (and therefore salad dressings containing them), milk (because it contains its own sugar), coffee and tea (because they make the body release stored sugar), smoked meats, fish and sausages. It's claimed that once the Candida is under control you can gradually reintroduce the forbidden foods. Or you may benefit from desensitization treatment (see under cystitis – page 136).

You may also need to increase your intake of the B vitamins. (However, you should ensure that any B supplements you take are not derived from yeast. Yeast is a rich source of these vitamins so many tablets are prepared from it.) One of the B vitamins, biotin, seems to prevent Candida overgrowth – and this may be yet another reason why the lactobacilli usually do such a good job: they make biotin. Not surprisingly, natural yoghurt is an excellent source of biotin – and also, of course, supplies those lactobacilli. Some practitioners recommend supplements of lactobacilli, as *Lactobacillus acidophilus* in capsule or powder form, to provide the bacteria in a much more concentrated form.

Unfortunately these are expensive, so first see if yoghurt does the trick for you.

Vitamin B_6 and B_{12} are necessary for a healthy immune system, as is vitamin C. The vitamins A and E, and zinc are also said to be important. Vitamin A helps keep the mucus membranes in good condition, so obviously you need adequate amounts if your vagina is to stay healthy. A vitamin A deficiency, it is suggested, may also make for a sluggish immune system, as may a deficiency of vitamin E and zinc. A zinc deficiency may also slow down healing. That's why, say some alternative practitioners, all thrush victims need supplements.

But the benefits of supplements – for thrush, or any other condition – are far from proven. The medical world, by and large, doesn't believe in them. And, among alternative practitioners, some do and some don't. And those who don't – and here orthodox and alternative practitioners seem to agree – say that a good wholefood diet can provide all the vitamins and minerals we need. There are possibly two exceptions: vegetarians – particularly vegans who eat no dairy produce or eggs – may not be getting enough vitamin B_{12} or zinc. And if you start off your anti-thrush diet by avoiding fruit you may need extra vitamin C.

The supporters of vitamin and mineral supplementation, on the other hand, say that because supplements are safe there's every reason for everyone to use them. They claim that even a marginal deficiency may impair your resistance to disease – so why not correct it? And supplements do seem to help some people. Take Karen, for instance:

I managed to obtain complete relief . . . with a vit. B complex. I developed thrush one summer and embarked upon several courses of nystatin suppositories. Several courses, because it kept returning. It seems to be linked to my period cycle and as my period finished so the thrush started . . . I took a normal recommended dose of the B complex (I had a horror of taking too much of anything) in the last week of my cycle and during my period – and have never had the problem since. There has been an occasion when I have felt the familiar itching, but a couple of B doses saw it off.

But though at the recommended doses (for RDAs see Chapter 2) supplementation doesn't seem to produce any adverse reactions, there have been a few reports that, at higher doses, supplements can cause side effects. What's a high dose? Unfortunately there's no simple answer: practitioners with experience of supplementation usually prescribe doses well in excess of the RDAs with no problems. Even so, most of them accept there's an upper limit which they should not exceed – as a general rule. But they break that rule for individual patients whom, they say, can safely be given yet bigger doses and indeed, that they need them if they're to get better.

Other practitioners, however, won't touch supplements, believing that changes in diet are the best way to achieve, and maintain, a healthy balance. On a more mundane level, if you take supplements regularly, they'll make a big hole in your bank account!

So use your common sense. Start off by modifying your diet – and give it several months before you decide whether it's working or not. If it isn't, ask for advice from either a doctor with experience of nutritional medicine, or a qualified naturopath. It could be that your diet is still deficient in some way and they'll be able to advise you on how to correct it. Try the modified diet for a few more months. If you still have no joy, ask your practitioner whether he thinks supplements might help – and follow his advice. Don't forget, different people have different needs and it takes a professional to design a programme of supplements suitable for *you*. Whatever you read in books about the virtues of 'megadoses', don't allow yourself to be too impressed: megadosing is strictly for the experts. As discussed in Chapter 2, we don't yet know nearly enough about them.

POSTSCRIPT: CANDIDIASIS

This is a severe, systemic Candida infection which, some

alternative practitioners believe, is to blame for all manner of ills: depression, anxiety, migraine, menstrual problems, fatigue and tummy troubles.[4] Needless to say this suggestion hasn't made the slightest impression on orthodox medics. They would point out that, since anxiety and depression are disorders of the mind, they may be particularly responsive to any therapy the patient believes is going to work. The other conditions, too, are thought sometimes to have a psychological component (see Chapter 4 on menstrual problems and Chapter 13 on migraine, for instance). But, whatever the reasons, some amazing cures have been reported after patients have been treated by the anti-thrush diet.

Other forms of alternative treatment

I've heard of several other alternative thrush treatments but they quite often include dietary changes as part of the regime – as is usual with holistic medicine.

HOMOEOPATHY

One medically qualified alternative practitioner who uses a number of different therapies in his practice says that homoeopathy is the treatment of choice for vaginal infections. And it may achieve very quick permanent results.

'I have been suffering from thrush . . . intermittently for the last 12 years,' a *Fitness* reader wrote in a letter to the magazine. 'Recently I took a course of homoeopathic treatment from a qualified practitioner and the month's course resulted in a long-lasting cure – something which, despite repeated visits to the doctor, orthodox medicine had failed to achieve.'

HERBS

Herbalists say thrush responds well to their remedies. The treatment programme is likely to be two-pronged. The practitioner will give dietary advice and herbal medicines to be taken internally. Both are aimed at improving the patient's general health. She'll also be given herbal lotions to be applied to the vagina: Thuja, Calendula and Hydrastis (Golden Seal) are often used.

If the patient is already receiving herbal medications for other health problems and then falls victim to a thrush attack then she may only need the lotions: the practitioner will have already started working to boost her overall health. In such cases the thrush can be banished within a matter of days as a 1985 report on five patients in the *New Herbal Practitioner* shows. It also indicates that permanent relief is possible with herbal remedies. However the author of the report points out that all these women had acute rather than chronic infections. '. . . in cases of chronic infection . . . treatment would take longer, and appropriate medication and dietary suggestions, etc., would be given to correct the underlying imbalance.' Again, this is a job for the expert – you can't treat yourself.

ACUPUNCTURE

Treatment usually starts with dietary advice. 'You can help the body along,' said one acupuncturist, 'but if they don't take the dietary advice you're going to get very slow results.' It's also impossible to know in advance how long the treatment will take to have an effect but, as a rule, the younger and healthier you are, and the sooner you seek help, the quicker the results.

DEALING WITH STRESS

Some women find that their thrush strikes when they're under stress. This isn't surprising: there's plenty of evidence that stress affects the immune system. So if this seems to be your 'trigger', some form of relaxation therapy may help. You may, of course, be able to find your own way of relaxing – reading books or listening to tapes – but if you're a particularly tense person, you may need to consult a teacher of, for example, meditation or autogenic training.

The alternative approach to herpes

You can ask your GP to prescribe either Zovirax and Imunovir and both will almost certainly cut short your attacks. But, as I've explained, both these drugs are very new and their safety, particularly when used regularly, is still somewhat open to question. So it's best to use them only when you absolutely must.

SELF-HELP

Some sufferers report that witch hazel or surgical spirit, dabbed sparingly on the sores, helps the pain of active herpes. And, to avoid recurrent attacks – which are sometimes sparked off by stress – try some form of stress reduction.

Keeping the genital area well aired (cotton pants only) and clean may reduce the frequency of attacks and, as with thrush, you should avoid anything which may irritate the skin.

There are now quite a few books on herpes and most of them include a lot of advice on how to make life a little easier. There's also a self-help association (see Useful Addresses).

NUTRITION

It should come as no surprise that diet is now being used to tackle herpes. The general aim – as with thrush – is to increase the body's resistance to infection. So most of the same rules apply: eat foods that give you adequate amounts of vitamins and minerals. Supplements – especially those aimed at the immune system (see above) – may do some good, but see an alternative nutritional expert first.

There's one big difference. Many alternative practitioners now believe that herpes victims need extra *lysine* and that they should also reduce their intake of *argenine*. Both these substances are amino acids (the building blocks from which proteins are made). Scientists have discovered that, in the laboratory, lysine inhibits the growth of the herpes virus, whereas argenine has the opposite effect. In fact, without argenine, herpes can't grow at all. Lysine and argenine have very similar structures. The theory is that if you surround the virus with lysine, but deprive it of argenine, it is 'fooled' into taking up the lysine. But, as it can't use it, it stops replicating.

It's a neat idea and one which is backed by other, circumstantial, evidence. For example, people with recurrent herpes who eat foods high in argenine, such as nuts, chocolate, and seeds, are more likely to get an attack. So alternative practitioners believe that the logical way of controlling recurrent herpes is to eat lots of lysine-rich foods such as fish, chicken and milk, while steering clear of those with a high argenine content. They may recommend lysine supplements, too.

These seem to work – sometimes. In their book, *Stop Herpes Now*,[5] US specialists Dr Barbara North and Penelope Crittenden explain that the results of scientific studies on the benefits of high-lysine diets have been conflicting. One of the problems, they say, is that other substances in the diet may prevent the lysine being absorbed:

> . . . human studies on lysine inhibition of herpes seem to ignore factors which affect how well or how poorly lysine is absorbed from the food in the intestine into the bloodstream. The amount of sugar and fat present is very important, as is the amount of protein present in the stomach. These substances can inhibit the absorption of lysine. So, even though you may take lysine tablets, you may not absorb much if you take them with sugar (even fruit juice, for example), fat or protein. Taking lysine along with a regular meal of any kind, may, in fact *prevent* its absorption.

Which makes it almost impossible, one would think, to control your herpes by eating lysine-rich foods which are all high in protein and, in the case of milk, fat too.

As for lysine supplements: North and Crittenden say that 'thousands of people have reported that they get significant relief from their recurrent herpes by using lysine'. And they add: 'In a survey of over 4000 herpes victims, the only therapies which had any lasting benefit were lysine therapy and stress management.'

It's intriguing that these two methods should seem to be the most effective. Are they linked in some way? Could it be that lysine is simply a fancy placebo – that the people for whom it works are the ones who are convinced it's going to? Given the enormous difficulties facing lysine absorption, it's possible.

TACKLING HERPES THROUGH THE MIND

North and Crittenden implicitly acknowledge the possibility that lysine may sometimes work *via* the placebo effect. They devote a whole chapter of their book to the psychological approach to herpes, including the power of positive thinking and visualization techniques (see Chapter 11 on cancer). And, among their case histories, they include the story of Dana G, who 'tried lysine, but some people told her that it wouldn't really work, and it didn't . . . She tried listening to relaxation tapes for stress management but didn't see how that could affect a virus in her body. It didn't.' Then Dana joined a herpes support group. And there she met Jim, who told her that he'd shared her scepticism. But he went on: '. . . little by little I've started to feel more positive and even hopeful. In the group I've heard some success stories about ways to handle herpes. So, when I try them, like lysine or relaxing, I actually think that maybe they'll work, and they're beginning to!'

In many ways, the alternative treatment of herpes mirrors that of cancer. Much emphasis is put on diet and supplements but the feeling one gets is that these are just adjuncts and that what really determines success is the patient's attitude to his disease.

HOMOEOPATHY

There are a number of remedies for herpes including *nosodes*, the homoeopathic equivalent of vaccines. Nosodes are prepared from virus-infected tissue. (They don't contain any virus because they've been diluted so many times.) I can't tell you how effective they are, but as they appear to be quite safe there's no harm in trying them. Consult a medically qualified homoeopath for further details.

What if I don't have an infection?

So far I've assumed that if you have *vulvovaginitis* (the medical term for any discomfort in the genital area) you have an infection of some sort. But what do you do if the doctor takes a sample, and the lab report comes back negative – not once but several times? (One negative result, if you continue to have discomfort, is virtually meaningless, as any experienced doctor will tell you.) You know there's *something* wrong with you but where are the bacteria? What could be causing your symptoms?

I've already explained that psychological factors may be involved in recurrent herpes (they may have something to do with cystitis, too – see below). So is it so surprising that our emotions may affect our genital health, even when we haven't got an infection?

There is evidence for this. A report in the *Practitioner* in 1981 described ninety-two women who had vulvovaginitis but no evidence of infection. Most of them had already had drug treatment but it had proved useless. Nearly half of them had had their symptoms for more than two years, a quarter for more than five, and six for more than eight. They were all given psychological counselling.

During counselling it emerged that many of them had psychological problems. For example, quite a number felt resentful towards their partners – in one case the woman was angry because her husband was studying away from home while she worked to keep them both. Another woman had a boyfriend of whom her mother disapproved. A third was having problems settling down to the day-to-day responsibilities of married life: arranging repairs to the house, waiting around for the repair men to turn up, and so on.

The suggestion is that for these women a sore vagina was a subconscious excuse to avoid sex. And they didn't want sex because it might bring to the surface distressing emotions which they'd so far managed to keep buried. During counselling they were given the opportunity to explore their feelings – and 92 per cent of them reported that they'd been helped by the therapy. 'In many cases,' the author of the report, a psychiatric social worker, writes:

> the symptoms of vaginitis disappeared. The first step was to help the patient change her belief that she had an 'infection' to the understanding that she had a 'condition'. This led to her realizing that the condition was caused by an expression of feelings which, for various reasons, she had not wanted to acknowledge previously.
>
> As the vaginitis is a 'defence', protecting the patient from acknowledged feelings, she needs to be encouraged gently to seek these for herself.
>
> Practical steps, such as keeping a diary to note when symptoms are bad, help the patient to link for herself strong emotional reactions with specific situations and bouts of vaginitis. Patients usually recognize at some point a sense of 'choice'. Either they continue as before, or they sense they can let the symptoms go. To quote one patient who recorded her feelings at the end of counselling: 'Now I know I'm so strong, no way will it (the vaginitis) come back.'

So if you've been told you've no infection and you suspect some psychological distress, try keeping your own diary. If your suspicions are confirmed, you may benefit from counselling. You may not need many sessions: the patients described in the *Practitioner* report had, on average, only four each.

CYSTITIS

Cystitis is so common – it's estimated that nearly one in two of us has had it at some time – that its symptoms are all too familiar.
1. Needing to pass water frequently and *at once* – yet when we get to the lavatory, often only a trickle comes out.
2. A burning sensation during urination.
3. Aches and pains in the lower tummy and groin – and possibly the back, too.
4. Feeling feverish and sick.
5. Perhaps the most frightening symptom of all: the blood we may see in our urine and on the toilet paper when we wipe ourselves.

The word cystitis means bladder inflammation. Our bladders and urethras become inflamed and irritable. Even small quantities of urine irritate the bladder's sensitive lining – the more so because, when we have cystitis, our urine becomes more acid than normal. So the bladder keeps sending us urgent messages to empty it. It's the acid urine flowing over the sore urethra that produces the burning pain. If our cystitis is particularly severe, or we've had previous attacks which have scarred the urethra, it may start to bleed, too.

One attack is bad enough. But for many of us that first bout is followed by lots more. Each time we're stricken, the doctor gives us antibiotics and the problem clears up. After our first attack we probably breathed a sigh of relief and gave praise to the wonders of medical science. But the old hands among us know that antibiotics are no protection against subsequent attacks.

What causes cystitis?

Sometimes cystitis is caused by bacteria; it may also be due to a Candida infection. If you've been treated with antibiotics for one attack, a second – due to Candida – may follow because the drugs have wiped out the 'good' bacteria in the intestine: the Candida makes the most of this opportunity to multiply and, if given the chance, to find its way into your urethra.

In up to half of cystitis cases, however, no bugs are found. This may be because the urine did contain some bacteria but not enough, in the pathologist's view, to have produced symptoms. Of course it could be – as many specialists recognize – that there were lots of bacteria there to start with but they died off before they could be grown in the laboratory. Nevertheless there's no doubt that you can have cystitis without having an infection.

Apart from bacteria or Candida, what can start cystitis off? At the beginning of this chapter I explained how our whole genital area – and not just our vaginas – may come in for a certain amount of bruising during sexual intercourse. For some women, that bruising is all it takes. Others have found that certain foods and drink, or even standing in the cold, can set off an attack. And, according to a report in the *Lancet* in 1984, soap is a common culprit. For some of us, these triggers on their own may not be enough to cause cystitis. But add a few bacteria – those which may have found their way out of our anus and onto our perineum after a bowel movement or during sex – and you have the ideal recipe for an infected bladder.

The popular self-help approach to cystitis

Many sufferers have reason to be grateful to Angela Kilmartin, herself a former cystitis victim, who's done so much to spread the self-help message.[6] But for those readers who haven't yet come across her methods, I'll mention them briefly here.

COPING WITH ATTACKS

Avoid antibiotics if you can. Apart from possible side effects such as diarrhoea and nausea, antibiotics don't do you that much good. If you have an infection they'll clear it for the time being; but they won't stop it coming back. They may also, as I've explained, increase the likelihood of vaginal thrush or of subsequent cystitis due to Candida. And, of course, if your cystitis isn't caused by bacteria, antibiotics won't help.

This isn't to say you'll always be able to get by without them. If self-help measures don't do the trick – and pretty fast – you do need medical treatment. The danger is that, once bacteria have got into your bladder, the infection may spread to your kidneys, with serious consequences.

But provided you start right at the beginning of an attack, you may be able to abort it by doing nothing more than drinking lots of water – laced every so often with sodium bicarbonate (baking soda) to alkalinize the urine. Start by drinking one pint of water plus one teaspoon of sodium bicarbonate. Then every twenty minutes for the next three hours drink half a pint of water or, if you really can't stand the taste of plain water, very dilute fruit squash. On the hour, every hour, add a teaspoon of sodium bicarbonate to your drink.

Instead of bicarbonate, you can also use a mixture of potassium citrate which your chemist can prepare for you. But many women just can't drink the Mist. Pot. Cit. (as it's known) because it tastes so awful. Unfortunately, not everyone likes sodium bicarbonate either, because it can give you wind. There's a fairly new proprietary product, called Cymalon, which works in exactly the same way, doesn't cause wind and which tastes slightly fruity.

As the urine gets more alkaline and you begin to produce more of it (because you're drinking more), the symptoms should gradually go away. If they're not substantially better within 24 hours – or if you start to feel more ill in the meantime – get to your doctor as soon as possible because the chances are that you do have an infection that only antibiotics can cure.

PREVENTING ATTACKS

All the preventive measures I mentioned in the thrush

section (see pages 117–19) also help you to avoid cystitis. Many sufferers have found that personal hygiene before and after sex is most important. You should wash – preferably without using soap which may irritate the vulva and urethra – before and after sex. Angela Kilmartin recommends pouring cool water over the vulva both to wash it and to soothe bruised tissues. And always try to urinate after intercouse to flush out any bacteria that may be left lurking in the urethra. As one former sufferer commented:

'Soon after I started having sex, I also started having cystitis. Each time I needed antibiotics. Then I heard about Angela Kilmartin's advice. I've followed it religiously and I haven't had cystitis for nearly ten years.'

If your attacks are triggered by some foods or drinks, avoid them or limit your intake. Coffee, tea, alcohol, spicy foods and citrus fruits have all been blamed for cystitis. Sometimes, though, you may be able to include them in your diet if you drink lots of water soon afterwards to wash out your bladder. This applies particularly to coffee and alcohol, which tend to make you want to urinate more often – with the risk that your urine will become more concentrated and irritant unless you replace the fluid you've excreted.

Alternative medical treatment for recurrent cystitis

Orthodox medicine has nothing specific to offer the chronic sufferer. At best, all a doctor can do is recommend that you read Kilmartin's books and step in with antibiotics if the self-help approach fails. Alternative practitioners are also great believers in self-help. But they may suggest other treatment as well.

DIET

Sensitivity to foods

I've already mentioned that this is one of the causes of cystitis, and sometimes it's easy for you to know which foods are responsible for your problems. But this isn't always so and you may need professional help to pin down the culprits. Having nailed them, you'll then need advice on diet. Or it may be possible for you to be desensitized so that you can eat them without getting cystitis.

There are two desensitization methods. The first involves the injection, just beneath the surface of the skin, of one-in-five serial salt-water dilutions of the food. That is, the first injection will be a one-in-five dilution of the neat preparation, the second a one-in-five dilution of the first, and so on. At first your skin will produce an allergic reaction in the form of a weal. (The odd thing about this technique, and one which makes conventional doctors dismiss it, is that a *neat* preparation of the same food often doesn't produce any reaction at all! So orthodox medicine doesn't recognize food sensitivity as an allergy problem. And the alternative doctors – clinical ecologists – who practise desensitization admit they don't know how it works, either.) Eventually, a *neutralizing* dose, to which the skin does not react, will be found. This dose may also 'switch off' your cystitis.

The other method is based on the same principle but, instead of an injection, you'll be given drops to put under the tongue.

Neither method gives permanent relief so many practitioners prefer the drops, which the patient can use whenever she needs them. If the food to which you are sensitive forms a regular part of your diet you'll have to take drops at least three times a day.

Desensitization is by no means the answer to food sensitivity because it doesn't work for everyone – the more sensitive you are the lower the chances of success. But it can be useful. It may also help women who are sensitive to certain chemicals.

Other effects of food

Dairy products are said to encourage cystitis in some cases. A herbalist explained: 'The whole of the inside of the body, including the urinary tract, is lined with mucus membrane and it's well known that a lot of milk or dairy produce brings mucus membranes into a 'catarrhal' condition, where they secrete excess amounts of mucus. They're then prone to bacterial infection.' This belief crops up time and again in alternative medicine so there may well be something in it. Reduce your intake of dairy produce and see what happens.

Vitamins and minerals

You may think I've already said enough about the ways these may help us fight infections. Obviously, in cystitis, the same principles apply. Vitamin C, at a dose of one to three grams a day, is said to be particularly useful in urinary tract infections. One reason could be that it acidifies the urine and so makes it more difficult for bugs to grow (making the urine more alkaline – as happens if you take sodium bicarbonate – has the same effect, of course).

US nutrition specialists Drs Emanuel Cheraskin, W. Marshall Ringsdorf and Emily Sisley report that three grams of vitamin C a day has been shown to relieve symptoms in two to four days.[7] And they add: 'Those patients who reported any recurrence of symptoms were always relieved by a repeat course of ascorbic acid [vitamin C].'

Used in this way, vitamin C is merely a first-aid measure – it does not prevent recurrence. Taken regularly, however, many alternative practitioners believe it stimulates the immune system – and there's lots of evidence to suggest they could be right. So, again, worth a try, particularly if you think your diet may be deficient in vitamin C – if you seldom eat citrus fruits or drink fresh fruit juice, for example.

HOMOEOPATHY

Cantharis is the traditional homoeopathic remedy for cystitis and there is a little *scientific*, as opposed to anecdotal, evidence in its favour. This comes from a controlled clinical trial. 'The cantharis,' explained a medically qualified homoeopath who keeps close tabs on research, 'was statistically better than placebo in relieving cystitis in a very small number of patients. But the trial needs repeating.' One significant result from a small sample of patients is hardly likely to set the orthodox medical world alight.

REFLEX ZONE THERAPY

This has helped some women, including Felicity Peake, who wrote in the *Daily Telegraph* in 1983:

> For many years I have suffered from cystitis. In the past two-and-a-half years this had become an almost chronic condition, mitigated only by course after course of antibiotics and visits to hospitals arranged by different specialists.
>
> I was in despair of ever finding a cure when I heard of zone therapy . . . I attended a leading practitioner . . . that was six months ago. Since then I have taken no antibiotics. Two months ago, after laboratory tests, my GP pronounced me free of cystitis.

CYSTITIS AND THE MIND

If you have recurrent cystitis that nothing seems to shift, you may benefit from some form of psychotherapy. I've already explained how vaginal discomfort may respond to counselling, and elsewhere in the book I discuss how some migraines, cancers and menstrual problems are thought to originate, at least partly, from mental dis-ease.

A psychotherapist working with groups of women with cystitis and other health problems told me: 'I think a person can legitimately make themselves sick as an expression of a whole-life situation.' In some cases, the cystitis seems to be the only way a woman can express the unhappiness, the *emotional* pain, that she's felt – but not been allowed to experience fully – either earlier in her life or in the present.

I've got someone with cystitis who's been treated for over a year [this psychotherapist continued]. She's been going back and back to the people who are supposed to have the answers [the doctors], to make the pain go away. And this has been her whole approach to her life: the pain has always been denied. Everyone has always tried to make her pain go away. She's terrified of it . . . she doesn't really think she has any right to have suffered. And I'm saying to her: maybe you really need this pain. As painful as it is, I'd say her *existential* statement is that 'no one's going to take *this* pain away . . .' The thing that's coming out very strongly is that when she's been suffering emotionally in her life someone has always scurried in to say, 'There, there.' Rather than being able to tolerate her unhappiness and her pain, they've tried to make it go away.

That's where we got to yesterday: nobody had been able to make *this* pain go away. She could feel just that little bit of some kind of validation – some kind of satisfaction.

This woman 'hasn't been deprived, she hasn't been beaten,' the psychotherapist explained. 'But somewhere she's not been allowed the suffering we all have. Everybody suffers; children suffer. They have pain; it's real but part of the fiction of our modern culture is that somehow you can make it all go away.'

Another cystitis victim had definitely suffered as a child. Her father had died when she was quite small but while he was dying she and her mother had emigrated. 'Her mother couldn't deal with her own pain,' explained the psychotherapist. So the father's death was glossed over and she never had the chance to work through her grief. Her cystitis is now the way she allows herself to suffer, the psychotherapist believes. 'But she hasn't done the real suffering.'

The aim of psychotherapy is to get the woman to recognize and explore her painful feelings and to work through them. Then she may find that she no longer 'needs' her cystitis. And the results? 'It's not something with quick answers and it doesn't promise cure . . . At the same time . . . yes, people do get better over a long period of time . . . But it's a question to me not of feeling better only, but of feeling *more* . . .'

6. Contraception

Our modern, high-tech methods of contraception have proved less than ideal. Effective contraceptives they may be, but they have a number of side effects. Some of these are extremely serious. Some can be fatal. Fortunately they are also rare. Other side effects are not exactly dangerous. But they are certainly distressing – and quite common.

THE COMBINED ORAL CONTRACEPTIVE (THE 'PILL')

Major side effects

The combined Pill, which contains synthetic forms of the hormones oestrogen and progesterone (progestogens), is known to make the blood clot more easily. These clots (thromboses) may block blood vessels in the brain, heart or lungs. This can kill a woman or severely disable her.

Deaths from these, and other, circulatory problems are rare, statistically – the now-famous 1981 report from the Royal College of General Practitioners found that out of the more than 46,000 women studied, of whom half were on the Pill, only 65 had died from circulatory diseases. On the other hand, of these 65, Pill-users outnumbered non-users by more than five to one. Thus, though if you take the Pill you're extremely unlikely to die prematurely, the risk that you might is certainly increased.

The Pill has also been implicated in cancer – of both the breast and the uterine cervix (see also Chapter 11). The association between Pill-taking and breast cancer remains controversial: the studies that show an increased risk are vastly outnumbered by those that don't. (And some doctors point out that Pill-taking appears to *protect* women against ovarian cancer which, though rare, is very hard to treat.) In the case of cervical cancer, though there does seem to be a definite link with the Pill, some researchers believe the Pill itself is not to blame.

It's known that barrier contraceptives protect the cervix against cancer by preventing the man's penis from coming into contact with it. Though the idea that intercourse can be carcinogenic (cancer-producing) may appear somewhat bizarre, there's quite a bit of evidence to support it (see Chapter 11). Obviously, if you're on the Pill you're hardly going to bother with barrier methods as well, so your cervix is more vulnerable to cancer.

Though it's still far from clear whether the Pill is ever *directly* responsible for cancer, the possibility is there, nevertheless. We can't ignore it. This, and the known link with circulatory diseases, have cast a shadow over what once seemed a well-nigh perfect contraceptive. But many doctors argue that for some women it's still better to take the Pill than risk pregnancy. They have a point. An unplanned pregnancy can be fraught with all sorts of psychological and social problems. And even a planned one carries some risks.

This argument, however, takes no account of the fact that other forms of contraception are not necessarily that much less efficient than the Pill. Because the Pill is, in theory, almost 100 per cent effective, it's often assumed that it's the only thing which stands between us and the drudgery of numerous, unwanted babies. But this is a myth. Small families have been the norm in this country since the 1920s – long before the advent of the Pill.

Minor side effects

In *The Pill*,[1] Dr John Guillebaud lists seventeen common side effects associated with the Pill, including lack of periods and an increase in breast size (both of which some women might think an advantage!), breakthrough bleeding, cystitis, depression and migraine.

Some doctors don't believe that depression has anything to do with the Pill. It is, after all, a very common complaint, especially among women. But there is evidence that some women taking the Pill have reduced levels of vitamin B_6 and feel much better if they're given supplements of this vitamin. There's a sound scientific explanation behind this: vitamin B_6 is tied up with the production of certain substances in the brain which can affect our mood. However, it's only fair to add that not all women who are depressed while on the Pill have low levels of vitamin B_6.

If you suffer from migraine, you may find your headaches are worse on the Pill. Some women get migraines for the first time (see also Chapter 13). This, again, is believed to be due to changes in brain chemistry.

Side effects and the newer types of Pill

The Pill causes all sorts of alterations in the way our body chemicals go about their normal business. So it's hardly surprising that we should experience some problems. Newer Pills aimed at reducing these side effects have lower doses of hormones, but it's too soon to tell whether they'll cause less trouble in the long run. Some doctors believe they will, but others claim that any powerful hormone is bound to upset our metabolism – and our health.

THE PROGESTOGEN-ONLY PILL (POP OR MINIPILL)

The POP is also fairly new so, again, less is known about its side effects. Researchers are not prepared to say that the POP is safer than the combined Pill, though they think it may be because it seems to have less effect on body chemistry. But, as with the newer types of combined Pill, this belief is based mostly on educated guesswork. Perhaps the situation is best summed up by Dr Guillebaud in the second edition of *The Pill*. He writes: '. . . the picture is confused at present. All one can say is that the relative advantages of the POP over the lowest dose available combined Pills may not be as great as was once thought . . .'

Already, though, the POP has been shown to have two major drawbacks. One is that it just isn't such a good contraceptive as the combined Pill, particularly in younger women. The other is that it often messes up a woman's periods. Sometimes periods may stop altogether; or they may come too often, be unpredictable and/or too heavy. Dr Guillebaud notes this in his book but adds that 'many women adjust very well after a month or two to their new bleeding pattern'. Yet in a recent large study of women using the POP, over half the women who stopped taking it did so because of period problems. Perhaps if you've turned to the POP because other methods haven't suited you, you might be prepared to put up with periods here, there and everywhere. But for most women, irregular and/or heavy periods are tiresome, to say the least, and not something most of us would tolerate given the choice.

CONTRACEPTIVE PILLS: NEW EVIDENCE AND CHANGING OPINIONS

In her book *The Bitter Pill*,[2] Dr Ellen Grant, one of the first researchers to study the Pill in this country, presents evidence which on the face of it damns the contraceptive Pill beyond hope of redemption. She blames it not only for cancer, thrombosis and migraine, but also for food allergies, and hyperactive and dyslexic children.

Dr Grant is a clinical ecologist (see Chapter 2) and so has a particular interest in they way trace elements can affect our bodies. She believes that many of the Pill's side effects can be linked with the high levels of copper found in Pill-users' bodies. Both migraine and heart disease, for example, may be related to excess copper and there's some evidence that it also may be to blame for postnatal depression.

Dr Grant's views are not shared by many orthodox doctors. And some of her scientific arguments – especially where she tries to beat the orthodox at their own game – are so tortuous as to be incomprehensible However, much of her book is well argued and convincing. It should, perhaps, be taken seriously. Dr Grant is one of a growing band of doctors – clinical ecologists and specialists in nutritional medicine – who believe that we interfere with our bodies at our peril.

Interestingly – and perhaps significantly – even doctors with more orthodox attitudes haven't dismissed Dr Grant's evidence out of hand. In the doctors' newspaper, *General Practitioner*, Dr David Delvin, while criticizing Dr Grant for going 'over the top', commented: '. . . there's no doubt that some of the warnings [Dr Grant] gave years ago about possible Pill side effects have turned out to have at least a degree of truth in them. Only a fool would deny that there's a possibility that one of two of the dire predictions she makes in this book might just turn out to be right.'

There's no doubt that most doctors err on the side of caution when prescribing the Pill. Many women who may be especially at risk of one of the more serious complications are warned off it. And those who do take it are advised to have regular blood-pressure checks and cervical smears and to examine their breasts every month for possible danger signs. Sensible though these measures are, they hardly inspire confidence.

A few doctors indeed share Dr Grant's belief that the Pill is too dangerous to prescribe under any circumstances. One eminent (male) gynaecologist told me: 'I have always believed that Ellen Grant was right. If I were a woman I wouldn't stay on the Pill for very long. The evidence against it has been accumulating.' He added that he'd advise women to use barrier methods of contraception instead. For more about the reasons why, see below.

INTRAUTERINE DEVICES (IUDS OR COILS)

Unlike the Pill, IUDs don't seem to upset our normal body chemistry in any obvious way. However, high levels of copper have been found in the hair of women using the copper-containing types of IUD. Though these levels aren't as high as those measured in women on the Pill, they may reflect some sort of metabolic upset. In our bodies copper, and another trace metal, zinc, work against each other. Zinc is vital for the action of many enzymes, so the balance between these two elements may be crucial. Exactly what the significance is of high copper in IUD-users is so far not clear, though.

IUDs don't suit all women. They don't give such good protection against pregnancy: it's been calculated that if 100 women use an IUD for a year, up to four of them will become pregnant. That's too high a risk for some pople. Others may be put off because fitting the device can be very painful, though this seems to be less of a problem with the newer types of IUD.

An IUD may also be expelled – sometimes without a woman realizing – so she is then at risk of pregnancy. If she conceives with an IUD in place then she's more likely to have an ectopic pregnancy (where the embryo grows in one of the fallopian tubes) or to miscarry. IUD users complain more often of heavy periods and period pains than women who use some other form of contraception.

But perhaps the most serious problem is that an IUD can make you permanently sterile, particularly if you're young and have never had a baby. This is because women with IUDs are at increased risk of developing pelvic inflammatory disease, which can result in irreparable damage to the fallopian tubes so that the woman can no longer conceive. Two articles published in the *New England Journal of Medicine* in 1985 revealed that the risk of infertility was up to seven times more likely among IUD users than non-users. Women who ran the highest risk were those using the Dalkon Shield, which is, fortunately, no longer available (though there's currently concern that some women, unknowingly, may still have Shields that were fitted years ago). But even women wearing the safer copper-containing devices were still up to one and a half times as likely to be infertile as women who had never had an IUD.

A new type of IUD now being tested is said to be safer than existing ones. It contains a hormone – the same one as is used in several brands of combined Pill – which, it is thought, protects the user against pelvic infection. However, an earlier hormone-containing IUD was withdrawn from the market in the late 1970s because it appeared to increase the risk of an ectopic pregnancy. Some researchers believe the new coil will not have the same problems, but are they right?

VAGINAL RINGS, HORMONE IMPLANTS, SPRAYS AND VACCINATIONS

None of these are yet available to the general public, though hormone-impregnated vaginal rings are now nearing the end of their testing period. The ring seems relatively simple to use: a woman can insert it herself and it can be left in place at the top of the vagina for up to three months. It's probably safer than the combined Pill as the hormone only seems to affect the uterus and cervix and not the entire body. But the failure rate is nearly 3 per cent and the ring may also disrupt a woman's menstrual cycle.

Implants are less appealing. Though they offer excellent protection against pregnancy, they have to be inserted under the skin by means of a small cut done under local anaesthetic. And again, irregular periods may prove a problem for some women.

There have been promising reports of a new nasal spray which contains a synthetic hormone which prevents ovulation. This appears to be effective and easily reversible – the hormone stops working minutes after you've taken it. Because of this, the hormone in the spray may turn out to be safer than those in Pills because the latter remain in the body for a considerable time. Whether or not this proves to be the case, there's no getting away from the fact that the spray does interfere with our normal hormones, albeit briefly and reversibly. If the thought worries you, then you're unlikely to want to use the spray if and when it becomes available.

Anti-fertility vaccines, which scientists are now testing in animals, are also said to be reversible. I find it somewhat alarming, though, that one of the vaccines they're investigating is an anti-sperm antibody – a substance that inactivates sperm. It's well known that both men and women sometimes produce their own natural antibodies to sperm and are permanently sterile as a result. And, indeed, one leading researcher was quoted in the *Daily Telegraph* in August 1985 as saying that 'at present' he could not 'promise that any vaccine could be made reversible'.[3]

STERILIZATION: THE ULTIMATE CONTRACEPTIVE?

Sterilization is, of course, effective and, with modern techniques, relatively painless and free from side effects. However, there is some evidence – as yet controversial – that the operation can interfere with the blood supply to the ovaries and so with the production of hormones, leading to excessively heavy periods.

These days some sterilized women can have their fertility restored by a further operation to rejoin the cut fallopian tubes. All the same, success is by no means guaranteed, so sterilization remains very much a 'last resort' method of contraception.

VASECTOMY AND THE MALE 'PILL'

Though this is a book about women, I should perhaps say a little about male contraception. (The sheath I'll discuss in more detail later on.) Contraception is a shared affair, after all. Vasectomy is still quite popular and earlier worries that it might increase a man's risk of heart disease now seem to have been unfounded. But vasectomy, like female sterilization, is still essentially an irreversible procedure. Reversal operations are done by a few surgeons in this country and some claim quite good success rates. But results are unpredictable and there's no way of knowing in advance which men are going to be the lucky ones.

Researchers are still beavering away at one of contraception's most tricky problems: a Pill for men. So far they haven't come up with anything that works *and* is free from obvious side effects. The male reproductive system is much less easy to manipulate than the female one. Several apparently promising methods have had to be abandoned because they either caused permanent sterility or ruined a man's sex drive.

BARRIER METHODS: THE DIAPHRAGM, SHEATH, CUSTOMIZED CAP, AND THE SPONGE

I sometimes wonder why researchers spend all this time and effort on developing new methods of contraception when the sheath is such a good one. Some men say they don't like it because it cuts down on their pleasure during intercourse or, as a male friend of mine once put it, 'It's like having a bath with your wellies on.' Other men say it increases their enjoyment because it allows them to 'hold back' longer and this adds to their partner's pleasure.

But the sheath has other drawbacks too, which, though not serious, can put a damper on sex for some people. One couple I know used the sheath effectively and would have been quite happy to continue doing so were it not for two of its inescapable properties: 'It smells so awful,' they said, 'and when you put it down the loo afterwards, it always floats.'

But perhaps the main objection to the sheath is that it is

not, or so it is usually said, a very efficient method. In fact, used properly, sheaths very rarely break. If a sheath does come to grief it's often because it's been punctured on a woman's long fingernails! However, even if a sheath does let you down, you should still be protected against pregnancy, provided you also use a spermicide. Alternatively, you can buy one of the newer types of sheath which are made with their own spermicide incorporated.

Research seems to indicate that if you're set on making the sheath work for you, then it will. 'Several studies have shown that couples who were determined not to have another pregnancy have had failure rates of less than one for every hundred couples using them for a year,' report Drs Peter Bromwich and Tony Parsons in their book *Contraception: the Facts*.[4]

Evidence suggests that, used as per instructions, the diaphragm can be almost as effective as the sheath, even though estimates of failure rates vary wildly – anything from 2 to 15 per cent. The diaphragm can be quite a hassle to use and it is suspected that the failure rates get bumped up by those women who don't put them in properly or simply forget, in the heat of the moment, that they aren't wearing them! There's no doubt that more women would use the diaphragm if the method were simpler and less messy – if they could just pop it in and forget about it. A device is now being tested which seems to fit the bill. It's called the Contracap and is a custom-made cap which fits over a woman's cervix.

Before a woman is fitted with a Contracap, a plaster cast impression is made of her cervix. This is then used as a mould for the actual cap, which is made of a rubber-like material. Unlike the diaphragm, the Contracap has no spring to hold it in place, so the match has to be absolutely perfect. The really clever thing about this cap, though, is that it has a one-way valve – which is designed to keep sperm out but allows the passage of cervical secretions and menstrual blood. In theory, this means that, once in, it needn't be removed for up to a year. The other plus point about it is that it's intended to be used without any spermicide.

A prototype of this cap was abandoned because too many women using it became pregnant. The redesigned version is now being tested internationally – in this country at the Margaret Pyke Centre in London. If successful, it could solve quite a few of our contraceptive dilemmas. Walli Bounds, who is in charge of the London trial, has said of the Contracap: 'It is potentially very exciting. If it works it will provide a safe, non-invasive, no-mess method.' Unfortunately, very recent results suggest that the Contracap is still very unreliable and that further research is needed.

Quite recently, a new type of barrier contraceptive appeared on the market. This is the sponge, sold under the name 'Today'. The sponge is said to be very popular in the United States, where it's been on sale for some time. But it, too, has its drawbacks. It's expensive and not all that easy to insert – though experienced diaphragm-users will probably find it a cinch.

More seriously, it isn't a very good contraceptive: in trials conducted at the Margaret Pyke, nearly one in four women became pregnant. For that reason, the British Family Planning Association recommends it only for women who are spacing their families – presumably because they won't mind *too* much if they conceive – or for women who aren't all that fertile. Older women and breastfeeding mothers come into the latter category. Breastfeeding actually can be a very good form of contraception on its own, but I'll explain more about that later in this chapter.

POST-COITAL (MORNING-AFTER) CONTRACEPTION

Many experts believe this form of contraception is a useful back-up when barrier methods fail. Post-coital contraception is now becoming more widely available in this country – either from family planning clinics or general practitioners.

The idea behind it is to prevent the implantation of the fertilized egg. Because this form of contraception is used *after* sex, it can't stop fertilization. Some people therefore regard it as a form of early abortion, though, legally speaking, it isn't.

A woman who believes she may have conceived is offered two choices. She can either have an IUD fitted or take two combined Pills twelve hours apart. The first Pill must be taken within seventy-two hours though an IUD can be inserted up to five days after sex and still be effective.

Though post-coital contraception seems an efficient way of dealing with the odd accident, occasionally it doesn't work and a woman will become pregnant. A foetus and an IUD make poor partners – if the coil is removed it can trigger a miscarriage but if it's left in place, the woman is quite likely to miscarry anyway. As for the hormones in the Pill – so far it seems they haven't been shown to have any adverse effects on the baby, but neither have they been proved safe. As Dr Grant points out in *The Bitter Pill*, some researchers believe that female hormones in the Pill are capable of causing birth defects. Certainly, as we have seen, women using the Pill as their regular form of contraception are advised by many doctors to stop taking it at least three months before they try for a baby.

So if post-coital contraception fails, probably the best thing to do is to have an abortion.

CONTRACEPTION IN PERSPECTIVE: IS THERE A SOLUTION?

There are now definite worries about the Pill, which newer formulations haven't managed to dispel. Future hormonal methods of contraception are, or so it seems to me, subject to at least some of the same doubts. IUDs may well be satisfactory for some women – but certainly not for those who are planning a family. A barrier method, used assiduously, does give pretty good protection against pregnancy and is free from short- and long-term side effects. But existing barrier methods have considerable aesthetic shortcomings.

The Contracap may provide an answer to these but a sufficiently reliable version has still to be designed.

So where do we go from here?

NATURAL FAMILY PLANNING

Twenty years ago the whole idea of natural family planning was a bad joke. The term was synonymous with the rhythm method and we all knew how effective that was! Understandably, professional family planners steered well clear of it – except when advising couples who, for religious reasons, would consider no other method.

However, most people could see that the *principle* behind natural family planning was a good one. The idea is to have intercourse only at those times of the month when the woman is infertile – that is when there's no chance of an egg being around to meet up with a sperm. Both eggs and sperm have relatively short lives – twenty-four hours at most for the egg and up to five days for the sperm. Theoretically, fertilization is possible for a maximum of six days a month.

The trouble with the rhythm method was that it was a very crude way of calculating when this fertile period might occur and mistakes – pregnancies – inevitably happened. The method was crude because it was based on the *probability* of the egg being released on a certain day of the month but gave no guarantee in any one month that ovulation would, or had, taken place on schedule.

Let me explain this in more detail. First of all a woman must keep a record of her periods for six months or a year. Suppose her cycle is very regular and she menstruates exactly every twenty-eight days. It's known that ovulation occurs ten to sixteen days before the onset of the next period. So the first day that the egg might be released would be day twelve. Then subtract the length of time a sperm can survive – five days – and you can see that intercourse should be safe for the first week of the cycle.

Intercourse also shouldn't result in conception if the

couple wait until near the end of the cycle when the egg has died. Here, to be on the safe side, one has to assume that the egg was released only ten days before menstruation – on day eighteen. A day later it's dead and no amount of sperm can fertilize it. So from day nineteen to the end of the cycle are designated 'safe'.

By these calculations the couple can have unprotected intercourse for a mere sixteen days out of the twenty-eight. And for women with unpredictable cycles, the 'prohibited' times can be even longer. Take the example of a woman whose cycle length varies between twenty-five and thirty days. Her last 'safe' day at the beginning of the month must be calculated using the shortest possible cycle and her first safe day at the end of the month from the longest one. The answer? Unprotected intercourse is only safe up to day four and after day twenty. If her cycle happens to be a short one that means sex is possible for only nine days of it!

This is clearly unsatisfactory. Not only does it make for a limited sex life but it takes no account of the fact that a woman's cycle may occasionally be thrown out of kilter. Stress, illness, or even a holiday, may sometimes cause ovulation to be delayed so that it occurs later – in the so-called safe period.

So much for the rhythm, now more often called the calendar, method.

Improving the method: indicators of fertility

Fortunately, though, we've progressed. It's now possible to predict in any one month the likely day of ovulation. With the latest method, several different indicators of ovulation are used. One is the state of the cervical mucus, which a woman can test for herself simply by inserting her finger a short way into her vagina. During the first part of the cycle the mucus is sticky, opaque and relatively non-elastic. But, as ovulation approaches it changes: it becomes more copious and watery, shiny and almost transparent – and very stretchy.

The cervix not only produces a different sort of mucus at ovulation time. It also becomes softer and higher up in the vagina. The entrance to the cervix also opens up a little. Many women can easily find their cervix with a finger and, with a little practice, can use it to gauge when ovulation is about to occur. Once the egg has been released the entrance to the cervix closes down again and the cervix itself becomes harder and hangs lower in the vagina.

The other sign that ovulation has occurred is a rise in temperature that continues until a couple of days before the start of the next period. A woman will only notice this if she keeps a regular record of her temperature, taken first thing in the morning using a special thermometer with a large scale. (The temperature shift is too small to show up clearly on an ordinary clinical thermometer.) Each day's temperature is then plotted on graph paper designed for the purpose.

Using two or three of these indicators together, it's possible to predict accurately when ovulation is imminent and when it has occurred. In the first half of the cycle, the temperature gives no information about the likely day of ovulation and the other indicators must be used. The fertile period is said to begin as soon as a woman notices the presence of any mucus in her vagina or any change in the cervix itself.

Once this happens, a couple must abstain from intercourse – or use a barrier method – until the woman's temperature has gone up and stayed up for at least three days. Or, if they're using the mucus symptom, they must wait for four days after the last day on which fertile-type mucus was observed. For greatest reliability, these two signs should be used together and unprotected intercourse postponed until the later one. You can double-check your accuracy by feeling your cervix as well.

Proponents of natural family planning claim that this method is highly effective if couples follow the rules. In her book *A Manual of Natural Family Planning*,[5] Dr Anna Flynn, one of its pioneers, quotes a failure rate of just over one per cent. Other studies, though, have produced much higher failure rates – sometimes over 20 per cent. This, claims Dr Jonathan Drake, a London NFP teacher who, with his wife, has also written a book on the method,[6] is usually because the couples weren't given good enough training. 'The method effectiveness [that is, its success when all the rules are followed] is 97 to 99 per cent. There's no doubt about that. If you talk to people who have got pregnant . . . you discover that the majority knew they were taking a chance.'

But certainly, if you are to use the method confidently, let alone successfully, you need special instruction from a trained teacher. This is especially so if your periods are irregular, you're breastfeeding or approaching the menopause. Dr Flynn claims that natural family planning works just as well in all these situations, though you may need even more help to interpret the signs your body's giving you. Even so, the method is not the easiest to use – and this may partially account for its high failure rate in some trials. Many things can throw a spanner in the works: an infection can send the temperature up and so mask the rise that signals ovulation. A couple of drinks the previous evening can also give an abnormally high temperature reading. Vaginal infections and semen left in the vagina from a previous act of intercourse can make mucus signs harder to interpret. Stress may upset mucus patterns, too.

Dr Flynn believes all these difficulties can be overcome with correct instruction. But they do show just how complicated natural family planning is. Nevertheless there is now considerable interest in this form of birth control and those who practise it are enthusiastic. Dr Drake and his wife use it themselves, which is a pretty good advertisement. 'In principle,' he says, 'anyone can use it, though at this stage it's mainly people who *have* to use it because they've suffered untoward side effects from the Pill or IUD, who don't like using barrier methods and who are not yet of an age when sterilization is a possibility.'

Dr Drake has now taught the method to more than 200 women and couples and says that the only ones who find it difficult are those who are subfertile and so don't produce very much mucus or ovulate regularly.

Advantages and disadvantages

In Dr Drake's experience, most people opt to use barrier methods during the fertile phase. The method therefore seems to offer the best of both worlds: abstinence isn't necessary but barriers need only be used for part of the month. The first day on which unprotected intercourse starts getting risky is usually the sixth day of the cycle or perhaps the fourth day for women with unusually short cycles.

It's said, though, that as women become experienced in interpreting their mucus, they can have unprotected intercourse every other day from then on until the mucus first appears: this is so that 'left-over' semen doesn't mask any changes in mucus. (Dr Drake has found that it usually takes up to six months before a woman has this sort of confidence.) A barrier method must then be used until three days after the temperature rise that marks ovulation. However both Dr Drake and Dr Flynn advise against using a spermicide, as this can make the mucus signs more difficult to read. This of course poses an additional problem – you haven't got any failsafe if the barrier lets you down. If this happens at your most fertile time, there's a good chance you may get pregnant. And while you're learning the method, you probably won't have the confidence to abandon barriers for more than half your cycle. Yet you won't have that extra security of a spermicide. And even when you're experienced, you must still remember to take your temperature once a day. Mucus, according to Dr Flynn, must be checked several times a day.

Is it worth it? For those who would jump at the chance of using a barrier for only some of the month rather than all of it, or for couples who are prepared to abstain during the rather lengthy fertile period, it may be. You may also discover an unexpected bonus. Dr Flynn reports that 75 per cent of the couples using natural family planning said that it enhanced their relationship. Of course it could be that they had a good thing going to start with and the cooperation necessary for this form of birth control simply drew them even closer.

I spoke to two of Dr Drake's clients. As it happened, both

of them were pregnant – not, I hasten to add, because the method had failed! But the other side to the natural family planning story is that, because it helps predict ovulation, it can be used to help couples to conceive: both these women found that once they decided to get pregnant they did so quite quickly.

Catherine, who is thirty-one, used the method to prevent conception for about eighteen months. 'I was fed up with the alternatives,' she explains. However, she did use a diaphragm as well during the first two weeks of her cycles. She also had regular periods, which made her fertile time easy to predict. 'I was quite happy with the cap but it seemed ridiculous to use it all the time when it wasn't necessary. This method seems much more sensible. I found it fairly easy to learn but it does take a while before you're confident in it.'

The other woman, Sally, had only used natural family planning as a contraceptive for a couple of months before deciding to have a baby. But she feels that in the future she may go back to it. She has some reservations, though.'I think that if I was going to use it as a permanent method I would want to use some sort of barrier method for a longer time than Dr Drake thinks is necessary. And I probably wouldn't be happy with it if I had long or irregular cycles.'

Further streamlining – science gets in on the act

How nice it would be if there were a more accurate way of pinpointing ovulation – a test which a woman could use in her own home to warn her when her fertile time was starting. This would be a boon for all those couples who like the *idea* of natural family planning but who find it difficult to read the signs of fertility. And, as mucus testing would no longer be needed, the sheath or cap could be used with spermicide for added efficiency.

Scientists are now working on this one. By measuring a hormone known as luteinizing hormone it's already possible to predict when ovulation is close – and this is now being used in hospitals to help infertile couples conceive. But it doesn't give enough warning of impending ovulation to help couples *avoid* conception. However, a new test is being developed which will do just that. It is expected to be available over the counter within the next year or so. This test is designed to measure the changes in oestrogen and progesterone which occur in a woman's urine several days before ovulation.

A different sort of early-warning system has been developed by researchers at King's College Hospital in London.[7] This is a device which is strapped onto a finger and monitors the way the blood vessels expand and contract. Oestrogen and progesterone change the pattern of these oscillations and the researchers have been able to link the changes with the growth of the follicle – the pocket in the ovary which contains the egg. Further testing is still needed before the device is made available to the public but it does look promising.

Breastfeeding as a contraceptive

As I've already mentioned, it's possible to use natural family planning while you're breastfeeding even though you may not start having periods until you begin to wean your baby and you're unable to notice any particular change in your mucus. A good teacher, though, will be able to help you to predict when you're about to start ovulating again. Because this is quite a complicated subject, I won't go into it in any detail here. The important thing, though, is that if you feed your baby *on demand* and don't try to impose regular mealtimes on her, you'll be completely safe against pregnancy for some weeks.

Breastfeeding has proved to be a very efficient form of contraception in primitive societies where mothers often continue suckling their children for up to three years. And modern research suggests that it can work just as well in the affluent West.

The key thing, though, is that the baby must be exclusively breastfed, on demand, *day and night*. Research done by Dr Flynn and other workers shows that this sort of breastfeeding will stop a woman ovulating for six to eight months. However, since we usually start giving our babies solid foods at around the four-month mark, most of us won't enjoy such long-term protection. Nor, I suspect, are we prepared to tolerate too many night feeds for longer than is absolutely necessary! But perhaps just one feed at night plus a late evening and early morning one might be enough to swing the balance in our favour: the research also suggests that, provided a woman feeds her baby at least six times every twenty-four hours, she won't ovulate. And the results of a study done in Edinburgh showed that, on average, breastfeeding mothers don't ovulate until thirty-six weeks after their baby is born.[8] But this is only an average and you can't depend on it as a guide: you might be one of those women who ovulate much sooner than this.

For practical purposes a breastfeeding woman can assume she's infertile for the first ten weeks after her baby is born. After that she needs to be alert to signs that ovulation may be on the way. If you have just had a baby and would like to try this method, *don't* do so until you've obtained some sound advice from a professional NFP teacher.

No one is sure exactly how breastfeeding works as a contraceptive. What is certain, though, is that her baby's sucking in some way depresses a woman's levels of luteinizing hormone (LH), the chemical that triggers ovulation. Regular, frequent feeds thus ensure that there's never enough LH around for ovulation to occur.

THE FUTURE or IS CONTRACEPTION REALLY SUCH A PROBLEM?

I don't think contraception will be problematical in the future. Not because the scientists will have developed better and safer hormonal contraceptives – I don't believe that any hormonal contraceptive will ever be entirely safe. But I'm convinced that science will eventually come up with such good ways of keeping track of our own natural fertility that there'll be less need to design drugs and devices that interfere with it.

Maybe one or both of the two new tests I've discussed will make natural family planning more attractive to more people. If not, it's still unlikely to be the end of the matter. There's now so much interest in NFP that I'm sure researchers will keep trying until they've got the problem licked.

Even then, of course, barrier methods will still be needed – for some of the time, at least. Whether this prospect appeals or appals depends on your point of view. It's up to you to weigh up all the possible risks and benefits of the existing methods and those likely to be available a few years from now. Which is more important: convenience and the knowledge that you're very unlikely to get pregnant; or safety and a slightly increased chance that you might? Only *you* can make that decision, based on the way your life is now and your hopes for it in the future.

7. Pregnancy and Childbirth

In this chapter I'll be discussing some of the ways alternative medicine may help you when you're planning a family, pregnant or giving birth. In many ways the alternative approach, based as it is on gently helping nature take its course, is particularly suited to the birth process which, after all, isn't an illness but a normal part of many women's lives.

Of course, having a baby can still be quite risky – for some women. If you have diabetes, for example, or kidney disease, or have had a baby suffering from Rhesus disease (where the mother's blood is incompatible with the baby's and attacks it), you'll need extra-special orthodox medical care. This doesn't mean that you can't try some of the alternatives as well. But you should do so only with your doctor's approval.

In fact *any* woman who's pregnant – no matter how healthy she is – needs the back-up of the medical profession. Serious problems seldom crop up. But *if* they do, then you'll need the kind of the treatment that only a medical specialist can give. This could save your baby's life. And though the chances of a mother dying in childbirth are extremely remote, a few women, even today, owe their own lives to modern medical skills.

However, until fairly recently, medical intervention tended to be used not just in 'life or death' situations but, in many hospitals, almost as a matter of routine. This was based on the assumption that, at worst, orthodox medical methods couldn't do any harm, and that they might reduce even the slight risk associated with a normal pregnancy and labour. That was enough, some doctors felt, to justify their use. How the women felt about it all didn't really enter into the equation.

In the last few years, though, women – and many of their doctors – have been questioning the wisdom of this approach. They're realizing that a woman's experience of childbirth – whether she sees it as a positive event and whether she feels in control of what's happening – can affect her ability to cope with the discomforts of pregnancy and labour, and to bond with her baby when it's born. A faultlessly managed high-tech labour, where her efforts are made to seem less important that the sophisticated workings of medical machinery, may sap her confidence as a woman and mother. Alternative medicine gives her the chance to reclaim some control. It also has some remedies for one or two of the more serious complications of pregnancy and labour (I'll be mentioning these later in the chapter). But it's really geared to the prevention and cure of chronic conditions, rather than to the treatment of acute ones. So in a full-blown obstetric crisis, alternative practitioners usually, very wisely, take a back seat.

CAN YOU PLAN FOR A HEALTHY BABY?

Recently, we've seen an increasing emphasis on the idea that producing a healthy baby isn't just a matter of luck. Many people now believe that our lifestyles, both before and after we conceive, may influence our babies' health; that we should eat sensibly and avoid, as far as possible, anything that might harm the foetus, such as drugs, cigarette smoke, alcohol, and environmental pollutants.

The most risky time for a foetus is in those first few weeks after conception. If any substance vital for normal development is lacking then, irreparable damage could result. A toxic chemical, like the drug thalidomide, for example, could have a similar effect. The results of this particular drug, which, at the time, was specifically recommended for pregnant women, so shocked doctors that they're now extremely cautious about prescribing any medicines at all in pregnancy.

What things are dangerous?

In 1983 the *New England Journal of Medicine* made an attempt to put some of these worries in perspective – in a lengthy review written by two acknowledged experts in the field. They wrote that, although many substances are suspected of causing congenital abnormalities, for most of them proper evidence is lacking. Out of a list of thirty-eight environmental 'suspects' which includes the heavy metals lead, cadmium and mercury, food additives, alcohol, cigarettes, coffee and organic solvents, only mercury and excessive amounts of alcohol have been shown to cause foetal deformities. Among the drugs – now that thalidomide is no longer available – it is really only anticonvulsants, anti-coagulants and some types of anti-cancer drugs for which the possible link with birth defects is at all convincing. Even Debendox, the drug prescribed for morning sickness and claimed by many to have led to the birth of deformed children, has not been shown convincingly to have harmful effects.

But doubts still remain. Not just about drugs like Debendox but about the many other possible teratogens (substances capable of causing birth defects) in our environment. And the authors of the article concede that, as far as the unborn child is concerned, it's impossible (and always will be) to be certain that *anything* in the environment is entirely safe.

Of course, foetal deformities are only one end of the spectrum. Toxic chemicals may have other effects. They may kill a baby in the womb. Or they may interfere with its growth so that it's born perfectly formed but underweight. These low birthweight babies tend to have more than their fair share of health problems. Or a baby may be born prematurely – and premature babies, too, face extra risks. There's fairly good evidence that the drug heroin, for example, can lead to both stillbirths and low birthweight babies. The journal also cites research which shows that heavy coffee drinkers may be more likely to have small babies.

Smoking and drinking

But the real hazards, as far as the medical profession is concerned, are smoking and drinking. Women are usually urged to give up both during pregnancy.

There's pretty good evidence that heavy smoking may cause harm during pregnancy. So far there's little suggestion than it can lead to congenital abnormalities; but it does increase a woman's risk of giving birth to a low birthweight baby. It *may* also increase her risks of miscarriage, and it's been estimated that a pregnant woman who smokes heavily is more than twice as likely as a non-smoker to lose her baby at or near birth. However, it's far from certain whether it is the smoking itself, or something else about women who smoke, which is the key factor here.

Oddly enough, for you'd think by now that there could be no doubt that drinking during pregnancy should be taboo, there's still considerable controversy about the dangers of alcohol. The *New England Journal* article mentioned above concludes that only women who drink 'relatively' large amounts of alcohol during pregnancy, or who are particularly sensitive to its effects, are at risk of giving birth to small or deformed babies.

Since that article was published, several other studies have appeared. But the results are still conflicting. One, from a group of doctors at the Charing Cross Hospital, London, found an association between the amount a woman drank and her chances of having a low birthweight baby.[1] But other researchers have criticized this study on a number of grounds. And, to muddy the waters even further, a survey of over 1200 pregnant women published in 1984 showed that even if a woman drank every day her baby was no more at risk than if she were teetotal. In fact the drinkers on average produced heavier babies than the non-drinkers![2]

Conclusion? One leading researcher in the field puts it like this: 'There is fairly good evidence that there is a thing called foetal alcohol syndrome which is associated with frank alcoholism in the mother and there's some evidence that it can also result from fairly heavy 'binge' drinking during pregnancy. But the evidence that lesser amounts of drink can have any effect is extremely scruffy.'

The ultrasound debate

There are a number of medical reasons why an individual woman might need an ultrasound scan – doubts about the age or size of the foetus, for example, vaginal bleeding, or a suspected foetal deformity. But many authorities believe there's no justification for offering scans to all women 'just in case'. Despite the fact that scans seem logical enough – experienced operators claim to be able to spot up to 90 per cent of foetal abnormalities during the second three months of pregnancy – of the few scientific studies done of the technique most have failed to show any medical benefit. Yet in many hospitals scans continue to be routine: it's estimated that at least 70 per cent of all pregnant women in this country are given one or more.

This enthusiasm for ultrasound is all the more worrying because no one knows if it's really safe. Most doctors think it is, pointing out that it has been used for the last twenty-five years and no one has yet been able to show that scans have any adverse effects on the baby. Others recall the story of X-rays: these were used widely in pregnancy from the 1920s on but it was not until the mid-1950s that a link between X-rays and leukaemia in children was suspected – and 1975 before this link was proven to everyone's satisfaction. These worries are fuelled by laboratory work which suggests that ultrasound is capable of damaging chromosomes and cell membranes and of interfering with the way the cells grow and divide. Animal research, too, suggests that ultrasound can affect the growth of the foetus.

None of this experimental work proves that human babies are at risk but it does raise doubts. Many investigators are now calling for better trials to try to settle the issue. But, in the meantime, what should a pregnant woman do if she's offered a routine scan? To try to answer this one, I spoke to a very pregnant woman doctor who works at one of the main centres devoted to research into the health of foetuses and newborn babies. 'I'd only have a routine scan if it was part of a controlled trial,' she told me. 'Otherwise, no.'

How important is diet and do we need extra vitamins and minerals?

Doctors are also divided over what sort of advice they should give women about diet during pregnancy. They all agree that junk food should be avoided and many will recommend a wholefood diet as providing the best balance of vitamins, minerals and trace elements needed by the mother and the foetus. But should they go any further?

Many doctors prescribe iron and folic acid supplements during pregnancy. But, though properly controlled scientific studies have shown that this increases the level of haemoglobin in the blood, so far they have provided no evidence that this is necessarily a good thing! However, according to most research, these supplements don't seem to do any harm and medical habits are hard to break.

Paradoxically, other doctors are unwilling to prescribe any other form of vitamin or mineral supplements, for the very reason that they don't believe there's enough evidence to support them. Some of their colleagues, however, say that the case for extra vitamins and minerals, though not watertight, is sufficiently strong to make supplements a must – if not for all women, at least for those at risk.

NEURAL TUBE DEFECTS

The current controversy over vitamins and minerals is focused on neural tube defects – a group of related abnormalities ranging from spina bifida to anencephaly (when the foetus's brain fails to develop). There are some indications that these conditions are linked to poverty and/or poor diet: during the Depression in the United States and in post-war Berlin, the proportion of affected babies increased sharply.

More recently, scientific studies have provided additional support for this theory. For instance, women who later gave birth to a spina bifida baby were found to have reduced amounts of vitamins such as folic acid, vitamin C, riboflavin and vitamin B_{12} in their blood during pregnancy. Another study, conducted in South Wales, showed that most of the women who had spina bifida babies ate lots of fat and carbohydrate but very little fresh fruit and vegetables.

A further study done in the same area looked at the effect of folic acid supplements. This trial was well designed though small – only 123 women were included. Two out of the sixty women prescribed folic acid had a baby with a neural tube defect compared with four out of the sixty-three women in the control group. This result easily could have been due to chance alone. So the researchers then took a closer look. They tried to find out whether the women who'd been prescribed the folic acid had actually taken it. It turned out that of the forty-four women who most probably *had* taken their tablets, none had had an affected baby compared with six (nearly 9 per cent) of those that either hadn't been given the supplements or probably hadn't taken those they'd been prescribed.

Obviously this study, despite its suggestion of a positive effect, wasn't ideal. The difference between the two groups of women rested on whether they really had taken the supplements. There was also the possibility that those who had were in some other way different from those that hadn't bothered to.

This is also one of the reasons why many researchers are sceptical about the results of the most famous vitamin trial: the one reported by Dr R. W. Smithells and his colleagues in 1981. These appeared to show that a multivitamin and mineral preparation taken before and after conception helped protect women who'd already had one child with a neural tube defect (NTD). Only one out of the 200 women who took the supplement, compared with thirteen out of 300 who didn't, had an NTD baby. Looks convincing, doesn't it? The trouble is that the women who took the supplement were very different from those that didn't. They tended to come from a higher social class, and to have had fewer previous miscarriages. Both these factors suggest that they were less at risk anyway – supplements or no supplements.

There are, as always, some animal studies which lend support to the idea that vitamin supplementation is important. For example, a modest amount of vitamin A – equivalent to about 4000 IU in humans – may reduce the risk of NTD. On the other hand, the animal work also suggests that supplements might be dangerous: both vitamins A and D are known to cause birth deformities when taken to excess.

In humans, too, supplements may not be as safe as is often claimed. In 1984, a doctor reported in the *Lancet* that a woman who had taken a multivitamin preparation had given birth to a baby with several severe birth defects. The Committee on Safety of Medicines (the government's drug safety watchdog) had also received eight similar reports. This suggests that supplements might be unsafe. 'In view of the theoretical possibility,' this doctor concluded, 'that vitamin supplementation, whether or not preventing neural tube defects, might harm the embryo/foetus, it is important to establish safety.'

So far this has not been done.

Other specialists, too, have cautioned that the risks and benefits of supplementation in pregnancy remain an unknown quantity.[3,4] Hence the British Medical Research Council has organized a new controlled trial.

Other evidence: how good is it?

Foresight, an organization devoted to the promotion of 'preconceptual' care, has no doubts that smoking and drinking alcohol – no matter how moderately – are *always* risky during pregnancy. Furthermore, even though the evidence is far from conclusive, it's convinced that NTDs *can* be prevented by supplementation.

But Foresight goes even further. It claims that *most* congenital abnormalities and miscarriages could be prevented by proper attention to diet, and by avoiding poisons – some self-inflicted ones like alcohol and cigarette smoke and some environmental ones such as lead – both before, as well as during, pregnancy. (For a more detailed discussion of miscarriage, see Chapter 8.)

Foresight believes that preconceptual care should start several months before a couple plans to conceive. There are two main planks to this argument. One is that a deficient diet and toxic chemicals may harm the egg and the sperm as well as the embryo. The other is that our bodies take time both to correct vitamin and mineral deficiencies and to eliminate poisons; if a woman doesn't begin to tackle these problems well in advance of conception, the damage may already have been done.

Most of Foresight's advice to prospective parents hinges on diet and, to that extent, is safe enough. But the organization does advocate extra vitamins and minerals as well. The doses of vitamins A and D are similar to the ones now being tested in the MRC trial and are unlikely to cause any harm. The Foresight supplement also contains all the other 'trial' vitamins – though in different, and mostly larger, doses than those being used by the MRC. It includes, in addition, several other vitamins and biological compounds not being tested.

Foresight advocates mineral supplements for those couples 'whose hair analysis reveals that they have low normal levels of essential trace minerals or minerals just below this'. As I explained in Chapter 2, hair mineral analysis is a very new technique, is often unreliable, and should never be used on its own to diagnose mineral deficiencies. A person's medical and dietary history must also be taken into account and it may be necessary to do blood tests to confirm or refute the results of the hair analysis. I gather that all hair analyses are interpreted by someone who is said to understand the technique. Nevertheless, many orthodox scientists remain highly sceptical of its value. Certainly, on current evidence, no lay person has a hope of making sense of the results. And many critics say the same goes for those who have experience of the technique!

That criticism apart, how good is the evidence that mineral deficiencies are an important cause of birth problems?

As with vitamins, most of this evidence comes from animal studies, though some research has indicated that at least one mineral, zinc, may also be linked with birth complications in humans. A deficiency of zinc has been reported to be associated with haemorrhage during labour, with smaller, less healthy babies, and with miscarriages and congenital abnormalities.[5] A few researchers have found that the iron supplements routinely prescribed in pregnancy lower zinc levels even further and so, they say, may increase these risks. Some alternative-minded doctors have taken this possible hazard seriously enough to stop prescribing iron to women in their care. Really, though, this isn't such a big step: as I mentioned earlier, there's no evidence that most women need extra iron anyway.

But three studies published in September 1985 in the *British Journal of Obstetrics and Gynaecology* seem to have scotched the zinc argument. They show pretty conclusively that, although zinc levels in the blood do fall during pregnancy, this does not mean that women become zinc-deficient. It's merely due to the fact that our blood increases in *volume* when we're pregnant, *diluting* the zinc but not reducing the total amount present in our bodies. One of the studies – of more than 400 Chinese women – showed that the average blood zinc levels were similar both for women with underweight babies and for those whose babies were of normal weight. Nor was there any link between low blood zinc and either miscarriage or deformed babies.

Two of the studies showed that iron supplements had no effect on zinc levels. Furthermore, one of them cited evidence that zinc supplements have been linked with premature births and stillbirths. One of the articles also demonstrated that hair analysis wasn't a reliable indicator of zinc deficiency.

An accompanying editorial in the same issue of the *Journal* asks: 'Is there convincing biochemical evidence of widespread zinc deficiency in pregnancy; and if there is, does it have any harmful effect on the foetus?' And the author answers:

> Evidence is accumulating, and [these] three papers . . . confirm, that the answer is no . . . Although many foetal abnormalities can be induced in animals by gross zinc deficiency . . . the evidence linking zinc insufficiency with harm to the human foetus is, to say the least, insecure . . . within the range of zinc concentrations found in the general pregnant population there is no good evidence.
>
> . . . Much better evidence must be produced before British doctors should be persuaded to provide zinc supplements for pregnant women.

Some alternative nutritional experts also believe that extra magnesium may be necessary to prevent an unduly painful labour and that low magnesium may be a cause of some premature births. Foresight chairman Mrs Belinda Barnes claims there has been a recent increase in the number of babies born with thalidomide-like 'limb reduction' deformities – due possibly to smoking and insecticides. Smoking may cause a deficiency of vitamin B_2, says Mrs Barnes, and insecticides, she adds, may lead to a manganese shortage. There's some animal research which shows that a lack of either vitamin B_2 or manganese can give rise to this type of deformity.

Some research now being done at Reading University by Professor D. Bryce-Smith, one of Foresight's leading supporters, indicates that the toxic metals lead and cadmium may be to blame for some stillbirths.[6] Lead is a common environmental pollutant – it gets into our bodies from tinned food and from petrol exhaust fumes. Cigarette smoke is a rich source of both cadmium and lead, so this could be one reason why smokers' babies are more at risk. Smoking may also damage sperm: in one study men who smoked produced sperm that were less lively than normal.[7] But none of this has cut much ice so far with the scientific establishment. If anything, there's even less evidence for these claims than there is for the importance of zinc.

What the statistics tell us

In its booklet *Guidelines For Future Parents* Foresight claims that 'Sadly . . . the figures prove that the unborn child in the 1980s is at greater risk than the unborn child of yesteryear.' This is patently untrue. Stillbirth and infant mortality rates have been falling steadily for most of this century and this drop was particularly rapid in the late 1970s. A baby is *less* likely to die now than ever before.

The figures for congenital abnormalities tell a similar story: the proportion of babies born with neural tube defects has dropped sharply since the mid-1970s and is still falling. Although screening programmes to detect foetuses with NTD – with the option of aborting them – may be part of the explanation, most researchers believe that this has had only a minor role and that some other influence is at work.

Could it be diet? Many people – not just Foresight and its supporters – suspect it might be, because there's no doubt that many of us are eating more healthily now. But, as I've explained, we don't yet *know* that diet is at the root of birth defects and we certainly lack the evidence to prove that vitamin and mineral supplements make any difference at all to the average middle-class Westerner.

As for the supposed increase in limb reduction deformities mentioned by Mrs Barnes: *Birth Counts*,[8] a comprehensive report of the statistics of pregnancy and childbirth, shows that there *was* a big jump in 1969 – from 154 to 324 per year – but this could have been due, at least partly, to changes that year in the way these deformities were defined. Since then, the level has remained fairly constant at around 250 to 300 a year. Of course, it would be wonderful if we could prevent these problems, even though they do affect only a tiny minority of babies. But because their number *is* so small, doesn't it seem rather unlikely that smoking and insecticides are the culprits?

Some types of abnormality – Down's syndrome and cleft lip and palate – are just as common now as they were ten years ago. Foresight believes this shows just how much need there is for their sort of advice. But we don't know whether it will really make any difference. And as far as supplements are concerned, as we've seen in the case of zinc, these may do more harm than good. Nevertheless, Foresight is absolutely committed to its approach. But in the absence of reliable studies to back its claims, many obstetricians feel that the organization's hard-hitting approach is irresponsible, that it will frighten women who haven't been eating as Foresight advises, or taking supplements, or who have been drinking and smoking, and who then become pregnant unexpectedly.

Mrs Barnes concedes that her campaigning might upset some people but she's unrepentant. 'I'd rather a mother was a little bit worried than her baby was born without limbs,' she says. But, as I've tried to show you, there's no reason – yet – to suppose that such worries are at all justified. So is it really fair to frighten people into thinking they are?

Foresight is now doing a survey of couples who follow its advice which, it hopes, will prove the strength of its claims. When I spoke to Mrs Barnes, about 200 couples had taken part in the Foresight programme. None of the babies born so far was deformed. Mrs Barnes hopes that, eventually, the survey will include 5000 couples so that any positive result will be statistically significant. 'I do not think,' she asserts, 'that we'll get any abnormalities. I should be absolutely shattered if we did.'

But Foresight has as yet no proper follow-up system for its couples and depends on their writing to report the outcome of their pregnancies – not a very satisfactory way of conducting a meaningful study. A further criticism is that the couples are, by definition, atypical: predominantly middle-class, intelligent, motivated people. Seasoned researchers point out that to carry any weight, the survey would have to be controlled – with similar numbers of matched couples not following the regime. It isn't. Even if the results are good and the number of deformities very small, it's only proper research, along the lines of the MRC vitamin trial, which could give us the answers we need.

Unfortunately, it could already be too late for this type of research. Quite a number of people – including doctors – are so convinced of the need for extra vitamins and minerals that they're refusing to take part in controlled trials. The other problem that worries researchers is their suspicion that many women in the control group may still follow a special diet and take vitamins just to be on the safe side.

Planning for a healthy baby: let's keep a sense of proportion.

Most babies are born alive and healthy and most stay that way. Your chances of having a dead baby or of losing him or her in the first week of life are about one in a hundred. As he or she gets older, the risks are even smaller. The likelihood of your having a deformed baby is also pretty remote: only two babies in a hundred have any defects at all and half of these have the kind of problem which is either so mild that it doesn't need any treatment or is one that can be corrected by surgery.

I know this isn't much consolation if you're unfortunate enough to have a baby which does die or which is severely deformed. And you may think that, next time round, you'll try harder to give your baby the best possible start. So, though the evidence against moderate smoking and drinking is far from conclusive, most specialists agree that these habits are better avoided.

It remains to be seen whether the results of future research will provide better evidence that marginal deficiencies of vitamins and minerals or small amounts of common pollutants are at all dangerous during pregnancy. (It is these we're talking about, not the severe deficiencies or poisonings that cause obvious illness.) For now, there's certainly no harm in switching to a wholefood diet (if you haven't done so already) and if you're still worried about possible deficiencies you might like to include more of the foods that contain minerals like zinc and magnesium (see page 59). These are simple and safe measures and in keeping with the current medical philosophy that the less you interfere with you body during pregnancy, the better.

Despite the claims of Foresight and continuing research, we really know very little about many of the things that can go wrong and even less about what we can do to prevent them. That, at least, is the view of experienced researchers. So let common sense be your guide and remember: the statistics are overwhelmingly in your favour.

YOUR HEALTH IN PREGNANCY

Keeping fit

Whether or not you plan to have an 'active' birth, you should try to make sure you're as fit as possible during pregnancy. Labour – even if you go through the entire process lying down – is just what it says: jolly hard work. Carrying a baby for the previous nine months is no joke either if your body is out of condition. All that extra weight puts new stress on your back and legs. The hormonal changes that occur during pregnancy have profound effects on your entire body. There'll be more blood in your circulation so your heart will have to work harder. In later pregnancy your lungs, too, will have a tougher job as they fight your uterus for space. Your blood vessels and intestines will become somewhat less efficient: this may make you more likely to develop varicose veins and to become constipated. Your ligaments – the sheets of tough fibrous material that hold your bones together – will be more flexible so you're more likely to strain your joints, particularly those in your back.

In short: if you're unfit when you begin pregnancy and do nothing to put it right then, by the time your baby is due, you're going to feel as though you'd been trampled by a herd of buffalo! Take a look at some of the heavily pregnant women waddling dejectedly through the antenatal clinic and you'll get the picture. Compare them with pregnant athletes or with women who've been doing yoga. *They* don't waddle and I'll bet few of them complain of nagging backache or of feeling so tired that everything is an effort.

Specialists agree that regular exercise is important during pregnancy. Research has shown that athletes usually have easier pregnancies and labours than other women: they're only half as likely to need a Caesarian section, for example. That doesn't mean you should start violent exercise when you're pregnant – this would be the worst time to take up jogging, for example. But gentle exercise – walking, swimming or yoga – is fine. It'll help tone up your body and may prevent the postural problems that cause so many aches and pains. And here's another thought to spur you on. Many women have found that regular exercise – during pregnancy as well as after the birth – have helped them get their shape back that much more quickly.

Interestingly, there's also some evidence that pregnancy can make you fitter than you were beforehand – once the baby is no longer holding you back, of course! Some world-class athletes have achieved some of their best performances shortly after giving birth. No one is quite sure why. But in his book *Sport and Medicine*,[9] Dr Peter Sperryn offers one or two explanations. 'The change from a younger, less mature woman to a more mature and strongly motivated one may play a major part,' he writes. 'There is also the suspicion that 9 months of continuous progressive cardiorespiratory stress coupled with a sophisticated form of weight-training plays a part!'

Aches, pains and other problems

MORNING SICKNESS

Because of possible danger to the foetus, your doctor may

well be reluctant to prescribe any drugs to help you combat sickness. Fortunately, for most women, this problem (which can strike at any time of the day – forget that 'morning' bit) almost always passes of its own accord by about the twelfth week of pregnancy. Nevertheless, while it's around it can make life pretty miserable and there are a number of natural remedies you might like to try.

Some nutrition experts believe that morning sickness can be due to a deficiency of vitamin B_6 and, possibly, of zinc as well. There's a bit of evidence to back this suggestion so it might be worth including in your diet more of the foods that contain these substances (see pages 57-9). This may be enough to put things right – provided, of course, you can keep the food down long enough! If not, or if you find that these dietary changes aren't enough, you may need supplements. But because, during pregnancy, one needs to be extra-careful about taking pills of any kind – even vitamins and minerals – it's as well to ask your own doctor, or consult a medical nutritional specialist first.

Homoeopathic remedies are also reputed to be useful for morning sickness. And, as far as we know, they're safe. According to a leaflet *Homoeopathy in Pregnancy and Childbirth* published by the Society of Homoeopaths, an organization for lay members of the profession, 'Homoeopathic remedies cannot cause side effects to either mother and baby . . . This is because only a very minute amount of the active ingredient is used . . .' But only remedies with a potency higher than about 24X have *no* active ingredient (see Chapter 1), so many homoeopaths believe that lower potencies should not be used at all in pregnancy. Others say the reverse is the case and recommend using only the sixth potency! This difference of opinion stems from the fact that scientifically oriented practitioners believe that the theoretical risk associated with taking even tiny amounts of a potentially poisonous substance (which many low-potency homoeopathic remedies contain) is greater than that of the higher 'energy' levels which are claimed to exist in high-potency remedies.

All very muddling for the lay person. On balance I'd go

with the scientific reasoning and stick to high-potency remedies. But first, I'd consult an experienced medical homoeopath, preferably one with a special interest in pregnancy. For morning sickness, he or she may well recommend Nux Vomica. This is indicated if your vomiting comes in spasms after breakfast and you also have a tendency to be constipated. Constant and persistent vomiting, with excessive salivation, is said to respond well to Ipecacuanha.

Herbalists also have some remedies for morning sickness. But, because some herbs can be dangerous during pregnancy, you should *never* try to treat yourself.

There's been some interest recently in *acupressure*: using the fingers to stimulate acupuncture points. Several such points are linked with morning sickness and some pregnant women have reported that this technique did relieve their nausea – at least for a short time. Some traditional acupuncturists, however, believe that any stimulation of points is inadvisable during pregnancy because of the risks of causing a miscarriage or premature birth. Acupuncture is, after all, also used to induce labour (see page 189). As one practitioner said, 'If I really thought a woman was suffering badly with morning sickness, I'd suggest acupressure; but I wouldn't give that advice routinely to all pregnant women.' So if you feel you do need this sort of help, consult an acupuncturist who should be able to advise you whether this treatment is safe for you.

One or two old theories about morning sickness have been given a new airing recently. One, which is now backed by some research, is that women who feel sick are less likely to lose their babies.[10] The reason is that they tend to produce more of a pregnancy hormone known as hCG. But if you happen to be someone who's never had a twinge of nausea, don't worry. The research also suggests that some women are just more sensitive than others to this hormone. They may be making adequate amounts but don't react to it.

Another idea is that morning sickness may have a psychological component: you feel sick because you expect to or because you're worried about being pregnant. There may be an element of truth in this. When the drug Debendox (see page 163) was withdrawn from the market, the number of women complaining of sickness dropped by over a third.[11] This suggests that for some women the knowledge that there was no treatment was enough to cure their problem! And, if we're to be honest, good old mind-over-matter may be behind the apparent success of some homoeopathic remedies, too, especially if they're prescribed by a practitioner who inspires confidence. Don't forget that no one knows how homoeopathy works. Nor can we be sure that, when remedies seem to have an effect, it's not something else entirely which is bringing about the cure. As I explained in Chapter 1, there have been some scientific trials to test homoeopathy – but not in pregnancy.

CONSTIPATION

Many women suffer from constipation in the first part of pregnancy. This is probably due to the high amounts of progesterone in the blood which have a relaxing effect on the intestine, making it less efficient. The best way to treat constipation is to avoid it – by eating a diet high in fibre. If you eat wholefoods, which you should be doing anyway, you're unlikely to get very constipated. In addition, you need to drink lots of water. If constipation does develop, you can often cure it by adding a little bran to your diet. But don't overdo it. Too much fibre can be almost as bad as too little! Occasionally a homoeopathic remedy seems to help: Nux Vomica is often recommended.

PILES AND ANAL FISSURES

These are often the result of constipation so, again, prevention is the key. But a tendency to piles may also be made worse in late pregnancy by the baby's head pressing on the veins in the pelvic area. Regular exercise throughout pregnancy will improve the circulation and help guard against piles.

If you do develop piles or a fissure (a tear in the lining of the anus), there are several homoeopathic remedies that can be taken either as a medicine or applied to the affected area. Homoeopathic Aesculus (horse chestnut) or Hamamelis (witch hazel), for example. There are also some herbal remedies but you should consult a medical herbalist to find out more about those. A yoga teacher told me that pelvic floor exercises (see Chapter 10) may help, too.

VARICOSE VEINS

The hormone progesterone has a direct relaxant effect on the lining of blood vessels. This, plus the reduced circulation to the legs, makes varicose veins more likely. And constipation tends to makes things worse: all that straining increases the pressure in the leg veins. If you do get varicose veins and they're not too severe, they may disappear after your baby is born. But they'll probably come back the next time you're pregnant; the more babies you have the greater the chance that your veins will stay that way.

Doctors very seldom suggest any treatment for varicose veins during pregnancy other than wearing elastic support tights. These are frightfully impractical as you have to put them on first thing every morning before getting out of bed. They're not all that attractive either. Very bad varicose veins can be treated – once you're no longer pregnant – with either injections or surgery, but results are unpredictable and the problem may recur.

So the best course is to try to avoid varicose veins by taking lots of exercise and eating a high-fibre diet. You may also like to discuss with your homoeopath or herbalist whether you could take some of the remedies mentioned above for piles. These may help prevent varicose veins, too. So may pelvic floor exercises, and some of the inverted yoga postures (see also Chapter 10). But you should only practise these postures if you've been doing yoga for some time, and have an experienced teacher; and don't attempt them if they cause any discomfort. Unfortunately, once the veins have become badly damaged, there's probably little that any form of alternative therapy can do.

VAGINAL INFECTIONS AND URINARY TRACT INFECTIONS

See Chapter 5. If you do decide to try alternative treatment during pregnancy for either of these conditions, first check with your doctor that it's safe to do so. Extreme changes in diet, for example, are not advisable when you're pregnant. Better still, ask your alternative practitioner to discuss your case with your GP before advising any treatment. (A reputable practitioner should do this, anyway.)

HEADACHES

The treatment of headaches during pregnancy is similar to that at any other time (see Chapter 13 for details). However, a very severe headache at the front of the head is a potential danger sign. It may herald eclampsia (see page 184) and you should seek medical advice as quickly as possible. If you try to treat it yourself – whether you take an aspirin or use an alternative remedy – you're wasting valuable time. So don't.

STRETCH MARKS

There's no orthodox medical treatment for stretch marks and I've seen no convincing evidence that alternatives work either. It's sometimes said that your skin is less likely to mark if you don't put on too much weight but the modern view is that weight-watching during pregnancy is definitely not on. The other preventive measure often recommended is to keep the skin lubricated either with lanolin or a cream containing vitamin E. While this will certainly help to keep the skin in good condition, it's unlikely to prevent stretch marks.

Most doctors believe that a predisposition to stretch marks is inherited: this could explain why some women go through several pregnancies without developing them while others get marks the first time they become pregnant. But there could be another reason: diet. Skin and the tissues under-lying it need adequate amounts of zinc, vitamin B_6 and vitamin C to stay healthy. If one or more of these ingredients is deficient in your diet, the tissues will be tend to form small tears when they're overstretched. If you suspect your diet may be inadequate, or you got stretch marks in a pre-vious pregnancy, it might be worth getting some nutritional advice.

Some people believe a vitamin E deficiency may also be to blame and recommend taking this vitamin internally. While this makes more sense than rubbing it on the skin, there's no evidence that it will prevent stretch marks. And, anyway, it's a bad idea to take extra fat-soluble vitamins during pregnancy.

Incidentally, I've heard of no good evidence that stretch marks can be cured once they've developed.

BACKACHE

Low backache is a very common problem during pregnancy. When you consider all that extra weight you're now hoicking about it's not too surprising. The other factor that tends to make pregnant women more prone to backache is that their ligaments are now softer and their joints more flexible and more liable to strain.

Posture, as I mentioned earlier, is all-important. Many pregnant women automatically try to compensate for their 'bump' by hollowing their backs – something that nature never intended. So the first step towards preventing and cur-ing backache is to stand – and sit – as upright as possible. You should also avoid putting undue strain on your back when lifting heavy objects (and that includes your toddler, if you have one). Bend your knees – not your back – when you want to pick something up. You should also make sure that your mattress is firm enough to support your back while you're asleep.

If, after all this, you're still suffering, you may benefit from *osteopathic* treatment. Some osteopaths take a particular interest in expectant mothers and the British School of Osteopathy in London runs a special clinic for them. Many women have reported pain-free pregnancies and easy deliveries after osteopathy. Even women with a long-standing back problem from a previous pregnancy can be helped.

Chiropractic may also be useful. Judy, who is in her late thirties, is expecting her second baby. 'There was something about my first pregnancy,' she says, 'that gave me a very bad back. I put on three and a quarter stone and that put an awful lot of strain on it and I had a lot of back problems afterwards. And I haven't got a very good posture anyway. I went to an orthopaedic surgeon and he diagnosed disc trouble. I did some exercises and it appeared to clear up. But within two months I'd conceived – and I was soon crawling round on my hands and knees.' She then consulted a chiropractor recommended by a friend. He said the problem was that one side of Judy's pelvis was tilted and that there was nothing wrong with her discs! The treatment started and Judy began to feel better quite quickly. 'I still get backache,' she admits, 'but I'm coping. This isn't an alternative treatment as far as I'm concerned; it was the only thing I could do.'

INSOMNIA

Many pregnant women find sleeping a little bit more difficult than usual, especially in the last few weeks of their pregnancy. Your doctor may prescribe sleeping tablets if you get really exhausted. These are quite safe if taken according to instructions but you may prefer to get along without them if you can. So what else can you do?

Simple relaxation – with or without the aid of a tape – often works wonders. And if you've been doing yoga throughout your pregnancy, you may well find that you're able to use some of its relaxation techniques to bring on sleep. There are several homoeopathic remedies, too, including Cocculus, Coffea and Lycopodium. To find out which one is most likely to work for you, you need to consult a homoeopath.

HIGH BLOOD PRESSURE (HYPERTENSION)

Doctors always worry when a pregnant woman's blood pressure goes up because this may be the first sign of a condition known as pre-eclamptic toxaemia (PET). This is potentially very dangerous for the baby and if it is allowed to develop unchecked (eclampsia) may threaten the mother's life as well.

PET is characterised by one or both of the following symptoms: high blood pressure, and proteinuria (protein in the urine). It may also be accompanied by oedema (swelling) though this, on its own, doesn't indicate that you have PET – one in three pregnant women has oedema to some extent. Once it has developed, I'm afraid, there's no place for alternative medicine. But there have been some suggestions that this condition can be *prevented* – yes, you've guessed it – by diet.

Research has shown that trying to restrict weight gain in pregnancy (common advice from both doctors and midwives) has no effect on the likelihood of PET. But there's as yet no evidence that a special diet – over and above a healthy, adequate one – makes any difference. At least that's what the majority of medical researchers believe. They point out that, whatever her social class, a woman's chances of PET are the same. Yet if PET was really due to diet, you'd expect there to be some difference since diet *does* vary with social class.

If your blood pressure is only slightly raised and you have no other symptoms your doctor will probably do no more than keep a close eye on you and recommend that you rest. If your blood pressure increases further – or you get other symptoms – you may be asked to come into hospital for more rest, and tests.

But before things get to this stage, what about trying some of the alternative treatments for raised blood pressure, for example relaxation? A study published in the *Lancet* in 1984 showed that both relaxation therapy and relaxation with biofeedback (a technique which reinforces the relaxation training) were able to reduce blood pressure in mildly hypertensive pregnant women. Out of the women who'd been given the therapy fewer than a third had to be admitted to hospital. But two-thirds of a control group of women – who hadn't had the therapy – needed to be admitted. *Acupuncture* is also said to be useful for relaxation and to be able to lower blood pressure but because of its possible dangers during pregnancy it's probably best avoided.

Some homoeopathic remedies may also work. Wendy wrote to tell me that her high blood pressure of 160/110 responded to *homoeopathic* Belladonna (Belladonna itself is the active ingredient of deadly nightshade and poisonous) by coming down to a normal value of 110/70. She adds: 'When I was in hospital near term my BP refused to go down and hovered around 160/100 and 140/95 despite bed rest, so I took Belladonna for five days. My BP came down to 120/60 at one point and I was allowed home.' That doesn't, of course, mean that Belladonna is the right remedy for everyone. Wendy hit upon it by chance when she began taking it for another problem. Nor should you take it without consulting a qualified homoeopath.

BIRTH

There's such a wealth of information available about natural childbirth – just look at all the leaflets and books produced by the National Childbirth Trust (NCT) and the Active Birth Movement (ABM) – that you may wonder what else there is to say about it all!

I'm going to leave the details of these two approaches aside. If you do want to know more you can read some of the books listed in the Bibliography. In this section I want to look at some of the other ways you can be helped to give birth naturally: many of these methods can be used in conjunction with NCT or ABM techniques as well as with more conventional medical ones. I'll also be discussing some aspects of the medical and more common alternative approaches to labour that don't seem to me have been fully covered in existing books on birth. Usually this is because there's now some new research to consider or because research that did exist then wasn't included in the books available at the time.

Preparation for labour

The best preparation is to stay healthy and relaxed. Diet and exercise, mentioned earlier, are obviously very important and relaxation will help keep you calm and in control when the big day arrives. Nearly all childbirth teachers, whatever their affiliation, incorporate relaxation training into their classes. If you still find it hard to relax, there are a number of special tapes available. These will give you the bit of extra support you may need to practise regularly.

Practice is terribly important, too, if you're planning to use NCT-type breathing techniques or the yoga-based exercises recommended by the Active Birth Movement. Some other ways of giving birth naturally also require preparation and I'll discuss these under Pain Relief (see page 191-5).

However, no matter how well you prepare yourself, don't expect too much. Labour *is* usually a stressful and often a painful experience. That doesn't mean that the pain will be unbearable: your particular method may well work for you but, if it doesn't, then you shouldn't feel bad about asking for drugs. On balance, a labour made relatively pain-free by drugs may be better for you and you baby than a painful one managed under your own steam. This is because stress can actually make a labour more difficult and there's nothing more stressful than pain. Stress is also harmful for the baby, too. Animal studies have shown this quite clearly. And one could argue that human mothers, by virtue of their greater intelligence, are even more susceptible to stress.

Does preparation help to reduce pain? Some researchers believe not. The results of a study published in the journal *Pain* (and quoted at length in the NCT's own magazine *New Generation*) showed that childbirth classes don't affect the pain itself but do decrease a woman's emotional reaction to it. But the doctor who did the research insists that, despite this, the pain is still considerable. He also reports that women feel more severe pain when their expectations of labour are 'violated' by the experience itself.

And even the NCT now recognizes that labour can be painful. 'It is unrealistic and unreasonable to imply that most labours are pain-free,' an NCT teacher writes in the same issue of *New Generation*. 'I have taught many indignant second-time mothers who felt "conned" in a previous labour because there was no mention of pain beforehand. Worse still, some had been subjected to the bribery of "if you do your breathing properly, you won't feel any pain". That's enough to make anyone feel both pain and guilt.'

Guilt is a powerful emotion. The results of one study actually suggest that couples – both men and women – who have failed to have their baby naturally may be more likely to suffer psychiatric symptoms after the birth. Hence the need for an open mind about all these self-help techniques.

Labour

INDUCTION

I'm starting off with induction because for many women this is how labour begins. Although the enthusiasm for induction appears to have waned in recent years, in many hospitals it's still routine for women whose babies are overdue.

The evidence: when is induction necessary?

A few years ago, many people thought induction could save babies' lives. Now they're not so sure. No matter how keen the doctors are on induction in a particular health region, the proportion of babies born dead or who die shortly after birth remains the same. Of course this could also be interpreted as showing that, at any rate, induction does no harm. But is this any reason for doing it?

Other research, it's true, has shown that induction

does save some babies – but only very few. The vast majority would have been all right anyway. But because of that slight doubt it's best never to refuse an induction point-blank. First find out the doctors' reasons for suggesting it. If you have pre-eclampsia, for example, or your baby seems not to be growing properly, you may decide that you'd rather it were born straightaway – just to be on the safe side.

But the research also suggests that there's no good reason for inducing labour in a woman whose baby is simply over-due. A survey done at the Dulwich Hospital in London[12] revealed that all 'late' babies – provided they're healthy – can be left to arrive without any help. And some of these babies were up to four weeks behind schedule! So much for the one- or two-week rules imposed by some hospitals.

For such babies induction, even if not dangerous, isn't a good idea. Induced labours tend to be more painful and longer than natural ones; this may mean that a women needs an epidural or extra pain-relieving drugs. If she has an epidural, then she is more likely to have her baby delivered by forceps or, possibly, according to some evidence, by Caesarian section.

ALTERNATIVES TO MEDICAL INDUCTION AND AIDS TO AN EFFICIENT LABOUR

Do-it-yourself

No, I don't mean the old-fashioned remedies of castor oil and a hot bath – though these may work if you're absolutely ready to go into labour. I'm talking about something completely different: nipple massage!

The idea that nipple stimulation can bring on labour isn't a new one. But until recently it was regarded as just another old wives' tale. It isn't, though: it's based on sound science and research is now proving that it often does the trick. Stimulation of the nipple leads to increased levels of a hormone known as oxytocin in the bloodstream. Oxytocin makes the uterus contract. Not surprisingly, it is also released during breastfeeding.

A study published in the *American Journal of Obstetrics and Gynecology* in 1984 showed that women who'd massaged their nipples were 70 per cent more likely to deliver their babies on time than those who hadn't. But the rub – if you'll excuse the pun – is that, to be effective, nipple stimulation has to be practised for at least three hours every day!

Acupuncture

Acupuncture can be used both to induce labour and to make contractions which have already started more efficient. Sometimes shiatsu or acupressure may be enough to get labour started. Traditionally, or so it's said, women in labour used to clutch at bedposts. I'd always thought that that meant they were in excruciating agony. Not necessarily, say acupuncturists: they were, without knowing it, pressing on points in the hand which directly relate to the uterus. This would help speed up their contractions and so shorten their labours. Today not many of us have bedposts. The modern equivalent, recommended in some circles, is to grip a couple of combs instead. However, because relaxation is so important during labour, you should only do this during contractions and not between them.

Homoeopathy

Homoeopathic Caulophyllum is said to make for an easier and quicker labour, though one woman who'd tried it warned: 'If you take too much you have the most phenomenal Braxton-Hicks contractions.' These are the 'practice' contractions that many women notice in late pregnancy and they can be quite painful.

Herbs

Herbal remedies, because they're potentially so powerful,

should only be taken on the advice of a trained medical herbalist. One such specialist I spoke to warned against the current fashion for taking raspberry leaf tea. This is said to help labour along. But, said the herbalist, before she would prescribe it she would need to know the patient. 'It can be as wrong as it can be right,' she explained. One group of women who'd used it found that some of them were having very long labours indeed. It all depends, the herbalist added, on the state of a woman's uterus to start with. A herb which makes labour easier for some women can have the reverse effect on others. Some herbs used to bring on labour can also be used to treat a threatened miscarriage. So you can see how important expert advice is.

PAIN RELIEF IN LABOUR: THE MEDICAL APPROACH

I'm not going to discuss this in much detail except to say that all the usual forms of pain relief have advantages as well as disadvantages. Some women swear by gas and air – others find it's not nearly effective enough. Some women like the effects of pethidine; others say it makes them feel 'woozy' and out of control. And many women have been delighted to find that an epidural really did abolish pain while leaving them conscious and alert. But for others an epidural took away some of the satisfaction of childbirth – they were unable to push their baby out and had to have it delivered by forceps or even Caesarian section. They felt cheated.

But perhaps the biggest drawback to a drug-aided delivery is that the drugs can affect the baby. There's no evidence that they do any lasting damage but pethidine in particular may make a baby so drowsy at first that it sleeps all the time and doesn't want to feed. This can be a blow to the mother and she and her baby may take a bit longer to get to know each other. If this 'bonding' process is delayed it may be some time before she really feels much for the baby. The drugs in an epidural, too, may affect the baby for a short time after birth.

ALTERNATIVE FORMS OF PAIN RELIEF

Acupuncture

This is said to give some pain relief for between 60 and 95 per cent of women. At least some part of the effect is due to its ability to relax the mother. Acupuncturists who attend hospital deliveries often find that the staff are amazed that it works so well. 'A common comment,' said one practitioner, 'is, "You wouldn't believe she was in labour!"' The baby, too, appears to benefit: acupuncturists claim that you can always spot 'their' babies on the postnatal ward – they're calmer and cry less than the others.

If you want acupuncture for your labour, you need to find a practitioner quite early in pregnancy. This is partly because he or she will want to see you several times before the baby's due – to explain the technique and to keep a check on your pregnancy. The acupuncturist may also offer some treatment during pregnancy. Though needles are rarely used, moxibustion (where a pellet of a special herb is burnt just *above* the acupuncture point) or acupressure may, occasionally, be indicated. An acupuncturist is also trained to advise a woman about diet.

The other reason for finding your acupuncturist well in advance is that there aren't very many practitioners who are prepared to do this kind of work. This is because alternative practitioners, unlike ordinary doctors, are not yet able to offer much in the way of emergency cover. There aren't enough of them and, even if you go into labour during the day, many acupuncturists can't just down tools leaving their other patients unattended while they spend the next twelve hours or so with you.

Electroacupuncture – the needles are stimulated by a very low-voltage electric current rather than by hand – is often used during labour. This form of the technique tends to be more efficient: most women find that, with time, they need more stimulation. It therefore makes sense to get a machine – instead of a human acupuncturist who could get jolly tired –

to do the job. The other advantage of electroacupuncture is that it allows a woman to adjust the level of stimulation so that it is just right for her. Some machines are also portable so the woman can walk around while she's in labour.

Fees for acupuncture vary considerably. The consultations during pregnancy are charged at the acupuncturists' usual rates – £15 to £35 each. If you want acupuncture during your labour as well, this could cost you up to £200, although some practitioners charge considerably less. Fortunately, most acupuncturists set a flat rate for labour so you won't be faced with an unexpectedly large bill if yours happens to be an abnormally long one.

Bonnie had both her babies with acupuncture. She didn't find it at all hard to find a practitioner – she's married to one! 'With Stuart [her first baby] I was having contractions but things weren't happening fast enough and I was getting tired,' she remembers. 'I was getting to the point where, if acupuncture hadn't been available, I would've been thinking about the other options. When the needles went in,' she reports, 'there was a change of emphasis. The contractions weren't pain-free but I did feel isolated from them. I was better able to concentrate.'

But things didn't go quite as planned. 'By the time I got to transition and the second stage I was very tired and although the needles were still helping I was beginning to panic. And at about the same time there were signs of foetal distress. I ended up having forceps.'

Her second birth – at home – was a much better experience. 'It was only five hours from beginning to end. 'At first I felt I didn't need any pain relief,' says Bonnie. 'It was only about two hours before Nicky was born that I felt I needed any help. Panic overcame me at that point so Richard [her husband] got in with his needles.' She was also feeling sick. 'There's an acupuncture point for nausea,' she explains, 'and it went away just like that.' The pain also went. 'There was space between the contractions and they were pain-free right up to the second stage. Three pushes and he was out!'

Bonnie insists that having her husband as her acupuncturist made no difference to her commitment to 'go through' with the technique. 'I had it on the strict understanding the first time that if it didn't work I would have whatever the hospital could offer. I wasn't going to be a martyr to Richard's cause!' But she also believes that her second labour was easier partly because she was more fit than she'd been for the first birth. She'd attended Active Birth classes and practised the exercises.

It seems to me that acupuncture may well be worth a try, provided you don't expect it to get rid of the pain altogether. The best results are reported for women who've had one baby already – not surprisingly, as second or subsequent labours tend to be much easier. But acupuncture won't give you the kind of pain relief you'd get with a successful epidural – at most, it's no more effective than pethidine. Because of this it seems sensible not to pin your hopes on acupuncture alone, but to practise other techniques, such as breathing exercises and Active Birth routines as well.

Incidentally, acupuncture can be used to treat a postpartum haemorrhage. In practice though, say acupuncturists, they prefer to leave this potentially life-threatening condition to the medics.

Transcutaneous electrical nerve stimulation (TENS)

Some medically qualified acupuncturists believe that this technique gives better pain relief than even electroacupuncture. It's not widely available at the moment though more and more hospitals are now buying TENS equipment.

It's very simple: just a black box the size of a calculator, four electrodes and a small, hand-held switch. The electrodes are attached to the woman's back over the area where the nerves which supply the uterus emerge from the spinal cord. The switch is used to control the intensity and type of current used.

TENS is thought to work in two different ways: a low-frequency current stimulates the production of endorphins, the body's own painkillers; a high-frequency current blocks pain 'gates', preventing the nerve messages which spell 'pain' from getting to the spinal cord. However the doctors, midwives and physiotherapists who use it point out that TENS – or acupuncture or any other form of pain relief you care to mention – works partly by the placebo effect. That is, about 30 per cent of women will be helped for reasons that have nothing to do with the actual technique!

TENS isn't as effective as drugs. It reduces, but doesn't abolish, the pain and some women still find they need drugs as well. Often, though, they can get by on a smaller dose. Some practitioners believe that a combination of electroacupuncture on the ear and TENS provides the best relief – equivalent to pethidine – and a trial is now being planned to assess this formally.

Hypnosis

Hypnosis can also been a reasonably effective form of pain relief though its main role seems to be to *relax* a woman so that she *experiences* less pain. In a few women, however, pain may be abolished entirely so that it may even be possible for her to have an episiotomy (an incision in the perineum to prevent it rupturing during birth) without a local anaesthetic. But hypnotists are wary about trying too hard. 'If you take an authoritarian approach – if you tell your patients they will not be able to feel any pain – then perhaps half will have a pain-free labour,' said one. 'On the other hand you'll have 30 per cent who feel failures because they did have pain.'

Though a few hypnotists do attend the actual birth, this usually isn't necessary because they'll already have trained their patient to hypnotize herself. This isn't as difficult as it sounds. Most of us can learn the art. And forget all you've read about 'going under' and 'not knowing what's happening'. It's quite possible to be in a light hypnotic trance without realizing it. Fiona, who had a successful 'hypnotic' delivery, says she wasn't convinced that hypnosis was going to work because, during her practice sessions, she didn't feel the slightest bit sleepy and kept her eyes open the whole time.

But her baby – her third – was born after an easy and quick labour, though she did use a bit of gas and air as well. (Hypnosis may also be combined with an epidural.) 'My hypnotist said I wouldn't be disturbed by the internal examinations and I wouldn't feel any injections.' This turned out to be true.

And Lynda Turbet, who wrote about her experiences in *Here's Health*, reported that hypnosis worked very well for her. Her first baby was born by Caesarian section after a pregnancy complicated by pre-eclampsia. Her second arrived normally half an hour after Lynda reached the hospital. Up until then she'd been at home practising self-hypnosis. 'I concentrated on feeling calm and relaxed, and it was only two hours before the birth that I began to register the contractions as mild menstrual pain.'

Another advantage of successful hypnosis is that it seems able to reduce the amount of blood lost during the birth.

Some hypnotists will demonstrate this during practice sessions – by sticking a needle in the woman's hand. Not only won't she feel it – she won't bleed either.

The essence of hypnosis is training. Your practitioner will want to see you at least twice – and possibly as many as six times – during your pregnancy. If he or she doesn't happen to be your usual doctor he or she will, of course, charge for these sessions. The other important thing to remember is that successful hypnosis depends on trust. If you don't like your practitioner or don't have confidence in him or her, then hypnosis is less likely to work. So, if necessary, be prepared to shop around.

Getting ready: shaving, episiotomies and enemas

All these humiliating and sometimes painful procedures are gradually becoming less routine since research has shown they're seldom necessary. It's been known for some time, for example, that shaving doesn't reduce the incidence of infection after the birth. Some midwives, however, feel that shaving just the labia and perineum is a good idea from the point of view of hygiene as it makes it easier to cope with the postnatal discharge (lochia). If you have access to a bidet, though, this really isn't a problem anyway.

Similarly with enemas. Routine enemas are totally unnecessary as our bodies tend to prepare themselves – many women get diarrhoea shortly before they go into labour. The only time you may need an enema is if you haven't moved your bowels recently and your labour appears to be going rather too slowly. An enema may then help speed it up.

Recent research has also, one hopes, put the last nail in the coffin of the dreaded routine episiotomy. It suggests that probably only one in ten women *needs* an episiotomy – to help her baby out – and that, contrary to established medical opinion, an episiotomy doesn't necessarily heal better than a tear.[13] In fact one study revealed that women who've had the former are more likely to find sex painful for some months after the birth – though other research suggests that this may not always be the case.

Can you avoid an abnormal delivery?

Forceps deliveries tend to be more common when a woman's had an epidural anaesthetic and/or has been induced. And, though the evidence is not compelling, the same may go for Caesarians. Some authorities also say that Active Birth techniques make a normal delivery much more likely. This is not yet accepted by everyone, however, and recently two studies have shown that most women actually prefer to stay in bed when labour really hots up. There's clearly a need for more research.

There's also much debate about when a Caesarian section is really necessary. Should a baby which seems distressed in the womb be delivered by Caesarian, for example? Obstetricians are understandably worried about the implications of leaving it too late. But some studies have shown that the usual form of heart monitoring used to detect foetal distress can be inaccurate and may push a doctor into performing an unnecessary Caesarian. More recent research, though, suggests that this problem is less likely if monitoring also includes examination of blood samples taken from the baby's scalp.

Some doctors believe that all breech babies should be delivered by Caesarian. Others – supported by many midwives committed to the natural approach – say they can be safely delivered vaginally. One way round this dilemma is to try to get the baby to turn before a woman goes into labour. Doctors may use a procedure known as external cephalic version. This involves pressing on the mother's abdomen – very rarely under general anaesthetic. Results are said to be good but some specialists still feel the technique is a risky one and that a Caesarian is preferable.

The Active Birth Movement claims that mothers can sometimes turn their babies themselves by adopting a position with the hips higher than the head and by visualizing the baby with its head pointing downwards. However, one of the Movement's leaders admits: 'It probably works as many times as it doesn't work.' Another method is to use either moxibustion or acupressure on the relevant acupuncture point: the little toes. Success rates of up to 90 per cent have been reported. However other studies have shown that nearly 60 per cent of breech babies turn round spontaneously anyway.

Pain relief during a Caesarian section

Many women now have this operation under epidural anaesthesia. This allows them to stay awake and cuddle their babies as soon as they're born. Usually a woman can have her partner with her too. From the medical point of view, an epidural is probably the best bet: general anaesthesia doesn't agree with babies so the bare minimum is usually given. Unfortunately very recent evidence has shown that this light level of anaesthesia may not be enough to give some women adequate pain relief.

One disadvantage of an epidural, of course, is that a woman may be a little *too* wide awake and, naturally enough, nervous about what's going to happen. Staff at Queen Charlotte's Hospital in London have come up with a simple and effective remedy for this: they play music to the mother through headphones. Nearly 80 per cent of the women who tried it said the music really helped them; only 5 per cent found it no use at all.

Caesarian sections can also be done under acupuncture, analgesia or hypnosis, though not many practitioners have the appropriate experience.

AFTER THE BIRTH

Treatment for a bruised perineum, episiotomy or tear

Homoeopathic Arnica is a favourite remedy. This can be taken both during labour, when it's said to help prevent bruising, and afterwards when it may help heal it. Arnica, homoeopaths say, also speeds healing of episiotomies and tears. Calendula ointment applied directly onto the scar may also alleviate discomfort. Ordinary witch hazel (Hamamelis) solution, bought at the chemists and diluted 1:3 with cooled, boiled water, sometimes works a treat, too.

Helen, who tried Arnica during her second labour, eleven years after the first, reports: 'I had a tear and several stitches. But the difference in me compared to a similar first delivery was fantastic. I had no bruising or swelling – sitting down was no problem at all – *no* afterpains of any kind. I felt so comfortable it wasn't true! Added bonus was no difficulty with bowel motions.'

Postnatal exercises

You can find details of these in any number of books. They're also discussed in Chapter 10. All I want to say here is that they're really important – particularly the ones designed to strengthen the pelvic floor.

You should do your pelvic floor exercises all through pregnancy, *immediately* after the birth (go gently at first, especially if you're at all sore) and for several months afterwards. Better still, *keep* doing them regularly for the rest of your life! A strong pelvic floor is the best defence against incontinence and uterine prolapse (see Chapter 10) which, once present, are hard to treat.

Breastfeeding

If you don't want to breastfeed you'll have to let the milk dry up of its own accord. Drugs are seldom given these days. So you can expect quite a bit of discomfort until your breasts have got used to the idea that their milk isn't needed! However, if you've been using hypnosis through pregnancy and during your labour, you may also find the same technique helps with painful, engorged breasts. Fiona, who didn't breastfeed any of her children, says that hypnosis made all the difference. 'Unlike the previous occasions my breasts weren't painful. Or rather,' she explains, 'I knew they were painful but the pain was way away above the corner of my room. I thought: "This is painful and uncomfortable but I'm not worried about it." That,' she adds, 'is what really convinced me that hypnosis works.'

You can also, of course, use hypnosis if you *are* breastfeeding and your breasts temporarily get engorged. Homoeopathic remedies are also worth a try but you'll need advice on which one to take. Another good remedy, according to herbalists, and easy enough to get hold of, is the humble cabbage leaf applied to the breast!

To increase your supply of milk, the best approach is to feed your baby whenever he seems to want to suck. Over a couple of days supply will catch up with demand. This method, advocated by several self-help organizations and those doctors and midwives who understand breastfeeding, very rarely fails. If it does you could try acupuncture, herbs or homoeopathy. For details consult a practitioner. You also need to eat a good diet and there's some evidence that vitamin B_{12} is particularly important during lactation.

Sore and cracked nipples are said to respond to Calendula ointment. And good, old-fashioned fresh air often helps, too – if you don't mind going around topless. Mastitis – the symptoms are an inflamed area on the breast and an increased temperature – may respond to alternative remedies, for example, homoeopathic Bryonia and Belladonna, but if you don't get better very quickly you'll need to take antibiotics. Your doctor should choose one that allows you to continue to feed your baby.

'Difficult' babies

A baby that continues to cry for no apparent reason can some-times be soothed with homoeopathic Chamomilla: the granules, obtainable from most health food shops, are sprinkled on the baby's tongue.

I've heard of several reports recently that fretful, crying babies respond very well to cranial osteopathy. It's thought that birth – particularly a difficult delivery – upsets the bones of their skulls which, for some reason, do not return to normal. I should add that this view is still not accepted by the majority of ordinary osteopaths – let alone orthodox doctors. However some mothers have been impressed by the results.

Patricia Kelly reported in the *Guardian* that after cranial osteopathy her own baby, Sally, changed overnight 'from the irritable little ratbag she was to the most adorable sweet-tempered child you could imagine'.

Another mother wrote in a local NCT newsletter that her baby, Victoria, slept very little and cried most of the time, despite being obviously well fed. After a few weeks she consulted an osteopath who specializes in the cranio-sacral technique (the correct name for cranial osteopathy):

She was able to tell that I had had a long labour from the shape of Victoria's head, which was flattened on top. I was told that the bones of the skull, which overlap during the birth process, had become temporarily jammed in Victoria's case due to the length of the labour. She would have grown out of it eventually, the osteopath hastened to tell me, but her screaming was probably due to headaches caused by bone overlap, which could actually be felt round the temples.

After treatment, Victoria got better immediately.

the results . . . were truly spectacular. The night after the first treatment Victoria slept through the night and continued to do so for the next three months . . . The crying and screaming fits stopped altogether and she became, and still is, one of the sunniest-natured babies around. Family and friends were totally amazed at the change in her.

Some other babies are miserable because they have an allergy to cows' milk. This can happen even in a breastfed baby because the allergenic (allergy-producing) substances in the mother's own diet get into her milk. The only cure for this is for the woman to avoid all dairy products – at least for the time being. Most babies grow out of their allergy as they get older. Other substances in a woman's diet may also affect her baby – a lot of fruit, for example, or alcohol. Quite recent research suggests that smoking – by either parent – may also be to blame for 'colicky' babies.

Postnatal mental illness

This is a very complicated subject. Much has been written about it but no one really understands it. The cause is probably partly psychological – having a baby is an over-whelming experience for everyone and for some women it can be positively traumatic – and partly hormonal. The illness can vary from the relatively mild 'three-day blues', which are so common as to be considered normal, to the rare full-blown psychosis which requires admission to hospital. In the middle is postnatal depression. It's this I want to talk about here.

Postnatal depression is thought to affect between 10 and 15 per cent of all mothers, so it's quite common. Many of these women never seek help, though, because they're scared to admit to the fact that they're feeling miserable and depressed at a time when they should – or so they believe – be brimming with joy. Fortunately, this attitude is changing with greater publicity and with the formation of self-help groups. It's now recognized that postnatal depression is an illness and needs treatment.

A popular theory is that this illness is caused by extra sensitivity to the fluctuating hormone levels a woman experiences after birth. This ties in with the fact that there seems to be a very strong link between postnatal depression and the subsequent development of the premenstrual syndrome. But current thinking is that though hormones may play a part they don't tell the whole story. The fact that many women have been helped by progesterone doesn't, as Vivienne Welburn points out in her book *Postnatal Depression*,[14] prove that postnatal depression is caused by a hormonal imbalance. More recent research has suggested that the endorphins may have something to do with it but, again, the evidence isn't yet all that convincing.

Welburn concludes that mental and physical stresses are just as important. I agree. Society – that means all of us, doctors and nurses included – has some pretty unrealistic expectations of motherhood. The dream is lovely, the truth – often – quite the reverse. So maybe a change in all our attitudes, a recognition that having a baby is damned hard, usually unrewarding work, might help prevent at least some cases of postnatal depression. Mothers also need practical, as well as emotional, help, and postnatal support groups are now going some way to providing both.

Is there anything else that can be done? Some researchers have found a link between postnatal depression and previous use of the Pill and this, in turn, may be due to the higher blood copper levels seen in women on the Pill. This is based on findings which link excessive copper with other forms of mental illness.

Copper rises anyway during pregnancy so it could be to blame, Pill or no Pill. Another interesting finding is that a zinc deficiency increases the size of the copper overload and, as I've already discussed, some alternative practitioners believe that at least some pregnant women may be zinc deficient. In morning sickness, a deficiency of vitamin B_6 has been found to be linked with that of zinc (page 177) and even some orthodox medics believe that women on the Pill who get depressed may need extra amounts of this vitamin. So perhaps it might help in postnatal depression, too.

All this research has still to be confirmed. But it does seem as though diet could be important. Many alternative practitioners believe it is – and say the prevention of postnatal depression is one reason for their emphasis on good eating habits. At the very least, a healthy diet goes some way to fighting a new mother's main enemy – exhaustion.

TREATMENT FOR POSTNATAL DEPRESSION

This is similar to the treatment of any other sort of depression and is usually based on drugs. Occasionally a woman's GP may suggest a consultation with a psychiatrist but, unless he's interested in psychotherapy, you'll probably get drugs from him too. For more details of the treatment of depression read Chapter 14. Vivienne Welburn also discusses in her book some of the options available.

ALTERNATIVE TREATMENT

I'm not including psychotherapy here because, although it *is* still something of an alternative, you can get the information you need from Chapter 14.

Most alternative practitioners claim some success with postnatal depression and there are, for example, specific homoeopathic remedies for this form of illness. The most useful is said to be Sepia. The homoeopathic 'picture' is of someone who is weak, sad, tired and totally indifferent to her surroundings.

Some osteopaths – particularly those who practise the cranio-sacral technique – believe that treatment after childbirth can help prevent postnatal depression.

Acupuncture sometimes seems to have a dramatic effect. Sylvia went to an acupuncturist after nine months of depression. Drugs hadn't helped. 'At first I admit I didn't think it was going to work,' she says, 'but by this time I was willing to try anything. After five treatments I was great. I woke up one morning and it seemed as if someone had pressed the right button at last.'

Some acupuncturists say they see very little postnatal depression among their regular customers. Diet again? Or is the explanation more mundane? As one practitioner admitted, most of her patients come from the type of family where the father is prepared to take time off work to help with the baby so the mother should be under less stress. (Not that it always follows, of course.) 'If postnatal depression is a physical imbalance, I'd not think it would be too difficult to treat,' she added. 'But if it's related to psychological or emotional factors, as an acupuncturist you can't do much about them.'

8. Infertility

The treatment of infertility is fast becoming one of medicine's success stories. It can now help many women who, only a few years ago, would have had little chance of having their own babies. Ovaries that aren't working properly, if at all, can be kicked into action with drugs. Blocked or damaged tubes can sometimes be repaired: if this proves impossible then *in vitro* fertilization (IVF) can be used to bypass them altogether.

Male infertility is usually much less easy to put right. Although there has been some progress recently, infertility in men is still poorly understood and, for many couples, artificial insemination by donor (AID) remains the only answer.

Several excellent books are now available on the medical approach to infertility so I won't go into it in too much detail here. Instead I want to look at some of the reasons why, despite all the exciting developments in the field, the treatment of this distressing and common condition – it's thought to affect as many as one in seven of all couples – leaves a lot to be desired.

In this chapter, too, I'll be talking about miscarriage. One reason is that, as Dr Andrew Stanway points out in his book *Why Us?*,[1] as many as 50 per cent of infertile couples who do manage to start a pregnancy then lose that much-wanted baby because the woman miscarries. Another is that quite a number of 'normally' fertile couples lose all their babies this way. They feel just as bereft and devastated as those who are infertile. Maybe even more so, because they've had their hopes raised – and dashed – so often. A third reason is that, from the point of view of holistic medicine, infertility or miscarriage in a woman may be regarded as arising from the same source: some dis-ease (not necessarily the same thing as disease) of body or mind – or both – which prevents her having children.

HOW THE DOCTORS CAN HELP WHEN YOU CAN'T CONCEIVE

The diagnosis and treatment of infertility can be a long drawn-out and humiliating business, even when the medical staff are sympathetic – which, sadly, is not always the case. It's no fun being questioned about your sex life: are you having sex 'properly'? often enough? at the right time of the month? and so on. All the same, these questions are important and many couples have conceived after a bit of advice about the fertile period (see Chapter 6). Often it's useful for the woman to keep a temperature chart so she can see if and when she's ovulating and to use some of the other indicators of fertility mentioned in Chapter 6.

The causes of infertility: what we know and what we don't

Because, for most people, getting pregnant seems all too easy, those who go month after month without conceiving understandably worry that something is wrong with them. But there may not be: even for the most fertile of couples, pregnancy is a matter of chance. And the older you are, the less fertile you become: fertility declines quite markedly after the age of 35. If you smoke, you may also take longer to conceive, according to two recent studies.[2,3]

Doctors consider that any couple who fails to conceive after about one year of regular, unprotected intercourse may have a fertility problem. This assumption is based on statistics: about a quarter of all couples conceive the first month they try, 50 per cent will have succeeded by six months and about 85 per cent by a year. So if, by then, you're one of the 15 per cent who are still trying, you have some reason to think that all is not as it should be. That doesn't mean you're completely sterile – very few couples are. But it indicates that you have one or more problems which make conception more difficult.

The woman

Some people suspect they may be infertile long before that first year is up, though. Often this is because the woman has no periods at all or very infrequent ones. This suggests that she's not ovulating, or ovulating so seldom that her partner's sperm have never had a decent chance to get to grips with one of her eggs. Of course, it only takes one egg and one sperm to make a baby. But timing is crucial: an egg can only be fertilized if it meets a sperm within about ten hours of being released. If it happens to arrive on a day when the couple doesn't have sex – no baby.

Often, however, the couple has had no inkling that they might have a problem. The woman has been having regular periods and it's only when the investigations start that they discover that those periods are anovulatory – that is, no eggs are being produced.

Ovulation problems are usually treated with drugs. Depending on the results of tests which examine a woman's hormone levels, the doctors may prescribe either bromocriptine, clomiphene citrate, gonadotrophins or, more recently, luteinizing hormone releasing hormone (LHRH) or urofollitrophin. All these treatments have proved very successful. Though they don't work for everyone, most women – up to 90 per cent – will ovulate on one or more of these drugs and up to three-quarters of those will become pregnant.

Fertility drugs, like most potent medicines, can have side effects. Gonadotrophins, for example, used to be notorious because they often resulted in multiple births. But doctors have fiddled around with the doses to try to reduce this risk. These days only about one in five women who becomes pregnant on the drug produces more than one baby – and usually no more than two – but triplets still occasionally crop up.

Bromocriptine and clomiphene don't seem to be associated with multiple births but clomiphene may give a woman hot flushes and make her feel bloated; bromocriptine can make her feel sick. Only a minority of women are said to get these side effects and most probably don't mind too much, provided they get pregnant fairly quickly. And – at least with bromocriptine – they often do.

In about a quarter of women, infertility is due to damaged tubes. Sometimes this damage is deliberate – as a result of a sterilization operation which the woman later regrets. Or it may be the result of a pelvic infection. This can have many causes ranging from a burst appendix to a sexually transmitted disease such as gonorrhoea or chlamydia. IUDs can also lead to pelvic infection: recent evidence shows that this form of contraception is a real threat to fertility, especially in young women who've never had a baby (see Chapter 6). Usually a woman will know she's had a pelvic infection but not always, as there may be no obvious symptoms.

A condition known as endometriosis (see page 101) can often cause infertility. Though it's not clear exactly why, the scar tissue that develops may tether the tubes so that they can't swing over to catch the newly released egg. (It often affects the other parts of a woman's reproductive tract too.)

If the fallopian tubes have been damaged by disease, repair isn't at all easy though it may be possible. If endometriosis is preventing conception, danazol may be able to clear the tubes and also improve matters elsewhere so that fertility is restored. Unfortunately, though, this drug has several unpleasant side effects (see page 311) and many women find they have to give it up before it's had time to work.

Surgery, too, may be able to repair tubes damaged by disease. But only 5 to 20 per cent of these operations succeed. However, good results – a success rate of up to 80 per cent is claimed by some surgeons – can be achieved for operations to reverse sterilization. But success depends very much on the techniques used for the original operation and on the skill of the surgeon who's doing the reversal. Some fertility specialists believe that the best chance for a woman with blocked or badly scarred tubes lies in *in vitro* fertilization. While this may well be so, this treatment is not so far widely available on the National Health Service. And, even in expert hands, the odds are against pregnancy. The best success rates – of over 30 per cent – come only from the most experienced IVF teams and then usually only when two or more embryos have been implanted at the same time. So there's always a risk that a woman may have more babies than she bargained for.

Nevertheless, this *is* a promising technique and one that's being improved all the time. Many specialists believe that IVF could well prove to be the treatment of choice for blocked tubes – one day. But we're not there yet. There are very real ethical dilemmas associated with this research which must be resolved if IVF is ever to find a routine place in the treatment of infertility. I suspect that, for nearly all of us, this technique touches on our deepest feelings about the meaning and sanctity of life and this makes it almost impossible to discuss the subject rationally. Even those of us who believe in the right of every couple to have their own child may question whether this justifies manipulating what is, at the very least, a potential baby. On the other hand, if abortion is ethical under certain, well-defined circumstances, surely IVF is too. I don't know what the answer is: maybe there isn't one. At any rate a big question mark hangs over this research at the moment.

Cervical problems are yet another cause of female infertility and are estimated to affect up to a third of all infertile women. The cervical mucus of a normally fertile women is hostile to sperms during most of her menstrual cycle – it's thick and sticky and acts as a barrier to keep them out. But it changes when she's in her fertile phase. The thin, watery, stretchy mucus that many women notice around the middle of their cycle is designed to help the sperms on their way. But the cervices of some infertile women seem unable to let the sperm in at all even for those few days a month. Sometimes the mucus is obviously of the 'infertile' type – but not always. The mucus may look as if it should be fertile but it isn't. The sperms just don't manage to get past it.

The reasons for this are far from clear. The woman may be producing antibodies to her partner's sperms or the semen may contain its own antibodies which kill off the sperms before they can penetrate the cervix. There is evidence for both these suggestions. The important thing, though, is that, whatever the cause, the sperms never get within spitting distance of the egg.

Diagnosis of this form of infertility depends on the post-coital test. The couple is asked to have sex as near as possible to the predicted day of ovulation (when the sperms *should* have the best chance of getting through the mucus) and to come to the hospital as soon as possible afterwards. A sample of mucus is then taken and examined under a microscope. If the mucus is normal then the sperms can be seen swimming quickly and easily through it. If it's hostile they appear dead or clumped together.

If antibodies are found to be the problem – either in the man or the woman – then powerful immunosuppressive drugs may be prescribed to damp down antibody production. However, results are unpredictable and some doctors believe that these drugs are too risky to be used in infertility.

In vitro fertilization may also been used in the treatment of cervical hostility. Though this is a fairly new use of the technique there's no reason why it shouldn't work just as well in this condition as it does for blocked tubes. But the ethical problems, of course, remain the same.

The man

Gone are the days when infertility was regarded as the 'woman's problem'. We now know that, in about 40 per cent of couples, it's the man whose reproductive equipment isn't working properly. This doesn't mean he's impotent or 'less of a man'. Quite the reverse, perhaps: research has indicated that very 'macho' men may be more likely to be infertile than their more retiring brothers![4] (Some men *are* impotent of course and so, no matter how healthy their sperms, can't impregnate their partners. But this isn't a common cause of infertility and the treatment often hinges on psychosexual counselling, which is beyond the scope of this book.)

The usual cause of male infertility is a low sperm count. Although, theoretically, only one sperm is needed to fertilize the egg, in practice too few sperms – less than 20 million per millilitre of semen – seem to reduce the chances of conception though they don't rule it out altogether. A poor sperm count may be due to a number of things. Sometimes the fault lies in the man's plumbing; sometimes the problem is hormonal. Some men produce normal numbers of sperms but they're deformed, dead or such bad swimmers that they never make it to the egg. If, under the microscope, the sperms are seen in clumps then anti-sperm antibodies are probably to blame.

Mechanical, 'plumbing' defects in men, as well as in women, are sometimes the result of a sexually transmitted infection. Surgery may be able to correct them. But blocked vasa deferentia – the tubes that carry the sperms from the testes – are, like the woman's fallopian tubes, a tricky proposition for even the best surgeon.

If anti-sperm antibodies seem to be the problem, drugs may be able to deal with them but, as we've seen, there are good reasons why not all doctors are prepared to offer this treatment. Easier to treat are varicoceles – varicose veins at the top of the testis – and results are good.

There's a good chance of success, too, if the man's low sperm count is thought to be due to overheated testicles. Sperm production occurs best when the testes are at a temperature 2–3 degrees C below that of the rest of the body. But if a man wears very tight underpants or spends large parts of the day sitting down, he may be making himself less fertile! He should therefore change his style of underwear – loose-fitting boxer shorts are ideal – take more exercise and regularly bathe his testicles in cold water. 'Seemingly miraculous results' can be achieved this way, according to Dr Stanway. Though not strictly a medical treatment, this may be something your doctor recommends before he suggests going on to more drastic remedies. Another possible solution is to inseminate the woman artificially using her husband's semen (AIH). This sometimes succeeds where normal intercourse has failed.

If a man's problem is hormonal there's not too much that can be done at the moment, though recently there's been some promising research with the hormone known as LHRH (luteinizing hormone releasing hormone). This can be used to treat some types of female infertility as well, as we have seen, and is administered by means of a portable pump which the man or woman wears continuously for several months. LHRH can help even those men who have never had a normal puberty, who have a condition known as hypogonadotrophic hypogonadism. The results from one study suggest that up to 40 per cent of these men may become fathers following LHRH treatment.

Another recent development has been the application of IVF techniques. This method is useful for men who have either low sperm counts or large numbers of damaged or abnormal sperms. The method depends on the fact that these men still do produce some healthy sperms which can be concentrated in the lab before they're allowed to come into contact with the woman's egg. The technique takes much of the chance element out of natural fertilization because it gives the healthy sperms a head start. Pregnancy rates of up to about 33 per cent have been reported. But not all researchers get such good results.

For many infertile men, then, treatment is not the answer and AID may be the only possible route left for couples who are determined to have their own baby. Interestingly enough, research shows that couples who opt for AID are much less likely to split up than those who've had their babies the conventional way. Whether this technique actually helps cement a marriage is doubtful: AID couples have already proved their commitment to one another by staying together despite all the emotional strains that are an inevitable part of infertility.

But there is another problem associated with AID: its

effects on the children. Though AID children are in a some-what anomalous situation legally – they are not supposed to be registered as the natural offspring of their mothers' partners – in practice the law turns a blind eye. There is still, however, the moral debate about whether these children should be told of their origins when they're old enough to understand. This, of course, could create all sorts of problems and in the United States is already doing so. Some American children, on learning that they were AID babies, have felt genuinely 'fatherless' and have embarked on a (usually unrewarding) search for their biological fathers.

One, interviewed by the *Sunday Times* a few years ago, was quoted as saying: 'It's an obsession with me. I must find my father even if it's only to discover what kind of man sells his sperm and ultimately his own flesh and blood . . . How is a child produced this way supposed to feel about a father who sold the essence of his life so cheaply and to a total stranger?' Another girl quoted in the same article said: 'What upset my whole sense of being was that nobody knew who my "real" father was: as though half of me did not, does not exist.'

These may be extreme reactions but few of the researchers in the field are entirely happy with the situation. Some of them are also concerned that, as more and more babies are born as a result of AID, there's a real possibility that a natural half-, or even full, brother and sister might unknowingly commit incest. This isn't a serious threat at the moment but in the future, who knows?

For some couples AID may seem like the answer to all their dreams. But what will it mean for their children and their grandchildren? As one of the women interviewed by the *Sunday Times* pointed out when she, too, was con-sidering AID (her own husband was infertile): 'I came to understand my mother's decision to have a baby by AID. She was no thoughtless ogre but a woman who craved her own child. But me, how can I make such a decision? My child would lack two generations of fathers.'

HOW THE DOCTORS CAN HELP WHEN YOU MISCARRY

Miscarriage is a common event: it is estimated that approximately one in five diagnosed pregnancies ends this way and recent evidence suggests that at least 8, and possibly as many as 30, per cent of pregnancies come to grief at such an early stage that the woman didn't even know she'd conceived. If the higher figure is correct – and the experts are in some doubt about that – it would mean that half of all pregnancies end in miscarriage. A more conservative estimate would suggest that about one in three does.

A woman who has one or even two miscarriages is usually not considered to have a medical problem unless these happen later on in pregnancy and there are indications that her cervix is too weak – 'incompetent' in medical jargon – to keep the baby in the uterus. If this seems to be the case then her doctors may suggest inserting a special stitch into the cervix to stop it opening up prematurely. But though this treatment seems logical enough, there is as yet no good scientific evidence that it works.

Many miscarriages of course occur quite early in pregnancy and a number of reasons have been put forward to explain them. For a detailed account of these, you might like to read *Miscarriage* by Ann Oakley, Dr Ann McPherson and Helen Roberts.[5] But the question of why babies miscarry is also central to the alternative approach to treatment so I'd like to discuss it in some detail here.

Many miscarriages seem to be due to some abnormality in the baby: either in its chromosomes as, for example, in Down's syndrome, or in its anatomy – spina bifida, for instance. For this reason, doctors often reassure women who've had a miscarriage that it was nature's way of getting rid of an imperfect foetus and therefore something for which they should be thankful.

But was the imperfection itself an accident of nature or was it caused by something over which we might have some control? We don't yet know for sure but there is evidence that environmental factors such as pollution and the food we eat may be to blame. Conventional medicine acknowledges this possibility – some toxic chemicals definitely seem to lie at the root of some foetal deformities. But most orthodox practitioners believe we still don't know enough about this aspect of miscarriage to do anything more than advise pregnant women to eat 'sensibly' and avoid obviously harmful influences such as drugs, cigarettes and alcohol. They may also warn against working with known hazardous chemicals during pregnancy. As we shall see, alternative practitioners, especially those interested specifically in nutritional medicine and environmental pollution, feel we can go much further than this.

Hormonal factors may also be involved in some miscarriages. But trials aimed at testing this idea haven't provided much support for it. Nevertheless some gynaecologists still prescribe hormones in an attempt to prevent miscarriage: quite probably the very same doctors who reject alternative medicine because it doesn't have a sufficiently sound scientific basis! This wouldn't matter so much if hormones were known to be safe, but they're not. They may actually damage the foetus: this was certainly the case with diethyl stilboestrol, an artificial hormone used in the 1950s. This was found many years later to be responsible for vaginal cancers and various other reproductive problems in the female children born to mothers who'd been given it during pregnancy.

There may be some hope, though, for women who have repeated miscarriages. As recently as 1985, a team of doctors working at St Mary's Hospital Medical School in London reported on the results of a controlled trial of an immunological treatment.[6] There is some evidence that women with this particular problem react adversely to the part of the foetus which comes from its father. Their immune systems recognize it as foreign, much as they would do a transplanted organ. This obviously doesn't happen in a normal pregnancy because in some way – no one is quite sure how – the foetus is protected from the mother's immune system. It seems, though, that in a normal pregnancy the woman produces antibodies against her partner's white blood cells. Many women with a history of recurrent miscarriage don't.

Researchers are still puzzling over why antibodies *against* the father's cells should be able to protect the baby when they might be predicted to have the opposite effect. A couple of theories have been suggested but neither of them really fits the bill. However, the fact is that they do. So the researchers have stimulated the production of these antibodies in the women who don't make any, simply by injecting them with a preparation of their partners' white blood cells.

For the trial the women were divided into two groups. One group was given an injection of their partners' cells and the other received a similar injection containing their own cells. Neither the women nor their doctors knew which injection was which. The trial was thus 'double blind' and controlled for the placebo effect. This is an important aspect of many trials but particularly so in miscarriage. Previous research has shown that *any* treatment seems to 'cure' a fair number of women, and as many as 70 per cent of women who've had three miscarriages will go on to have a successful pregnancy without any treatment at all! It's been suggested that the doctor's sympathy, care and understanding may be responsible. So the placebo effect may indeed be at work even when no treatment is offered.

The St Mary's researchers believe that the comfort and encouragement they give all their patients may definitely reduce stress and so help the baby's development. There is a considerable amount of evidence from research on animals that stress is indeed harmful during pregnancy and some that suggests the same may be true for human mothers too. So you can see how hard it is to interpret the results of any treatment for miscarriage. Hence the necessity for rigorous controls in this recent trial.

In fact the cure rate – the number of successful pregnancies – was much higher in the women given active treatment, the injection of their partners' cells. Nearly 80 per cent of them but only 37 per cent of the control group went on to have a normal baby. (Compared with the 70 per cent 'spontaneous' cures mentioned above, this success rate for the control group seems rather low but might be due to the fact that some of the women in the trial had had up to eight miscarriages.)

Clearly the active treatment was having an effect over and above that of the placebo. And so far it seems safe, though some questions remain to be answered: for example, why did 10 per cent of the foetuses grow more slowly than normal? Because the basis for the treatment is still so poorly understood some doctors feel it's still far too early to talk of a breakthrough.

WHY MEDICINE DOESN'T HAVE ALL THE ANSWERS

Despite all these exciting medical techniques doctors sometimes have to admit defeat. Estimates vary, but it seems that at most 60 per cent and maybe as few as a third of couples conceive following treatment. Medicine cannot help another third and about 12 per cent of infertile women and up to 10 per cent of infertile men have no obvious defect which could account for their failure to have a baby. As for miscarriage: although the new treatment described above may well help many couples suffering from recurrent miscarriages, it won't be the answer for all of them. And it will do nothing to prevent the 'one-off' miscarriages which, on present evidence, seem unlikely to have anything to do with antibody levels.

For the couples whom medicine has failed the realization dawns that their childlessness is probably a permanent state of affairs, but often only after they've been subjected to lengthy – and sometimes unpleasant – tests and treatment.

Carol and Pete Thompson are typical. Carol wrote: 'Pete and I have been trying unsuccessfully for just over seven years now and have experienced numerous tests and investigations over approximately a five-year period, resorting to drugs and AIH.' Later they told me in detail about their treatment.

'My sperm count was on the low side,' explained Pete. 'It wouldn't have been impossible for us to conceive but it would've relied on Carol being perfectly OK. There was no problem with her ovulation and her tubes weren't blocked. The only thing they were worried about was that there seemed to be a problem with the build-up in her endometrium.' (The endometrium, or lining of the uterus, normally grows and becomes well supplied with blood during the second half of the menstrual cycle in preparation for any fertilized egg. If this mechanism isn't working properly, the egg may not survive long enough for pregnancy to become established.)

At first the doctors suggested the 'cold baths' treatment mentioned earlier in this chapter to try to get Pete's sperm count up. The count improved and Pete began to feel more hopeful. But after about nine months Carol still wasn't pregnant, so interest switched to her. 'I had all the usual tests,' she said, 'and they didn't seem to reveal too much. They said I had to have a D and C and that would cure everything.' But – still no joy.

Carol's next investigation was a laparoscopy – an operation, sometimes done under a local anaesthetic, which allows the doctor to look inside the pelvis to check that all is normal. Result: nothing wrong. 'I then had hormone tests,' Carol went on, 'but I think they must have done them at the wrong time of the month because they got odd results.' A friend then recommended another specialist so off they went to see him – and all the tests had to be done again. 'He decided,' said Pete, 'that my sperms weren't swimming as fast as they should.' There was a suspicion that Carol's cervix might be hostile to Pete's sperms but, after two post-coital tests, the specialist changed his mind.

At that point, only two things appeared to be at all wrong: Pete's sperm count remained on the low side and there was still some concern that Carol's endometrium wasn't functioning properly. So they were both put on a drug – the same one: tamoxifen. This sometimes works for women who aren't ovulating. Its use in male infertility is much less well established (only a few well-informed specialists appear to know about it) but recent evidence does suggest it may boost a man's sperm count. Further trials are now planned to test this more thoroughly.

Tamoxifen didn't agree with Carol. 'I had a lot of pain around ovulation and really felt sore, bloated and generally quite awful.' She also gained weight. 'I stuck it for about six months and then because it obviously wasn't working I felt I just couldn't go on with it any more. But it took quite a while to lose the weight I'd put on.'

The Thompsons still aren't sure why they haven't had a baby yet but they are certain that conventional medicine isn't able to help them. More about that later, though.

Of course doctors don't always get it right; that would be too much to expect. But some seem to have more success than others, particularly in the tubal surgery department. A specialist who isn't all that good at mending tubes should ideally refer you to someone who is, but he may feel there's no point. This is what happened to Pauline, who is now in her mid-thirties.

'My problem,' she wrote, 'was blocked fallopian tubes following gonorrhoea which I had when I was twenty-nine and which was undetected for a while. The first hysterosalpingo-gram [where radio-opaque dye is introduced into the reproductive tract and viewed with X-rays] hurt and confirmed my worst fears that the tubes were blocked at the exit of the womb.' She then had a laparoscopy which revealed that her tubes were very badly blocked at both ends. 'My only chance of pregnancy was a test-tube baby.' At the time (1979) Pauline was working in the US and the best IVF teams were in the UK. 'I cried intermittently for eighteen months,' Pauline remembers.

In 1981, she finally returned to the UK and consulted a specialist at a London hospital. 'The doctor going over my notes said I had only a two to five per cent chance of an operation working, so another laparoscopy was a waste of time. But I insisted and, in 1982, the second tube was shown to be free. At this point I wondered about the American doctor's findings: had they been correct – they must have been – why would he lie or how could he have missed it?'

Pauline also tried some alternative methods: I'll come back to her story later. Here I'd like to talk about some other possible causes of infertility – which may be involved in miscarriage, too. Many doctors don't bother to mention them. This may be because they don't really believe in them: some of the problems I'll be discussing haven't been studied enough to give the sort of cast-iron scientific evidence on which many doctors like to base their treatment. Others are regarded by most specialists as being of minor importance. They may occur in a couple who also have a readily identifiable 'medical' difficulty and one which the specialist feels he can treat. Any other less obvious cause for a couple's infertility tends to get ignored once the medical machine has whirred into action. And, of course, there are some doctors who believe that all of what I'm about to tell you is a load of old rubbish. But I think they may be wrong – and a growing number of other doctors and alternative practitioners are sure they are.

INFERTILITY AND MISCARRIAGE: THE ALTERNATIVE APPROACH

Mind over matter?

'After my husband and I had been trying to conceive for about two years (tests had shown I had a blocked fallopian tube and my husband a low sperm count) . . . we started applying to adopt a baby and didn't think much more about trying other ways to become pregnant. We successfully adopted a baby girl and then I became pregnant and gave birth to a boy fifteen months later!' It does happen. More often, some people believe, than can be explained by chance alone. Even doctors who are absolutely committed to high-tech solutions will admit that they've seen couples adopt a baby and later have one of their own.

Just luck? Perhaps. But perhaps not. The possibility that our minds may influence our fertility can't be discounted, according to a recent medical textbook[7] which devotes several pages to 'Infertility as a psychosomatic disorder' and 'Adoption as a cure for infertility?' The author of this section – a psychologist working at a London hospital – concludes that there is no watertight scientific evidence that infertility is ever *caused* by psychological factors. But he concedes that once a couple have realized they have a fertility problem, whatever its cause, then they become stressed. Stress can have a profound effect on a woman's menstrual cycle: previously regular ovulation may become irregular or infrequent, or stop altogether. So conception becomes even less likely. Many specialists are well aware of this problem, of course. Hence the advice given to many couples after prolonged investigation to 'go away, forget about it and relax'. Easy to say; far from easy to do!

A few researchers, however, do believe that psychological problems may occasionally be the sole reason for a couple's failure to conceive. They have hypothesized that, because our nervous systems and the workings of our hormones are known to be linked in a variety of complex ways, our emotions may be able to affect our reproductive systems. They may do this not only by interfering with ovulation, as discussed above, but also by altering the chemical environment of the vagina, so that it becomes hostile to sperms. Or their fallopian tubes may go into spasm so that they're unable to carry the egg to the uterus. Stress, as we've seen, may perhaps have a role in miscarriage, too.

There's very little evidence to prove this, unfortunately. This is mainly because we're now talking about the sort of emotions that most people keep to themselves. They may even bury them so deep in their subconscious that they're unaware they have them. For example, in the literature there are reports of several women who've been unable to conceive until they've decided to give up rewarding careers. The implication, of course, is that their wish to start a family was conflicting with an equally strong desire to continue with life as it was. A perfectly natural dilemma and one that many of us have to face. Of course, most of us do conceive despite the pressures, but it says something about the society in which we live that for some women the decision to have a baby may be such a hard one to make both on the conscious and the subconscious level.

Some conflicts about motherhood, so the theory goes, are even more deep-seated than this. They may only be revealed after intensive psychotherapy or under hypnosis. These techniques don't lend themselves to the kind of large-scale controlled trials that might be able to provide the evidence we're looking for. So all we have to go on is case histories which, as any die-hard scientist will tell you, are interesting but prove nothing. Still, they do suggest, at the very least, that our unconscious motives may – sometimes – stand between us and the child our conscious selves so desperately want.

Take a small study published in 1966 of nine women suffering from recurrent miscarriage. All had cervical stitches inserted. Result? Five of them developed post-partum psychosis, a particularly severe form of postnatal depression, and three others needed psychotherapy during pregnancy.[8] It would be rash to draw conclusions from such a small uncontrolled trial but might it not just be possible that these women had a profound desire *not* to be pregnant?

RELAXATION, COUNSELLING AND HYPNOSIS: UNDERSTANDING
THE MOTIVES AND REMOVING THE BLOCKS

Though most orthodox practitioners may not believe that infertility is ever solely a psychosomatic disorder they would probably agree that a tense, anxious couple is less likely to conceive than happy, relaxed one. They also know that talking to couples about their problem and their feelings – 'counselling' – is very important. But all this takes second place to the medical treatment and, unless you're very lucky, the only advice you'll get on relaxation is to do it!

Truly holistic practitioners, on the other hand, whether

they're medically qualified or not, make relaxation an integral part of their treatment. Techniques differ (see Chapter 1) and some suit some people better than others. Pauline, mentioned above, took up yoga before she returned to England for more conventional medical treatment. The Thompsons received advice on how to relax using tapes.

Because relaxation is usually only a part of the treatment you'll receive if you consult an alternative practitioner and because the holistic approach is just that – a treatment of the *whole* person – it's not possible, or appropriate, to try to draw conclusions about how effective relaxation is as a treatment for infertility. It's just part of the 'package'.

Similarly, with hypnosis (see Chapters 1 and 14). At one level hypnosis is simply another way of getting someone to relax and it always goes hand in hand with the excellent counselling that is the hallmark of the best alternative practitioners. However, hypnosis may be able to achieve what ordinary relaxation can't: it can reveal aspects of a person's mind that would normally remain hidden and which may have a bearing on her infertility. One practitioner I spoke to described how he asks his clients, under hypnosis, to find 'that part of their subconscious mind that controls fertility. If they cannot find it at all then we can create it. If we do find it then we can make it so that it does its job better.'

Sometimes it happens that a client doesn't have any 'fertility part' but does have one for infertility. It's then necessary to find out why. This usually involves regression – taking the person, while under hypnosis, back through her life to try to find out what it is that has made it important for her – at a subconscious level – to remain childless. It may be that, as a child, she felt unloved or rejected. Not necessarily because her parents were unloving but because she misintepreted their behaviour.

One woman, for example, who had a history of repeated miscarriages, revealed under hypnosis that she'd been inconsolable when her parents left her for a short while to visit relatives abroad. She'd thought they weren't coming back. They did, of course, but it was the painful moments of separation and the subsequent weeks of loss – and not the joyful reunion – that remained fixed in her subconscious. But – again under hypnosis – the therapist was able to help her write the happy ending of the story into her subconscious. He asked her to visualize her parents' return and how they cuddled her and gave her presents. Under hypnosis, this experience became as real to her as if it was happening there and then. When, during a subsequent session, she was again regressed, it was this happy time – and not her previous distress – that she remembered.

Another woman had been infertile for ten years after having a baby which had died shortly after birth and which she had never seen. Since that time her periods had been scanty and there was very little sign of fertile cervical mucus. A short while after hypnosis she had a heavy period and around the middle of the following month began producing masses of fertile mucus.

It would be nice to be able to report that both these women went on to have normal healthy babies. But they didn't. The first one again lost hers, albeit at a later stage in pregnancy. The other woman lost contact with her practitioner about two years ago and he believes that, had she become pregnant, she would have got in touch.

But this approach does seem to work for a few couples who, after several years of infertility, *have* had a healthy baby. And this particular practitioner claims quite good results by combining his methods with AID. Women who've failed to conceive after one or two years of AID alone have become pregnant when hypnosis was used as well. This suggests that some psychological factor might have been getting in the way of conception. 'I can't prove anything,' this practitioner admits, 'but I've come to the conclusion that there are a number of people who are turning off their fertility and they can be made to turn it on again.'

Is he right? It's hard to say. His results are hardly impressive even though many of the women he sees are potentially fertile anyway – either because they've already had a baby in the past or have been accepted for AID. In theory they could conceive at any time – a criticism which he accepts. But he adds: 'The patients themselves say they feel marvellous. They say, "I don't mind carrying on because I feel so good." So even if they don't get pregnant there are some compensations.'

Can our diet and environment affect our fertility?

In February 1985 *Here's Health* published two accounts of successful alternative treatments for infertility which, the magazine claimed, 'will be heartening to those people who have been abandoned by the medical profession and consigned to the ranks of the "infertile".'

The first story was of Sue Bradley, who had suffered five miscarriages before consulting a medical doctor who is also a practitioner of nutritional medicine and clinical ecology. Such doctors believe that many of our modern ills are caused by deficiencies in our diet, food allergies and toxic chemicals in the environment (see also Chapters 1 and 7). The doctor's diagnosis was that Sue was suffering from certain mineral imbalances and was slightly allergic to some foods.

He put her on a diet free of additives and advised her to take large doses of supplements for up to four months before trying to conceive again. When she did become pregnant, everything was going well at twenty-nine weeks, the time she spoke to *Here's Health*. 'I felt enormous disbelief after the previous five miscarriages, and was very worried about this pregnancy,' she told the magazine. 'But this time everything seems to be progressing successfully.'

The other couple – Audrey and Ray Woolacott – had a baby with the help of IVF – not exactly an alternative technique! Still, the Woolacotts did use alternative medicine, in the form of nutritional supplements, after the first IVF attempt failed. They consulted Foresight, the society for pre-conceptual care (see Chapter 7). After four months of taking the supplements recommended by the Foresight doctors, Audrey returned to the clinic for a second go at IVF and this time it worked. The Woolacotts now have a healthy daughter, *Here's Health* reports.

Heartwarming stories – yes. But they tell us nothing about the effectiveness of the nutritional approach to infertility. As we've seen, recurrent miscarriage often responds quite well to any form of treatment, particularly if the doctor is kind, caring and goes out of his way to give a couple the support they need. And this is something Foresight doctors – and many other holistic practitioners – are extremely good at. As for IVF: the treatment fails more often than it succeeds. Maybe nutritional therapy did help the Woolacotts. But it might have been simply a matter of luck.

The same might be said of Felicity who, at the age of forty-four, now has a healthy baby following two miscarriages, the first when she was forty. Interestingly enough, Felicity didn't turn to nutritional medicine because she wanted a baby but mainly for bad periods and PMS. Gynaecologists had been unable to help her but after nutritional therapy – and some other alternatives – she felt much better. The baby came as a bit of a bonus, though in holistic as well as in hormonal terms, it's perhaps not too surprising. What better proof that Felicity's reproductive system was working as it should? Felicity reports: 'Life has *never* been better and I am extremely healthy generally.'

Nutrition hasn't so far provided a baby for the Thompsons. They were advised to go on a pretty rigid diet by their alternative practitioner and to take vitamins and minerals as well. Eighteen months later Carol still hadn't conceived though they did feel better for their new regime. 'After a while on the diet,' Carol explained, 'both Pete and I began to feel much more healthy and we now admit we couldn't go back to our old eating habits – we are now near-vegetarians, but eat the occasional chicken or fish. We are still hopeful,' she added, 'that things may work for us soon!'

As discussed in Chapter 2, nutritional medicine has some scientific basis. But though population studies do suggest that diet may help prevent disease, most of the research that might take this further has been done on animals. There is some evidence from human studies but this isn't so good: nearly all of it is either anecdotal – based on case histories – or comes from uncontrolled trials, so the results are not accepted by many doctors. That doesn't, of course, mean we should dismiss this approach – far from it. But nutritional medicine doesn't yet have the scientific community's seal of approval. This is for very good reasons: scientists aren't just a bunch of stuffy reactionaries; important new discoveries excite them just as much as they do other people. But scientists know that it is all too easy to misinterpret promising results unless they've been subjected to proper objective testing.

Having said that, what do we know about the effects of nutrition and other environmental influences? Before reading this section you might find it useful to refer to Chapters 2 and 7 (on eating for health and pregnancy respectively). These provide a detailed background of the links between dietary deficiencies, environmental toxins and the problems of pregnancy. Here I'm going to take a closer look at how this evidence may possibly help to explain infertility and miscarriage.

WHAT GETS INTO OUR BODIES FROM THE WORLD AROUND US: NOT ENOUGH OF SOME THINGS, TOO MUCH OF OTHERS?

A good, balanced diet is an essential foundation for a healthy pregnancy. There's abundant evidence that when people are living at starvation level, their fertility and their ability to carry a healthy baby to term is affected. That doesn't apply to most of us, of course. But some nutritional experts question whether even the average middle-class diet – let alone that of people living in less affluent circumstances – really is all that 'good' or 'balanced'. Certain vital components may be deficient or lacking. And other substances which end up in our bodies, either from the food we eat or from the world around us, may have quite harmful effects on our ability either to conceive or to maintain a pregnancy.

Good and bad minerals

Zinc appears to have a role in preserving fertility, according to a number of studies. Biochemist Dr Jeffrey Bland, a leading US exponent of the nutritional approach, cites evidence that some women with a long-standing fertility problem may be suffering from borderline hypothyroidism – that is, their thyroid glands are slightly below par.[9] Further research has suggested that this may be due to a zinc deficiency. Adequate amounts of zinc are also necessary if a man is to produce normal amounts of healthy sperm. Diets which are only moderately deficient in zinc may lead to a reduced sperm count which can be improved if zinc is given in the form of supplements.[9]

Reduced levels of zinc have also been implicated in foetal abnormalities (see Chapter 7). A woman is more likely to miscarry a defective foetus than a normal one, so adequate levels of zinc may help, some investigators believe, to guard against miscarriage. However, as I explained in Chapter 7, the latest research seems to have largely demolished the hypothesis that zinc deficiency is a problem during pregnancy.

Nor is there yet much support for Foresight's claims that other nutritional deficiencies, and the adverse effects of common environmental pollutants, cause many of the early miscarriages found to be due to deformities and/or chromosomal defects. There's a little evidence – so far, from laboratory work – that inadequate selenium levels may lead to chromosome damage, according to Foresight Chairman Mrs Belinda Barnes. And Professor D. Bryce-Smith, of Reading University, believes he has evidence that the toxic heavy metals lead and cadmium may have adverse effects on the foetus. The lead in our bodies comes largely from petrol and the lead-based solder often used to seal food cans (though some manufacturers have apparently changed to safer sealing methods); cadmium from a number of sources including cigarette smoke. Incidentally, if your diet contains adequate amounts of zinc, this may help offset the bad effects

of these heavy metals. But I must again stress that none of
this research has been confirmed so far.

Vitamins

Vitamin B_6 may have a role in curing 'unexplained' infertility
in women. One study, published in 1979,[10] revealed that
twelve out of fourteen infertile women conceived following
treatment with this vitamin. Vitamin B_{12} has also proved
useful in some cases. But it is doubtful whether deficiencies
of either of these vitamins are at the root of many cases of
infertility.

Another B vitamin, folic acid, is said to protect against
recurrent miscarriages (it may also have a role in preventing
birth defects – see Chapter 7). Again, though, there's not too
much evidence to support this claim. In any case, nearly all
pregnant women in the UK are prescribed folic acid, usually
combined with an iron supplement, as a matter of course.

Adequate vitamin C levels may also be involved in preventing neural tube defects (see Chapter 7) and hence, by
implication, may help stop some miscarriages. This vitamin
has also been used to treat certain types of male infertility: it
appears to reduce the clumping of sperms due to antibodies.

Although all these vitamins have the reputation of being
'safe', side effects have been reported with large doses of
some of them, albeit rarely (see Chapter 2). It is just these so-
called 'megadoses' that alternative practitioners sometimes
advise. Yet they report few, if any, problems. This may be
because they monitor their patients very closely and are able
to step in to correct any imbalances which the vitamin
therapy itself may cause. But one has to bear in mind that this
is a relatively new area and we can't know for certain that
such treatment is always entirely safe.

Vitamin E is one of the alternative practitioners' favourite
'fertility' vitamins. But the evidence in its favour is extremely
slim and most medically qualified nutritional experts don't
believe there is much to be gained by prescribing it. Moreover, vitamin E is one of the fat-soluble vitamins and may

occasionally cause side effects at doses of as little as 100 IU a day.

Alternative practitioners sometimes also prescribe vitamin A – another fat-soluble vitamin – for infertility. Massive doses of it are sometimes recommended. If taken for only short periods of time – a month or less – these appear to have no side effects on the woman, at least. But because vitamin A can be teratogenic, or damaging to the foetus (see Chapter 7), it would be extremely unwise to take supplements if you were trying to conceive or thought there was any chance that you might be pregnant. So, as you can see, it may not be the most appropriate vitamin for an infertility problem.

There is some evidence, however, that a *little* extra vitamin A may help prevent neural tube deformities (see Chapter 7) and a trial has been set up to test this idea. In the meantime, if you're pregnant don't take these supplements without advice from someone who is properly qualified to understand the implications. If you're infertile and have been taking vitamin A, ask your practitioner when it would be safe for you to try again to conceive. And remember, vitamin A can be toxic in doses above 5000 IU a day for some people and above 25,000 IU for many.

The same goes for another fat-soluble vitamin, D, also sometimes recommended for women planning a baby because of its important role in the healthy development of bones. But vitamin D can cause side effects at daily doses above about 1000 IU. As Dr Carl Pfeiffer, a leading expert in the field, has pointed out: 'Vitamin D requirements are not uniform, and what may be appropriate for one individual may be toxic for another.'[11]

Other nutritional supplements

If we know little about the benefits of extra vitamins, we know even less about some of the other supplements sometimes prescribed by alternative practitioners for infertility. A popular one contains extracts of various animal glands. Even the practitioners who recommend these supplements seem to have no idea how they're supposed to work other than to suggest that they give your own glands – the ones that are involved in controlling fertility – the right 'starting' materials for hormone production. But since these 'building blocks' are present in abundance in all but the most deprived diets, any benefit must be marginal.

WHAT CAN WE CONCLUDE FROM THE EVIDENCE?

There's no doubt that gross malnutrition can have an effect on fertility. The question is: is it possible to suffer a degree of malnutrition while being 'well fed'? So far, sound evidence that marginal dietary deficiencies exist or that they are a key factor in infertility is lacking, though they may be for some people. And though some toxic chemicals may cause miscarriage and other birth problems, we do not know to what extent, if at all, everyday exposure to substances such as lead and cadmium is to blame. On the other hand indiscriminate, uninformed vitamin supplementation may also be risky.

For this reason I think it's sensible not to jump to the conclusion that extra vitamins and minerals are the answer to your problem. First of all, find out if your diet is adequate: it may be, particularly if you eat wholefoods, don't drink, smoke, or drink excessive amounts of coffee or feel you're under stress – all these things can deplete your vitamin and mineral levels.

If you're in any doubt, consult either a doctor with an interest in nutritional medicine or a properly qualified naturopath. A good one will probably first recommend certain changes in your diet. These may be enough to correct any deficiency. If not, a small amount of extra vitamins and minerals should do it. If your practitioner prescribes supplements in doses well above the recommended daily allowance (for a discussion of RDAs see Chapter 2) he or she must be prepared to check you regularly to make sure you're not suffering from any side effects and to change your treatment, if no improvement is seen. Above all, remember that 'megadose' therapy of the fat-soluble vitamins may be risky, and should be avoided at all costs if you're pregnant or trying to conceive.

What else can alternative medicine do?

The nutritional approach to infertility has probably the most evidence to back it yet, as we've seen, even that's still far from convincing. Nevertheless I believe that's where you should start. This applies just as much to those couples who are undergoing orthodox medical treatment as to those who have switched completely to one or more of the alternatives. Infertility and miscarriage, particularly of the 'unexplained' sort, are such complex problems that *anything* you can do to improve your general health may increase your chances of having a baby. In fact the nutritional approach to health, as I explained in Chapter 2, isn't really an alternative at all. All professionals – alternative and orthodox – agree that good nutrition is fundamental to health. Where they differ is in how they define it! A good holistic practitioner, whatever his or her particular expertise, will start off by grilling you about your eating habits and may suggest some changes in your diet before going on to more specific treatment.

Because none of these experts 'specializes' in infertility in the way that some orthodox medics do, and because they see infertility as just a symptom of a more general health problem, it's impossible to give you any idea of just how effective these other alternative methods are. Even more so because many practitioners use several techniques and nutritional advice usually goes hand in hand with the treatment.

ACUPUNCTURE

Many of the practitioners I spoke to claimed some success in curing infertility but few of them had had many patients with this problem. Acupuncturists trained according to the traditional Chinese school believe that infertility is often the result of an emotional disturbance. This ties in with some of the other evidence already mentioned but doesn't, of course, mean this explanation is the correct one. Nevertheless, acupuncture does seem to have helped some people to conceive. One acupuncturist estimated that about 30 per cent of women could be treated and that those with irregular ovulation responded particularly well.

Another was more cautious. Although she has a fairly busy practice she had treated only two patients with this problem. One conceived but miscarried. The other was six months into an apparently normal pregnancy after conceiving the day after one of her acupuncture sessions. 'Obviously she was extremely uptight,' the therapist explained. 'I gave her five or six treatments before she became pregnant. Acupuncture relaxed her enormously.' But the woman had also taken one dose of clomiphene and had had conventional treatment for one blocked tube. 'Several factors could have contributed to her pregnancy, of which acupuncture was one,' conceded the therapist. Other acupuncturists also spoke of the calming effect of their technique and that it had proved effective in infertile women who were obviously anxious.

It does seem that acupuncture may sometimes help, though it's probably unlikely to do much for women with blocked tubes. One practitioner who practises several different therapies – and who is also medically qualified – said he would plump for the nutritional approach first for both infertility and miscarriage. For infertility he would also try acupuncture 'provided there are no mechanical problems. If there are, those should be put right first.' Another reported that he had also successfully treated about six women for recurrent miscarriage. (But bear in mind the high spontaneous cure rate mentioned earlier in this chapter.)

HERBS

Again, medical herbalists will want to know about your diet and they'll use herbs to try to correct any imbalances. 'I certainly don't believe in taking these large quantities of vitamins and minerals,' one herbalist said, 'but then we have other tools.' Like many acupuncturists, herbalists will often aim to reduce nervous tension – and this sometimes seems enough to allow conception, provided the fallopian tubes aren't completely blocked. Sometimes the effect is almost immediate and the woman conceives right away. Sometimes it seems to take three to six months for the herbs to have an effect. And sometimes nothing happens at all.

It's the same with miscarriage. Sometimes the treatment seems to work – sometimes it doesn't. Did it work for Barbara? She had had a pretty chequered reproductive career, starting with infertility investigations and an operation for fibroids. She then had two normal babies followed by three early miscarriages.

'My gynaecologist could only (eventually) offer a hystero-salpingogram (see page 219); there was no treatment available.' Meanwhile a close friend who is a qualified medical herbalist prescribed a herb which she felt could help Barbara conceive. 'This I took before conception. When a new pregnancy was confirmed, she prescribed another medicine to help prevent miscarriage.' Barbara didn't, in fact, take the second herb for very long but, she concludes: 'Whether or not these medicines were 'effective' (and I'm well aware of the theories about physician-dependence, placebo effect, etc. and that the statistics were in my favour by now), I am now twenty-eight weeks into this pregnancy.'

As Barbara recognized, it's almost impossible to tell whether any cure was really the result of the herbs or whether it would have happened anyway. However, in favour of herbalism, it must be said that many women who try this method for infertility have already had most of the things medicine can give them, including drugs like clomiphene. If they then get pregnant, it's clearly against the odds. And, as explained in Chapter 1, herbalism has quite a bit of science to back it.

HOMOEOPATHY

One very experienced medically qualified homoeopath told me: 'I do get some good results with infertility but I also go for nutrition. And if there's a mechanical problem, it needs the assessment of a gynaecologist.' This doctor, incidentally, is one who looks at her own practice with an extremely critical eye and believes that homoeopathy needs to be put on a much sounder scientific footing. That apart, homoeopathy – in my estimation at least – seems no more or less effective than any other alternative. I've heard from patients who have conceived after a homoeopathic regime and those who found it was no help at all.

'I'm thirty-three years old, married with a year-old daughter,' wrote Rebecca. 'Having previously suffered an ectopic pregnancy and then a miscarriage, I despaired of ever having a child. Feeling extremely low, mentally and physically, and getting no help from allopathic medicine, I turned to homoeopathy and have never looked back.'

Elizabeth, who has a hormonal problem which prevents conception, consulted a homoeopath for two years but eventually the practitioner had to admit defeat. She'd also previously tried both reflexology and acupuncture. 'All things considered, I have had no help from alternative medicine . . . The only solution appears to be experimentation with the normal fertility drugs,' she concludes.

OSTEOPATHY

Osteopaths don't, they would be the first to admit, have much of a track record in the treatment of infertility. Some will even deny that osteopathy has anything to offer women with this condition. But others report the odd, unexpected, cure in women who've consulted them for some other problem. One osteopath said with a somewhat puzzled frown: 'I can't explain it. But I'm sure it's more than coincidence.' One or two theories have been put forward, though, to do with the effects of the manipulation on either the spinal nerves supplying the reproductive system or, more indirectly, on the pituitary gland. But the evidence, such as it is, suggests that if it works it does so only for women with either irregular ovulation or unexplained infertility.

Does alternative medicine *really* work?

I have to say I don't know! I certainly think there's a lot to be
said for a healthy, balanced, wholefood diet but that's part
and parcel of most alternative therapies. I believe that stress
and tension may sometimes stop a woman conceiving and
just may provoke a miscarriage. But both these factors may
resolve themselves without any help from alternatives. On
the other hand, because of his or her reassuring approach, an
alternative practitioner may help to speed things up.

But infertility and miscarriage are notoriously fickle conditions. No matter how many miscarriages a woman has had
she still has a chance of having a healthy baby. And recent
evidence from the United States suggests that as many as 40
per cent of infertile couples will conceive eventually with or
without medical treatment.[12] Actually the odds are slightly in
favour of letting nature take its course: the same study
revealed that 60 per cent of the 'successful' couples conceived
either without any treatment at all or so long after it that the
doctors believed their efforts had nothing to do with conception.

THE END OF PAULINE'S STORY

Remember Pauline, the woman with blocked tubes who'd
been told she had little chance of ever conceiving? I'd like to
end by telling you how things worked out for her. Her story
doesn't prove alternative medicine works – any more than
does any of the other evidence I've mentioned in this chapter
– but it does make you think.

After one of her blocked tubes was found to be clear,
Pauline consulted a palmist ('I figured I had nothing left to
lose') who recommended a one-day-a-week 'fast' when she
should eat only vegetarian foods. She was told she should
keep this up for three and a half years! But later that same
year she saw her medical specialist again. He looked at her
most recent X-ray and decided that her blocked tube could

be treated. He prescribed danazol, which Pauline took for four months. She also took vitamin E supplements.

By January 1983 both Pauline's tubes were clear. But at that time she didn't have a boyfriend. And the specialist still wanted to operate because her tubes still weren't perfect. The operation was booked but, in the meantime, just at the beginning of a new relationship, Pauline conceived!

She couldn't believe it. 'I'd never been pregnant before – I was thirty-five years old. During my younger years, from seventeen to twenty-three, I used no birth control and even though my relationships weren't regular, I never conceived.' She now has a healthy son. 'So if you dismiss this and think I'm a crank (who's to judge?) . . . *something* helped me apart from the four months of danazol tablets. It's all very interesting wondering how and why!'

I don't think Pauline's a crank – far from it. She showed great perseverence and had a sufficiently open mind not to dismiss conventional medicine though, at first, it seemed to have failed her. I wouldn't like even to guess what tipped the scales: was it the danazol, the yoga or the diet? Or was she more relaxed with the new boyfriend than with any of his predecessors? Could it have been a fluke?

We'll never know.

9. The Menopause

The concept of oestrogen replacement therapy is an affront to my sensibility. The implication is that if I must have something replaced it is because I have lost something, I am deficient in something. It is viewing me (or any menopausal woman) from entirely the wrong perspective. The term 'replacement' implies in this context that I will be replaced to where I was when I was menstruating. Why? I don't want any more children and I'm glad to be through with the nuisance of menstrual periods – I've had them for over thirty-five years and that's long enough. I've been looking forward to this freedom from conception and sanitary measures.

I accept that I'm a healthy woman whose body is changing. No matter how many articles and books I read that tell me I'm suffering from a 'deficiency disease', I say I don't believe it. I have never felt more in control of my life than I do now and I feel neither deficient nor diseased.

(Rosetta Reitz: *Menopause. A Positive Approach*[1])

It is important to remember . . . that the post-menopausal ovary is not a dead structure but continues to secrete hormones, oestrogens and androgens for many years after the menopause . . . Therefore the idea that the menopause is associated with 'oestrogen deficiency' is probably not tenable for most women who reach a natural menopause.

(Drs Anne Anderson and Ann McPherson:
The Menopause[2])

. . . there is a sufficiently large aggregation of evidence to call into question the 'deficiency disease' concept. It appears that the 'menopause' has been used as a catch-all explanation for the distress experienced by women over a significant proportion of the life span.

(Dr David J.Cooke[3])

Get the message? During the menopause, our hormone levels are certainly changing. But we do not suddenly, or even gradually, become hormone-less. (I'm not talking here about women who have a surgical menopause; their problems are somewhat different and I discuss them in more detail in Chapter 4, in the section on hysterectomy.) Our bodies continue to make female hormones, albeit in lower amounts.

For simplicity, from now on I'm going to use the word 'menopause' to describe that time in our lives which many women call 'The Change' and which doctors have labelled 'the climacteric'. Medically, menopause is an inaccurate term because it refers only to the stage at which periods actually stop and not the several – maybe many – years on either side when our hormone levels are altering. Still, when we say we're in our menopause that's what most of us mean, so I'll stick to it.

The good news about the menopause is that – or so it seems – it's what we make of it that's important, not what our hormone levels happen to be doing at the time. It's estimated that although nearly all women do experience some 'menopausal' symptoms, for most of them the severity of those symptoms doesn't depend on hormones. More important are one's general attitude to one's health, one's lifestyle and one's ability to cope with those changes in life which are an inevitable part of growing older.

I hope that doesn't sound too glib: I don't mean it to. Heaven knows, it can take a lot of courage and confidence to face what psychologists call 'stressful life events' – children leaving home; parents, friends and partners becoming ill, dying even. But as sad and irrevocable as such things are, we *can* come to terms with them. Often, of course, we'll need help if we're to 'come through', and loving support from friends and family can make all the difference to the way we experience our menopause.

Rosetta Reitz, quoted above, talked to about 1000 women about their feelings and the way they coped. She found that for the vast majority – 95 per cent – hormone replacement therapy (HRT) just hadn't been necessary. Still, reports Reitz, they 'were more than "getting by" . . . These women were interested in nutrition and most receptive to the idea of the relationship of food and good health. And of greatest importance, they did not feel isolated, for they were women who gathered in groups to talk.'

Reitz admits that her sample wasn't representative of menopausal women as a whole. They came from similar areas and nearly all of them worked outside the home. And the idea of the menopausal 'workshop' – getting together to talk specifically about one's menopause – is still far too 'way out' for many of us stiff-upper-lipped Britishers. But there's no doubt that this sort of 'group therapy' can help enormously. It would do us all good to sit down and talk to other women about our feelings and our fears.

Rosetta Reitz has made the menopause into something of a crusade. Hers is an intensely personal view. But she's not alone in believing that there's more to menopausal problems than just physical changes. Many other researchers have discovered a strong mind-and-body link behind it all.

One study, for example, found that women from the lower social classes, those who had no outside work, or who had a 'restricted social network' (which I take to mean few relatives or friends close by), were more likely to have a difficult menopause. Other research suggests that menopausal women with family problems are particularly prone to mental illness at this time.

Dr Cooke describes a study of seventy-eight Scottish menopausal women. This was rather a complicated piece of research – of necessity because of the difficulty of trying to weed out psychological factors from all the other things that are going on during the menopause. Nevertheless, the results are interesting. They suggest that some women do have a worse time than others simply because, psychologically, they're more vulnerable. Not having a job *can* make your menopause harder to bear, as can having few people in whom you can confide. If, on top of that, something happens in your life that is stressful, these same psychological factors can affect the way you cope with it.

None of this may surprise you. To me it seems self-evident. But that doesn't mean it's true. It's still only a suggestion, a well-founded hypothesis, if you like. There still isn't proof that the state of one's mind and one's personal relationships can affect one's menopausal symptoms. And, given the enormous difficulty of this sort of research, there may never be.

So what do we do? Do we continue to believe that our hormones are to blame for all our ills – and therefore either beyond our control or treatable only by HRT? Or do we decide that, maybe, *we* can do something about them by changing the way we live our lives; by going out and making friends, by getting a job if possible, and by telling other people about our feelings?

Rosetta Reitz would say yes to all of this. But she also makes the point that for the menopausal woman to change her life in this way may be a big undertaking. All too often she sees herself only through society's eyes – as someone's wife or someone's mother. She has been trained to 'serve' other people and to put herself last. Then, with the menopause, comes new propaganda. She can no longer bear children and those she has are leaving home; so her role as mother is over. She is no longer sexually attractive; so her role as lover becomes harder to hang onto. If you really believe all this, your self-esteem can hit rock-bottom. And without it there's no way you're going to go out and forge an new life for yourself.

But as Reitz shows clearly and eloquently, this really *is* just so much propaganda. The menopausal woman is most definitely not on the scrap heap. The change of life brings many bonuses. But first you must reject your conditioning and start to value those qualities in yourself which make you the person you are. Then you may find that you've never had it so good.

It may seem a little strange for me to have started this chapter in this way, rather than leaping immediately into the pros and cons of HRT and its natural alternatives. But I believe that, before we even begin to think about treatment of any sort, we need to put it in perspective. Do we really need it or do we only *think* we do? Maybe some of our symptoms *are* due to fluctuating hormones but are they being made worse by the fact that we're feeling unloved, unwanted and worthless? If the answer is yes – or perhaps – then we may want to leave any treatment, especially HRT, aside for the time being while we take stock of our lives. Our bodies could be trying to tell us something very important and we should listen to them.

WHAT HAPPENS TO OUR HORMONES AT THE MENOPAUSE?

No one's quite sure! It seems, though, that gradually, over a number of years, our ovaries become less efficient at pumping out oestrogens. The most potent oestrogen, and the one which is around all during our childbearing years, is oestradiol. And at the menopause it's this hormone that's most affected: within a year of our last period our oestradiol will have fallen to only one tenth of the lowest level we experienced during our menstrual cycles.

As the oestrogens go down so our pituitary gland goes into overdrive – it hasn't yet got the message that the ovaries are going into retirement so it keeps producing increasing amounts of luteinizing hormone (LH) and follicle stimulating hormone (FSH) to try to get them working again. However, as I mentioned above, this doesn't mean that the ovaries have shut up shop completely. They may not be producing eggs, or much oestradiol, but they're still making other oestrogens and androgens – 'male' hormones which are linked with our sex drive. And our adrenal glands, which also produce androgens, continue to do so after the menopause. These androgens are actually converted into oestrogens (to which they're very closely related) in other parts of our bodies such as skin, fat and muscle.

After the menopause, the main oestrogen produced is oestrone. This isn't nearly as active as oestradiol but it is, nevertheless, a female hormone. Hence the assertion quoted at the beginning of this chapter, that the menopause is not, necessarily, associated with an oestrogen deficiency. In fact, Drs Anderson and McPherson believe that 'Oestrone . . . must provide the menopausal woman with a reasonable amount of oestrogenic activity.'[4] For many women, that 'reasonable' amount seems to be enough.

Oestrogen deficiency and its effects

Doctors are now agreed that very few menopausal symptoms are due directly to oestrogen deficiency: only hot flushes – and the night sweats that so often go with them – definitely are. Palpitations may be, though they could well also be psychological in origin. Atrophic vaginitis – a thinning of the lining of the vagina, which can make sex uncomfortable and vaginal infections more likely – and urinary problems, such as recurrent cystisis and incontinence, are also related to oestrogen deficiency. But there's a bit of a difference of opinion as to whether these are truly 'menopausal' symptoms: most doctors find these usually don't crop up until many years after the menopause is over. However, because some menopausal women do complain of pain during intercourse, some doctors believe that oestrogen deficiency is to blame and prescribe oestrogen-containing creams. Others dispute whether this is the best course of action and I'll explain more about that later.

Osteoporosis – a thinning of the bones and an increased tendency for them to fracture – also seems to be the result of oestrogen deficiency. But this isn't so much a symptom as a process. Bone loss occurs gradually, starting at the age of approximately thirty-five or forty (all estimates about the menopause are approximate!) when oestrogen levels begin to decline.

But although our risks of breaking a bone do increase somewhat after the age of forty-five, it's usually not until we're elderly that this thinning is sufficiently severe to cause significant problems. However, obviously it would be a good thing if osteoporosis could be avoided. This may be possible, as I discuss on pages 244-53.

Some specialists also believe that oestrogen deficiency endangers our hearts. This is based on statistics: before the menopause women are much less likely than men to get a heart attack: after the age of fifty our risk increases much more rapidly than a man's. But it's not yet certain whether this difference between the sexes is due to women's oestrogen protecting them or to something – possibly hormonal – that men have when they're younger which puts them more at risk and which they lose when they're about fifty.

In fact, the argument about the protective effect of oestrogen – and one which is often put forward in support of hormone replacement therapy – was thrown back in the melting pot recently. A new study showed that women who took the hormone for menopausal symptoms were 60 per cent *more* likely to suffer from either heart disease or a stroke (yet another result of a diseased circulatory system) than women who'd not had HRT.[5]

All the other 'menopausal' symptoms – like not being able to concentrate, feeling tired and depressed – are *not* due to oestrogen deficiency. But, of course, if you're having umpteen hot flushes a day and your sex life is non-existent because your vagina is playing up, you have every reason to feel run-down and unhappy. Whether that means you need HRT is another matter. Certainly if your *main* problem is sheer misery you probably don't. Something else is amiss and HRT won't put it right.

Hormone replacement therapy (HRT)

WHEN MIGHT YOU NEED IT?

For hot flushes

The only woman who might need HRT is the one whose life is being made unbearable by hot flushes. And many women find that, though they can cope with day-time hot flushes, the accompanying night sweats are just *too* much. Your bed is regularly soaked, your sleep is disrupted so you're exhausted. Your partner is also sick and tired of being turfed out of bed every night so that the sheets can be changed. Twin beds might be one solution to the latter difficulty but I can't see that it would do much for your relationship!

HRT *does* help with hot flushes. But why it should is still a bit of a mystery because the flushes aren't directly associated with oestrogen levels. After all, all women go through the menopause but not all have hot flushes. Nor do women who get very bad flushes have lower oestrogen levels than those who don't.

For a dry vagina

As I explained above, there's considerable doubt about whether HRT should ever be prescribed for this symptom. A dry vagina may well respond to oestrogen creams. But though this symptom may, in much older women, be a direct result of oestrogen deficiency, there's quite a bit of evidence that for younger women this isn't the case. 'Although women often complain of vaginal dryness at the menopause,' report Drs Anderson and McPherson, 'severe atrophic [thinning] changes do not usually occur until many years later.' So if it's not lack of oestrogen that's making our vaginas dry, what is it?

To put it crudely, not enough use. Regular sex – or masturbation if you don't have a partner or don't feel like intercourse – will help keep your vagina in good working order.

Rosetta Reitz, who devotes a whole chapter of her book to the joys of mature sex, reports, 'Sex is better when you're older.' Many women report an increased sex drive, she says – possibly due to the fact that their androgens have now got things pretty much to themselves. And women who enjoy sex keep on enjoying it. Reitz also makes the point that these women aren't going to be the ones who consult their doctors. Our doctors, she claims, (who are usually male) get a completely biased view of the menopausal woman's sex life because they only hear about the problems!

Even though the walls of the vagina may be thinner than they were during our fertile years, Reitz points out, 'there are many other factors involved in feeling discomfort or not. Women who engaged in regular masturbation . . . reported increased lubrication with a partner and the disappearance of vaginal pain due to dryness. Thinness of vaginal walls,' Reitz adds, 'does not automatically mean pain during intercourse.'

Maybe oestrogen creams also help. But if they do, I'd hazard a guess that it's partly because, once the initial dryness has been overcome, sex is once more pleasurable – and more frequent.

For osteoporosis

This is a bit more tricky. There's good evidence that HRT, started early enough, can prevent osteoporosis, and once bone changes have set in, can certainly slow them down and maybe even halt them. There's also some research which suggests that five years of HRT around the menopause can actually reverse these changes though this result isn't yet generally accepted. The trouble is that, to do any good in the long term, many people believe that a woman would have to begin therapy *before* her menopause and continue it into old age. In fact, a few studies have shown that once a woman has started taking oestrogens, if she then stops therapy her bone loss is faster than if she'd never had it.

But if long-term therapy is the only solution, what of the possible risks – of cancer and heart disease (see below)? It seems reasonable to suppose that they'd increase. The other problem is that some women seem to be more prone to osteoporosis than others. Though there are some techniques which can be used to spot which of us are most at risk, these are not widely available. (There are, though, other possible ways of predicting which women are likely to develop severe osteoporosis and I'll return to these later. Is it right to expose these women to risks from hormones they may not need?

In the United Kingdom, we don't yet have the choice, anyway. The cost to the National Health Service of prescribing hormones to all menopausal women would be prohibitively expensive.

IS HRT DANGEROUS?

Cardiovascular disease

I've already mentioned the fact that there's considerable doubt about whether oestrogen protects against diseases of the circulatory system. Some of the latest evidence suggests that HRT may increase the risk of both heart disease and strokes. This has certainly been shown to be the case with the oestrogens in the Pill though, of course, they're usually given in higher doses: you need only up to about 20 micrograms of ethinyl oestradiol (a synthetic oestrogen) to prevent hot flushes and even the lowest dose Pills contain half as much again. The other difference is that, whereas the Pill contains synthetic oestrogens, natural ones are sometimes, though not always, used for HRT. So far, though, there's no evidence that the natural ones are less or more safe.

There's also slight concern that the progestogens (synthetic progesterones) now usually given as part of HRT may increase the risks of cardiovascular disease (though the combined therapy does seem to be safer in other ways – see below). But because progesterones haven't been used for as long as oestrogens, we don't yet know if these fears are justified.

Cancer of the lining of the uterus

Menopausal women are more likely to get this form of cancer than those who are still fertile. But research has indicated that HRT using 'unopposed' oestrogens – that is, oestrogens given alone, without progestogen – more than triples this risk. This seems to be because oestrogen encourages the lining of the womb – the endometrium – to grow. This also happens during normal menstrual cycles. The difference, though, is that for the lining to be shed, progesterone also has to be present and most menopausal women don't produce enough progesterone for this to happen. Hence the endometrium continues to grow. This overgrowth, known as endometrial hyperplasia, is thought to be a forerunner of cancer. This doesn't mean that a woman with a hyperplastic endometrium *will* develop cancer, but she *is* more likely to.

For this reason all women on HRT, provided they haven't had a hysterectomy, are given a progestogen for several days a month. The disadvantage of this is that they will also have a regular monthly 'withdrawal' bleed as the progesterone levels decline. However, a new combined HRT regime seems to do away with this bleed while, it's said, still protecting against endometrial hyperplasia.[6]

Cancer of the breasts

It used to be thought that HRT carried no risk of breast cancer but recent studies suggest that it does. The most up-to-date information indicates that the increased risk may only be associated with long-term use of HRT – ten years or more. Some doctors believe this is 'reassuring' news for women because it means the benefits – or so they say – of HRT far outweigh the dangers. And some women I've spoken to say that they could accept almost any hazard in return for ten trouble-free years. Will they feel the same if they get cancer?

SHOULD YOU HAVE HRT?

Although the potential dangers of this form of therapy apply to all women, some are more at risk than others. Women who've had cancer of the breast, endometrium or ovary shouldn't have it and neither should those with liver disease. It's also not a good idea for women who smoke, have symptoms of cardiovascular disease such as high blood pressure, endometriosis or fibroids, or diabetes. Most doctors are – or should be – very wary of prescribing HRT under these circumstances.

What about the rest of us? I'd say that if you're getting very bad symptoms of a genuine oestrogen deficiency (see above) then HRT will probably help. But before asking for a prescription I think it would be well worthwhile trying one of the alternatives that I'll be discussing in the next section. If you're worried about osteoporosis, then HRT probably isn't the answer because there are several other things you can do which are much safer – things which, incidentally, the medical establishment is now paying some heed to!

THE ALTERNATIVE APPROACH TO THE MENOPAUSE

What can we do about osteoporosis?

Hot flushes and other menopausal symptoms tend to pass once the menopause is over, though quite a few women report they still get the odd flush ten or even twenty years after their last period. The risk of osteoporosis, on the other hand, increases with age.

But not all women seem to get osteoporosis to the same extent. Some of the differences are probably genetic: for example osteoporosis is not nearly as much of a problem for black women as it is for their white sisters. This could also explain some of the differences between women of the same race. But other factors are at work: fat women seem less at risk than thin ones; this could be due to the fact that they're producing larger amounts of oestrogen (because androgens can be converted into oestrogens in fatty tissue).

THE IMPORTANCE OF CALCIUM

For other reasons, though – mainly an increased risk of heart disease – being fat is not a good idea. But numerous studies now suggest that it *is* possible to eat your way to stronger bones without getting larger in the process! The key, it turns out, is how much calcium you get. Research has shown time and again that women whose diets are deficient in this element are more likely to have weak bones. It's even been suggested that one's calcium intake is at least as important as one's oestrogen level because the faster bone loss that's been seen *after* HRT (see above) hasn't been observed in women who were given adequate calcium supplements.

Now this may seem only common sense. Bones are, after all, made largely of calcium and everyone knows that it's important to get enough of it. But, as I explained in Chapter 2, there's considerable controversy about whether the current recommended daily allowances of vitamins and minerals really *are* enough. In the case of calcium, most people now agree that the RDA – 500 mg in the UK – is completely inadequate. According to an editorial in the *Lancet* in 1985 before your menopause you need 1100 mg a day and after it 1500 mg. But most of us don't get even 500 mg in our diet. 'There is sufficient evidence,' the editorial concluded, 'that a boost of dietary intake to the levels suggested above would at least reduce the rate of post-menopausal bone loss and, in addition, might favourably affect peak bone mass.' The second bit of this statement means that is we may be able to make our bones stronger to start with if we up our calcium intake before the menopause.

Before the menopause you may be able to get enough calcium from your diet by stepping up the amount of dairy produce you eat. But, because this is high in saturated fats and therefore may increase your risk of heart disease (see Chapter 2), it's probably better to take a calcium supplement – at least 500 mg and up to 1000 mg a day. In addition, say nutritional specialists, you'll need a magnesium supplement. This is because calcium and magnesium work together in our bodies and the balance between them is a very fine one: increased calcium levels can result in a magnesium deficiency and *vice versa*. Some specialists recommend dolomite as a good natural and balanced source of both. But there are indications that a specially designed mineral supplement may be better. Find an expert who can advise you on which one to take.

The interplay between calcium and magnesium could explain some of the negative findings about the importance of extra calcium. For example, in 1984, the *British Medical Journal* published a paper showing that calcium supplementation of up to 2000 mg a day had *no* effect on bone loss in postmenopausal women. But some nutritionists say this was because the women hadn't been given magnesium as well so the calcium couldn't be used properly.

What else can we do?

WATCH YOUR INTAKE OF ZINC

Severe osteoporosis – the kind seen in elderly women – has been linked recently to a zinc deficiency. This doesn't necessarily mean that a reduced zinc level is even partly to blame for osteoporosis: elderly people may often be zinc deficient anyway. But just in case, it may be prudent to get more zinc-rich foods into your diet (see Chapter 2) – I don't think, at this stage, there's any point in taking supplements.

GET OUTSIDE!

If our bodies are to use the calcium we give them they also need adequate amounts of vitamin D. This doesn't mean, though, that we should take supplements. The research indicates that most of us can make this vitamin well enough, provided we get sufficient sunshine. That means exposing at least 30 per cent of our bodies to the sun for at least half and hour a day, according to Dr Jeffrey Bland.[7] (However, light-skinned people should also be wary of too much sunbathing because this seems to increase the risks of skin cancer.) If you're dark-skinned you may need much more sunlight – evidence suggests that Asian people living in the UK are more prone to vitamin D deficiency than the lighter-skinned members of the population. Vitamin D supplements *may* be necessary for these people and for elderly women who don't get out much. But because this vitamin can be toxic in excess you need specialist advice.

TAKE MORE EXERCISE

But not too much! Sorry to be so confusing, but although exercise is good for us and can help strengthen our bones, vigorous regular exercise – the sort that athletes and some fanatical joggers go in for – can have the opposite effect. Trained female athletes and obsessive exercisers sometimes lose their periods and research has shown that this is because they become oestrogen deficient. Not surprisingly, their bones start to suffer. Fortunately this process seems to be reversible. Even so it's not a good idea to expose your body to this kind of stress. So exercise in moderation – three 20 minute sessions three times a week is plenty. (If you haven't yet reached the menopause and have been doing much more than this – and your periods start becoming irregular, or stop altogether – reduce your exercise regime to give your body chance to recover.)

EAT LESS MEAT

Though scientific studies haven't yet proved a direct link, it does seem as though people – both men and women – who eat lots of meat are more likely to get osteoporosis. It is thought that this may be due to overloading the body with protein. A balanced vegetarian diet, because it contains less protein, seems to protect against osteoporosis. A word of warning though: if you're a vegan and eat no dairy produce, you may actually be increasing your chances of osteoporosis because you may not be getting enough calcium and vitamin D.

CUT DOWN ON SALT

Many – but not all – experts (see Chapter 2) believe you should be doing this anyway because of the possibility that a high salt intake may be associated with an increased risk of heart disease. And recent animal research suggests that excess salt makes our bodies excrete more calcium – and phosphorus, another important constituent of bone – and so may speed up bone loss.

CUT DOWN ON COFFEE AND ALCOHOL

Caffeine encourages the excretion of calcium. So, if you can, give coffee a miss and use one of the cereal-based beverages instead. Alternatively, switch to decaffeinated coffee. If you drink a lot of alcohol, you're also more likely to get osteoporosis, though it is not yet known whether modest amounts have any effect.

DON'T SMOKE

Women who smoke seem to be more at risk of osteoporosis. They also tend to have an earlier menopause than non-smokers. While the one could follow from the other, research also indicates that smoking can reduce our oestrogen levels long before we reach the menopause and therefore may be having adverse effects on our bones while we're still fertile.

Alternative treatment for other menopausal problems

We've seen how the medical establishment is at last taking some notice of what alternative practitioners have been saying for years – that diet may make all the difference between a healthy and unhealthy postmenopausal women, at least as far as her bones are concerned. But orthodox medics are still really at the starting gate. Whilst they're convinced – more or less – that calcium and exercise can help prevent osteoporosis, most of them would reach for the hormones when confronted with a woman complaining of bad hot flushes or a dry vagina. They *know*, you see, that these problems are caused by an oestrogen deficiency.

But as I've tried to explain, the *severity* of these symptoms may be due to other factors and so may respond to less drastic treatment. And, almost all the alternative practitioners I talked to said that diet could help prevent them. If they did appear, they said, then a combination of diet, vitamin and mineral supplements, and one or more alternative techniques could treat them quite successfully.

NUTRITION

Sarah, who is fifty, first consulted a nutritional specialist about a year ago. 'I was getting the most terrible hot flushes. Actually,' she adds, 'they weren't that bad, but they were bad enough for me to feel uncomfortable and for them to be a nuisance. I didn't want to take hormones, which I knew would be the only thing my doctor would advise.'

Sarah's nutritionist recommended a change of diet and extra vitamins and minerals. 'Within a month I thought I was feeling better, anyhow, but I thought it might be my imagination. But within two months I had no hot flushes and I've not really had once since. I feel marvellous. Occasionally,' she admits, 'I do get a suspicion of a hot flush but I haven't been taking my vitamins in the same quantity or quite as regularly recently.'

Sarah has, however, religiously stuck to her vitamin C and E supplements. She also believes vitamin B_6 was especially useful. In addition she took evening primrose oil (see also pages 71-2) and kelp, which is rich natural source of many minerals.

Vitamin B_6 and evening primrose oil are often suggested for a whole host of women's problems though, as far as I know, they've only been shown to be of definite benefit in premenstrual tension and, in the case of B_6, depression – and then not for all women with these particular problems. Still, a moderate amount of these supplements might help correct any marginal deficiencies a menopausal woman might have and so make her feel healthier. The same goes for kelp.

Vitamins C and E

Some research has suggested that vitamin C and the related compounds known as the bioflavonoids might be a useful treatment for hot flushes. Vitamin C is also sometimes suggested for women on HRT because it encourages the body to metabolize oestrogen. However, vitamin C has also been shown, in women on the Pill, to *increase* the effective dose of oestrogen and thus, theoretically, to increase the risks.[8] Clearly we don't yet know enough about it.

Vitamin E is a popular alternative remedy for both hot flushes and atrophic vaginitis. Emrika Padus in her *Women's Encyclopedia of Health and Natural Healing*[9] cites quite a bit of evidence that this vitamin is useful for both these conditions. She also says that a dry vagina also responds well to vitamin E cream.

Rosetta Reitz is also a big fan of both vitamins. 'Many women,' she reports, 'have found relief in two days from taking 800 International Units of vitamin E complex . . . I have seen flashes [flushes] disappear completely when the vitamin E is also accompanied by 2000 to 3000 milligrams of vitamin C . . . When the flashes have subsided, usually after a week, the women reduce the vitamin E intake to 400 International Units.'

Bear in mind, though, that occasional research findings have suggested that vitamin E may be toxic in doses as small as 100 IU a day and that some specialists believe that doses bigger than this should only be taken under medical supervision. Dr Bland, however, reports that the studies which show a risk are in the minority and concludes that 'vitamin E is a safe substance to employ in supplemental doses for a long period of time'. I'd say that if vitamin E is going to work for you it should do so pretty quickly and at a relatively low dose, too. If you notice no improvement after a few weeks, there's probably no point in continuing with it.

OTHER APPROACHES

Homoeopathy and herbs

A combination of homoeopathy plus vitamin and mineral supplements was recommended by one medically qualified practitioner. 'The results,' he said 'are at least as good as those of HRT and have minimal side effects.' One of his patients, Alison, confirmed this.

'I was suffering mainly from hot flushes,' she says. 'But I was also feeling sick and dizzy.' The doctor prescribed a special mixture of homoeopathic and herbal remedies. These mixtures are somewhat controversial in alternative circles because many traditionally trained herbalists and homoeopaths say you shouldn't mix the two treatments – nor should you use more than one homoeopathic remedy at a time. Others say this doesn't matter because by using this 'blunderbuss' approach you're tackling several problems at once. Who's right? Heaven only knows, but it does make the whole business look, I think, a bit more dubious than it really is.

Back to Alison. The first mixture didn't work but the second one – which contained nearly twice as many herbs and homoeopathic remedies – did. 'As long as I keep taking it my hot flushes do stop,' she reports. 'If I don't take it they come back very rapidly.' I asked Alison's doctor why he thought the second remedy had worked when the first one hadn't. 'I don't know,' he said.

Perhaps the reason is, as homoeopaths and herbalists believe, that individual women respond differently – so each needs a slightly different prescription. This can make self-help almost impossible. However, some homoeopaths say that a few remedies seem to help quite a lot of people and are worth trying even before you go for a professional consultation. Homoeopathic Sepia and Lachesis are at the top of the list.

But it must be admitted that these natural treatments don't work for everyone and some women *will* do better with HRT

– if they choose to have it. 'I've had my failures,' one herbalist reported ruefully. 'And I've seen them have HRT and get better.'

Acupuncture

Acupuncturists report considerable success in the treatment of both hot flushes and atrophic vaginitis. One medically qualified practitioner told me that there is actually a good explanation behind this – for hot flushes at any rate. The flush appears to coincide with the release of follicle stimulating hormone and luteinizing hormone and, as I've mentioned, these hormones are present in very high levels during the menopause. Acupuncture, this doctor explained, can reduce the level of both these hormones. 'I've treated many women for this problem,' he says, 'and all except one have got better. The patients ring me up afterwards to tell me that their husbands think I'm a magician!'

CONCLUSIONS: HOW TO TACKLE YOUR MENOPAUSE

1. Look on it as a positive experience. If you find this difficult I suggest you read Rosetta Reitz's book. Although it does go a bit over the top – and I don't agree with a number of her views – much of her advice is sound.
2. Don't blame all your problems on the menopause. If you're feeling generally miserable the chances are that your life is not the way you'd like it to be. See if you can change it.
3. Take a look at your diet. Does it contain enough of the vitamins and minerals you need? Make sure you're getting adequate calcium, sunshine and exercise. If you still feel under par, perhaps you do need supplements. Consult a nutritional specialist about these.
4. Don't be beaten by a dry vagina. Think of what you can do to improve your sex life. Read some books on

technique if you think they'd help. And, to get you started, use a little lubricating cream such as K-Y jelly.

5. If your general health is good, your diet is adequate but hot flushes are still troublesome, consult an alternative practitioner. If you haven't already responded to dietary changes then acupuncture is probably the technique most likely to help.

10. Double Trouble: Uterine Prolapse and Incontinence

The bad news

These two conditions often – though not always – go together. A uterus which starts to sink from its moorings may also put pressure on the bladder. This may cause *stress incontinence* – the involuntary loss of urine when we cough or sneeze. A pregnant uterus can also press on the bladder so stress incontinence may occur during pregnancy. It usually goes once the baby's born. If your incontinence is due to a prolapse, however, you'll be stuck with it – unless your uterus can be lifted back to its normal position or removed altogether.

It is often said that these conditions are part of the price we pay for having children and growing older. So if you're young, healthy and childless, you may feel like skipping this chapter. But please don't. Although if you've never had a child you're unlikely to get a prolapsed uterus, this doesn't necessarily protect you from incontinence.

Surveys have shown that large numbers of women of all ages, childless or not, wet themselves from time to time. One, of college students, revealed that just over half had occasional 'accidents' and 5 per cent 'leaked' regularly.[1] Alarming, isn't it?

The other distressing fact about both prolapse and incontinence is that they tend to get more severe with time. The uterus may drop so far that it actually protudes from the vaginal opening. And incontinence may be eventually so frequent that a woman has to wear absorbent pads to catch the urine which may escape at any time.

There comes a point when the only remedy is surgery –

though sometimes the uterus may first be given a temporary, artificial support in the form of a *ring pessary* placed at the top of the vagina. The surgical treatment of prolapse ranges from repair operations, which strengthen and tighten the ligaments and muscles supporting the uterus, to hysterectomy. If you're incontinent as a result of the prolapse then the operation should put that right as well. Surgery may be used in other forms of incontinence, with the aim of strengthening the muscles which support the urethra and bladder.

Results from prolapse surgery are said to be good. But, when incontinence is the *primary* problem, success is somewhat unpredictable, the best results being achieved only by the most skilled surgeons. In any case, who wants an operation if she can avoid it?

Unfortunately, once you've got been told you need surgery, alternative medicine probably won't do that much for you: most of the practitioners I spoke to agreed that treatment of severe prolapse and incontinence is best left to the surgeon.

We're victims of evolution

Although other structures are also involved, our uteri and bladders get most of their support from the muscles of the pelvic floor which form a kind of hammock slung between the pubis in front and the coccyx (the base of the spine) at the back. This *pubococcygeus* muscle hasn't changed much since our ancestors walked on all fours. It didn't have to do much work then because our abdominal muscles took most of the weight of our internal organs. But once we took to two legs, these two sets of muscles reversed roles: it's now the pelvic floor that has to counteract the effects of gravity.

So if those muscles begin to weaken and sag, the organs in our pelvic cavity start to drop. Pregnancy tends to make things worse, of course. But you'll recall that some childless women – even those barely out of their teens – are already showing signs that their pelvic floors are giving way: incontinence may be common but it's not *normal*. It happens because those crucial weight-bearing muscles aren't taut enough.

Our pubococcygeus is to some extent beyond our control. Under normal circumstances it's always in a slight state of tension – if it weren't we'd all have prolapses and be permanently incontinent. But if it becomes weakened, then it is less able to cope with the extra pressures we put on it. For some of us, pregnancy may be the last straw. Chronic constipation and coughs may also contribute towards flabby pelvic floor muscles. And some women's muscles are so weak to start with that they can't fight back against even the occasional extra pressure from coughs, sneezes or giggles – so they wet themselves. This is a bad omen because if they do get pregnant – and certainly as they get older when *all* their muscles will become less efficient – their pelvic floors will tend to lose what little strength they have left.

The good news

We can tighten that muscular hammock by exercising it – provided we start before the structure of the muscles has been damaged. A lax muscle isn't necessarily a damaged one: it may have simply lost the habit of contracting properly. The purpose of exercise is to re-educate the muscles so that they 'remember' that they're supposed to be in a state of contraction all the time.

There's no doubt that exercise can help prevent both prolapse and incontinence. In fact, both alternative and orthodox practitioners say that if all women exercised their pelvic floors regularly then both these conditions would be very much rarer than they are.

What sort of exercises?

KEGEL EXERCISES

These are the best known (and if you've attended natural

childbirth classes, you'll probably have come across them already). Named after the American obstetrics professor who designed them, they are aimed specifically at the pelvic floor.

The object is to contract and relax the pubococcygeus muscle in a controlled manner, much as if you were clenching and unclenching your fist. Each time you 'squeeze' you should hold the contraction for about five seconds before relaxing again. Then repeat about four more times. That forms one exercise session. The experts say you need fifty sessions a day to keep your pelvic floor in trim. Sounds a lot? Not really, say the enthusiasts, because you can do this exercise any time, any place – when waiting for a bus, stuck in a traffic jam or while brushing your teeth, for instance. The opportunities, they claim, are virtually unlimited!

If you can exercise in this way, you'll certainly benefit. Kegel found that his exercises alone were an effective treatment for women with stress incontinence (provided they didn't have problems with prolapse, too) and enabled them to avoid surgery. A strong pelvic floor will also enhance your sex life because once you can contract and relax the muscles at will, you can use the same technique during intercourse. This will add to your man's pleasure and also to yours. In fact, it's said that you may even be able to bring yourself to orgasm through Kegel exercises alone.

There are some drawbacks, though. Many women find these exercises impossible – they can't find the right muscles to contract! This isn't so surprising: because we seldom need to control them consciously, most of us get by without being aware of their existence.

One hint, often mentioned in books on childbirth, is to put a couple of fingers in your vagina and then to tighten the vagina round them. (You can also do this during intercourse, when your partner's response will let you know if you're having the desired effect.) But this may be easier said than done. One doctor who specializes in psychosexual matters told me: 'Three out of four women really find it very difficult'

Another test is to begin to pass urine then try to stop in mid-stream. If you can, then you're using the correct muscles. But, again, many women can't do it – not because their muscles are weak but because they haven't got their pubococcygeus under *conscious* control.

And even when you've got the technique off pat, it's all to easy to forget to practise, particularly if you've just had a baby. Though postnatal Kegels are vital to get the pelvic floor back in shape, many of us forget to do them after a few weeks because so much else is going on in our lives at this time.

There is also the point that although these exercises are effective and, once you've got the idea, simple enough, they're not very exciting. It's all very well for childbirth teachers to tell us to use them to fill in time when we're bored anyway. But – traffic jams and toothbrushing apart – who's bored fifty times a day?

OTHER FORMS OF EXERCISE

'Your general fitness may be excellent,' writes Elizabeth Noble in *Essential Exercises for the Childbearing Year*,[2] 'but this has no relation to the integrity of these internal structures [the pelvic floor]. [It] is not exercised unintentionally during sports or calisthenics. Special efforts are required . . .'

Not so. Fortunately for those of us who like exercise but can't get to grips with Kegels, Ms Nobel is wrong. A report published in the *Lancet* in 1985 shows that practically any form of exercise, provided we do it regularly, strengthens the pelvic floor.

The research was carried out at Northwick Park Hospital, Harrow. The object was to discover if women who'd had a traumatic vaginal delivery – had needed forceps and/or an episiotomy, or who had torn when the baby was born – had weaker pelvic floors then those who either hadn't ever given birth or who had their babies delivered by Caesarian section. (If you have a Caesar, of course, your pelvic floor escapes the worst rigours of childbirth.) An inflated condom attached to a pressure gauge was used to measure pelvic floor strength: the women in the study were asked to contract their muscles around the condom. Those who'd had babies – their first in all cases – had given birth about one year previously.

The researchers were intrigued to discover that having a baby, irrespective of the way it had arrived, made no difference to the strength of the pelvic floor. Nor did the size of the baby or the mother's age. Those findings on their own are fairly revolutionary. We're often told that a traumatic delivery tends to weaken the pelvic floor and that the older we are or the bigger our baby the greater the risk of prolapse or incontinence in later life. So much for that belief!

What did make a big difference, though, was whether the women exercised or not. Women who'd done postnatal exercises were able to squeeze the condom with more force than those who hadn't. Women who exercised *regularly* were even better squeezers. But the really interesting thing was that very few – only three out of eighteen – of the exercisers used Kegels. Instead they went to keep-fit classes or regularly walked, jogged, swam or danced. One woman did yoga. 'It seems,' the researchers conclude, 'that any form of muscular exercise improves perineal [pelvic floor] muscle funtion. Our experience shows that pure perineal exercises are not extensively practised, either because women are not convinced of the benefit, or because they find them tedious. Perhaps more emphasis should be placed on exercise that women find interesting and fulfilling.'

'If you do any exercise in an upright position,' one of the researchers, a consultant gynaecologist, explained to me, 'you contract your perineal muscles.' But good as it is, general 'all over' exercise is only a *preventive* measure. It tightens weak muscles before they get a chance to sag. A sagging pelvic floor definitely requires the concentrated attention that only Kegels can give.

MORE ON YOGA

Yoga isn't as fashionable as jogging, keep-fit and the rest of them. It is a pity because yoga may be one of the best ways of keeping those perineal muscles in good shape. (Kegel exercises, incidentally, are based on yoga.)

Even a severely prolapsed uterus may respond to yoga, according to a medical textbook written from the yogic point of view.[3] 'Once a ligament is torn, it is difficult to reconstitute it without surgery, and extremely weak muscles will need persistent daily exercise over several months before they regain their full strength. Nevertheless, even in cases of severe prolapse, yoga therapy can be beneficial and may eliminate the need for surgery. Definitely mild or recent prolapse can be completely corrected in a few months, with the help of appropriate yoga practices.'

This is also the experience of a well-known London yoga teacher. 'I've known women who've been under the threat of the surgeon's knife for a hysterectomy and they've practised postures like the plough pose and have managed to avoid surgery.' Inverted postures, such as the plough, headstand, and shoulder-stand, are said to be particularly helpful because they reverse the effect of gravity. The authors of the book from which the above quote was taken say that incontinence also responds very well to yoga and that practising twice a day 'will bring noticeable results within a few weeks'.

You can pick up a few hints on postures from any book on yoga. But for the best chance of success you also must practise other, more advanced, techniques for which you need an experienced teacher. (See Useful Addresses.)

Other alternative therapy

Because prolapse and incontinence are largely mechanical problems they are best prevented by and, in their early stages, respond best to mechanical treatment – i.e. exercise. (Incontinence may be a symptom of other conditions that have nothing to do with the state of the pelvic floor but these are not nearly so common.)

So most alternative practitioners – naturopaths, osteopaths and acupuncturists – like their orthodox counterparts, start off by recommending an exercise regime.

Osteopaths may, in addition, work to correct poor posture, which may, in some cases, increase the tendency for the uterus to sink. 'But once the . . . support has packed up, there's not a great deal you can do for it . . . it has to be supported . . . I'd let that be dealt with by a gynaecologist,' said one, adding however, 'You can do a lot to prevent it happening again.' His therapy, he said, was 'complementary rather than purely alternative'.

Acupuncture may also help – but, again, only if the problem is dealt with in its early stages. None of the practitioners I contacted had treated many prolapses but their success rate was impressive. 'It's very easy to treat,' one reported. 'I've treated three and they were all treated very quickly. But the prolapses weren't very bad. One had had it only for about six weeks. She was fine after eight treatments.' Another said: 'I've treated it really quite well but only two or three times. It probably works best if you use Western medicine [surgery] as well.' But he stressed that if he'd had more experience, he might possibly have different views!

CONCLUSIONS

The message coming from all sides is prevention. And you're never too young to start. Specialists say we'd be doing our daughters a big favour if we taught them pelvic floor exercises while they were still children. Who knows? they might get the hang of them far more easily than we do. But any regular exercise, especially yoga, will strengthen and tone the muscles of the pelvic floor.

If you suspect your pelvic floor is weaker than it should be – if you begin to 'leak' occasionally – act promptly. Find a natural childbirth teacher or a physiotherapist who can teach you the Kegel routine. Step up your yoga, preferably with a teacher who is clued-up on pelvic floor problems. Do try to master these techniques because they will help. If this isn't enough, try osteopathy or acupuncture. But again, *don't* leave it too late. And, whatever treatment you have, you still need to keep exercising, now and for the rest of your life. Any muscle, even if it's been repaired surgically, needs regular use if it's to stay strong.

11. Female Cancer

I think the problem with so much alternative medicine is that the practitioners cannot offer evidence that what they're doing has any significant impact on the patient's disease.

(Professor Tim McElwain, cancer specialist, speaking on BBC-TV *Brass Tacks* programme: 'A Patient's Dilemma')

There are at least 80 non-toxic therapy measures designed to control cancer which have been extensively and effectively used, considering that in most cases patients only turn to this kind of help when all else fails.

(Brenda Kidman: *A Gentle Way with Cancer*)[1]

Alternative forms of cancer treatment have been in the news a lot in the last few years. What's been missing, though, from all this publicity, is an objective assessment of the methods. Instead, alternative and conventional medicine have been painted in black and white. If you watch television programmes which are on the side of alternatives – like the BBC-TV series *A Gentle Way with Cancer*, which featured the methods discussed in Kidman's book – you'll learn that conventional therapy is harsh, and often ineffective, and that it erodes a person's physical and psychological defences; on the other hand, therapy based on diet and other 'gentle' approaches is non-toxic and encourages a positive attitude, a will to live. This information is usually presented with dramatic stories of people who've beaten their cancer after following an alternative regime.

The typical 'anti' programme concentrates on recent improvements in the medical treatment of cancer and contrasts that with the lack of scientific evidence that alternatives have any effect at all on the disease. A bevy of obviously kind and respectable doctors is wheeled on to talk about the importance of testing *all* treatments in the proper scientific way. And then we learn about the darker side of alternative medicine: about a few practitioners – usually those with dubious or non-existent qualifications – who have been exploiting sick people with promises of cures that they can't hope to fulfil. After watching this sort of programme – a good example is the BBC-TV *Brass Tacks* on 'A Patient's Dilemma' from which the quote above was taken – you're left with the impression that the patient who turns to alternatives dies of his disease, sooner rather than later.

No doubt the producers of both types of programme are sincere. Those supporting the 'gentle' way are offering the patient hope – hope which may renew their will to live. And nobody would scoff at that. But the critics of alternative medicine would argue that it is cruel even to raise that hope when it rests on such shaky ground.

IS THERE A SOLUTION TO 'THE PATIENT'S DILEMMA'?

Both these viewpoints are extreme. Somewhere in between them there is, I believe, a common ground where conventional and alternative medicine can work together to produce the best chance of cure. I don't think alternative medicine should ever be used alone in the treatment of cancer but nor do modern medical techniques have all the answers either. I also think that one of the main benefits of the gentle approach – and one which scientific researchers are only just beginning to take an interest in – is its power to influence a person's mind, to change her attitude to her cancer. It's possible that the strength of a person's immune system may be linked to her psychological state so that if she has positive feelings about her treatment then the growth of her cancer may be arrested or even reversed. And even if alternative medicine seldom achieves such miracles – if it fails either to cure a patient or delay her death – it can make a big difference to the *quality* of her life, and of her dying.

This isn't to say that conventional medicine hasn't made great strides in the way it cares for the dying: the growth of the hospice movement has meant that these days more of those cancer patients who die do so with dignity and without pain. But hospices are only for the terminally ill. Patients with less advanced disease still get precious little in the way of emotional support. Their bodies are treated – but not their psyches. And as one woman who had turned to alternatives explained to me: 'The worst thing about having cancer is the loneliness. You can't talk to anyone about how you feel, because no one who hasn't had cancer really understands what it's like.'

In the rest of this chapter, I hope to give you some idea of how both forms of treatment can best be combined – in a truly complementary fashion. The gentle approach is, of course, a holistic one and so treats the patient rather than trying to cure the cancer. For this reason – with one exception – I shan't be discussing alternative therapies for specific, female cancers. Instead I'm going to talk about how the alternative approach is aimed at what its practitioners believe to be the roots of *all* forms of the disease.

Having said that, there is some evidence that different types of cancer may be more likely to occur under some circumstances than others. And the exciting thing is that though quite a bit of this evidence comes from mainstream medical research, it lends support to the sort of treatment regime recommended for years by alternative practitioners. However, most orthodox medics feel that while this information may tell us something about the ways in which cancer might be *prevented*, we're still a long way from being able to use it to treat the disease once it's developed. Surgery and drugs on the other hand, they argue, have an established track record and so should still be the first line of attack.

Are they right? After all, many cancer patients decide to try alternative methods because of growing doubts in the power of conventional medicine to heal them. Is their distrust justified? Is it based on facts – or fear: fear that not only is their cancer untreatable but that the effects of the treatment they may be offered will turn out to be worse than the disease itself? If we, as patients, are going to solve our dilemma, we need to know the truth about conventional medicine. If it's effective then there's little place for alternatives. If it's not, then the argument for the gentle approach becomes much harder to ignore.

CONVENTIONAL TREATMENT

Breast Cancer

IS EARLY DETECTION IMPORTANT?

We're often told that the treatment of breast cancer is more likely to be successful when the disease is discovered in its early stages. Hence the current interest in screening techniques, such as mammography, which can detect a cancer while it's still too small to be felt either by the woman herself or by a doctor examining her. But screening is not yet generally available, so the emphasis on early detection at the moment is on a woman examining her breasts regularly and being able to spot changes in them.

THE CASE FOR BREAST SELF-EXAMINATION (BSE)

It's often said that our depressing breast cancer statistics – one in every fourteen women will get the disease and one in thirty will die from it – could be improved if every woman examined her breasts at least once a month.

But the evidence in favour of BSE isn't all that impressive. By the time a tumour can be felt, it's at least 2 cm in size. And by then there's at least a 50/50 chance that the cancer will have already spread elsewhere in the body (metastasized), although those new malignant growths will be so tiny that they may not yet be evident (micrometastases). Metastatic breast cancer is very difficult to treat successfully (see pages 275-9). So though BSE may mean an earlier diagnosis it won't necessarily affect a woman's chances of cure. Some studies have shown that women who practise BSE and who find a tumour are likely to live for longer after diagnosis than those whose cancers are discovered accidently. But critics of the technique – and there are many of them – point out that this doesn't prove that it's beneficial. The diagnosis is merely brought forward so the women only appear to live longer.

We don't yet know whether this is so. But even specialists who support BSE admit that they're doing it more in hope than in expectation. Trials are now in progress which may help to remove this uncertainty, but they will take many years to complete.

THE CASE FOR SCREENING

As we've seen, even regular breast self-examination leaves a lot to be desired because it can't pick up the smallest tumours. Neither can a doctor examining a woman's breasts in the same way. Mammography – a simple X-ray of the breasts – on the other hand, can detect cancers when they're still as small as ¼ or ½ cm in diameter.

You might think, then, that the logical way of combating breast cancer would be for all women over, say, forty (when the risk of breast cancer seriously begins to increase) to have regular mammograms. Unfortunately it's not that simple.

For one thing, mammography, because of the X-rays, could actually *increase* the risks of cancer, though most experts now believe that a yearly mammogram carries very little danger. Another problem is that no one is yet certain which groups of women would benefit most from the technique. Initial studies in the US suggested that, though the technique could pick up most cancers in women over fifty, it was less effective in younger women, because of the different composition of their breasts. Later results, however, including those from a Swedish trial published in the *Lancet* in 1985, seem to suggest that mammography may also be a benefit in the over-forties.

But would mammography save more lives than the simpler – and cheaper – BSE? As with BSE, the technique may simply be revealing cancers earlier and so artificially prolonging the time between diagnosis and death. There's another reason for doubt – one based on current knowledge about how tumours grow and spread. By the time a tumour is picked up by BSE it has already doubled in size thirty-two times. A tumour which shows up on mammography has doubled thirty times. The difference in size may be quite large but the chances that that tumour has already metastasized are probably the same.

More trials of mammography are being done. But they're enormously difficult to set up and take a long time to complete. So it may be years before we know if the technique is really useful as a screening tool.

SURGERY

All breast lumps – whether benign or malignant – are usually removed surgically. Benign cysts are an exception to this rule: they're fairly easy to diagnose and are usually treated with simple aspiration, where the fluid in the cyst is sucked out. (Benign breast disease is covered in more detail in chapter 12.) But with other, more solid, lumps diagnosis is more difficult: the lump – or part of it – must be removed so that it can be looked at more closely in the laboratory. Most lumps, fortunately – about nine out of ten – are *not* malignant and once they've been taken out that's usually the end of the matter.

However if your lump does prove cancerous then you'll be advised to have further surgery. Just what sort depends not only on how advanced your disease appears to be – whether it has spread to the lymph-nodes in your armpit, for example – but also on your surgeon.

The results of a number of studies done over the last twenty years, and in particular several very recent ones, have suggested that, for many women, the mutilating mastectomy operation just isn't necessary. More conservative surgery, which removes the lump but leaves the rest of the breast more or less intact, may be all that's needed. A woman who has the less drastic operation will, it seems, live just as long as one who has had her entire breast taken away. She'll need additional treatment – in the form of radiotherapy – to eliminate any cancer cells left behind after surgery but, with modern techniques, the side effects are minimal and the end result in many cases is a normal-looking breast.

Despite this, according to a recent survey in the *British Medical Journal*, 85 per cent of all UK surgeons still do mastectomies as a routine. 'Surgeons,' the authors of the report concluded, 'do not appear to follow results of trials but use their own treatment.'

To be fair, though, to the majority of surgeons who still favour mastectomies, we still don't know for sure that conservative surgery is always just as safe as mastectomy. Most specialists do believe the evidence that mastectomy is no better at saving lives. But this isn't their only worry. They're also concerned that lumpectomy – even when radiotheraphy is used as well – may not be as good at preventing the recurrence of cancer in the affected breast. Recurrent cancer may not kill but it can be very difficult to treat. Often mastectomy is then the *only* solution. The latest trial[2] indicates that recurrence isn't a problem but the surgery used was slightly more extensive than a simple lumpectomy – some normal tissue was removed as well. Will lumpectomy prove just as successful?

There are doubts, too, about the length of the recent trials. Few patients were followed for even five years. Yet most surgeons believe that a woman can't be considered to be cured of breast cancer until she's survived without any evidence of the disease for at least twenty.

The other problem about lumpectomy is this: though surgeons agree that it will probably never be suitable for all women with breast cancer, there's still no consensus about which ones *would* benefit. Some US specialists claim that as many as 80 per cent of patients could be treated adequately by this technique. Some UK surgeons are more cautious and say that it's suitable for only one woman in five.

So at this stage, the picture is rather confused. No wonder surgeons are tending to stick with the tried-and-tested mastectomy. New trials are now being carried out to try to settle the issue. But it'll be at least ten years before we have the results.

For the present, what should you do if you've been told you have breast cancer? The first thing is to find a surgeon who is willing to perform lumpectomies – and who has a fair bit of experience in doing the operation. You'll then need to discuss with him whether lumpectomy would be suitable in your particular case. If he's in favour of lumpectomies in principle then he's likely to give you unbiased advice. If it turns out that a mastectomy may be the better operation for you, find out just what the surgery entails – there are several types of mastectomy and some are less mutilating than others.

You may also want to consider the possibility of breast reconstruction. This involves the insertion of an implant to replace the missing breast tissue. Sometimes this can be done at the same time as the mastectomy so you won't have to face waking up minus a breast. The latest evidence, though, suggests it may be better to delay reconstruction. A new technique, involving the gradual expansion of the remaining tissue, helps give the 'new' breast a more natural contour.

CYTOTOXIC CHEMOTHERAPHY

The object of chemotherapy is to eradicate the micro-metastases – the microscopic cancers which may form elsewhere in the body from malignant cells shed from the primary tumour in the breast. These are too small to be diagnosed clinically. But, as I've explained, more than 50 per cent of all women – some specialists believe as many as 70 per cent – will already have these 'silent' micrometastases by the time their breast cancer is diagnosed.

Your specialist will try to predict whether you're one of the women who are likely to have micrometastases. If you have cancer in the lymph-nodes in your armpit, for example, you're more at risk. Your breast lump will be carefully examined too: some types of primary tumour seem to spread more rapidly than others. Unfortunately, though, these are no more than educated guesses. A woman thought to be at low risk may still go on to develop secondary cancer.

This makes the specialist's job extremely difficult. Should he prescribe chemotherapy, which is a very toxic form of treatment, to all breast cancer patients because the majority of them *will* later be found to have secondary cancers? Or should he hold his fire? His decision is made harder by the knowledge that, if chemotherapy is to work at all, it needs to be given in very large doses which may cause severe side-effects in many women. The side effects of chemotheraphy include hair loss (alopecia), nausea, vomiting, diarrhoea and loss of sensation in the fingertips. These would all be bad enough if they lasted a few weeks. But the drugs may have to be administered for one or even two years.

Is it worth it? Well, most specialists now agree that only certain women will probably benefit. These are the ones who haven't yet reached the menopause and who also have 'positive' lumph-nodes – nodes which contain cancer cells. This suggests that the cancer may well have spread elsewhere, even if other secondaries aren't obvious. However, even in this selected group of women, results are not particularly good. At best, one in five women treated with cytotoxic drugs lives longer. How much longer? No one knows.

So chemotherapy hasn't yet proved its worth. Some specialists suspect that it never will – even when we have the results of newer trials. 'I think we're going to find there is an effect on increased survival,' one explained. 'But I don't think that's going to solve the problem of whether this treatment should be prescribed routinely because, unfortunately, the differences are not going to be very large.' By which he means that chemotherapy may help a few women live longer but it isn't going to do anything for the rest. Perhaps even more revealing is the fact that some investigators have abandoned trials altogether because of 'unbearable' side effects. One also has to bear in mind that chemotherapy may even, occasionally, kill the patient.

But we shouldn't write it off altogether. If a woman does respond to chemotherapy it may actually give her a few – possibly many – more years than she would have had otherwise. And, if she also happens to suffer few side effects from the drugs, it could be argued that the treatment was justified.

ENDOCRINE THERAPY

In the past, premenopausal women with breast cancer were advised to have their ovaries removed surgically or destroyed by radiotherapy. The reason for this is that many breast tumours – hence the secondary cancers they produce – are oestrogen-dependent. But a number of studies over the years have shown there's no justification for this drastic treatment. Though these procedures did delay the appearance of metastases, the women didn't actually live any longer.

Fortunately, there are now alternatives. It is now recognized that oestrogen-dependent tumours have oestrogen-binding sites on their surfaces. Prevent the oestrogen binding to those sites and you may be able to stop the cancer growing. There are now drugs which do just that. One is tamoxifen, which competes with oestrogen for the binding site. Another is aminoglutethimide, which inhibits the production of oestrogen so there's less available for binding. Both these drugs are relatively non-toxic. Initially, they were used mainly to treat advanced cases of breast cancer and produced good results in both premenopausal and postmenopausal women. Up to 30 per cent of patients go into a remission, which can last for one to two years. Preliminary results suggest that these drugs may help a minority of women with early breast cancer live longer, too. (There are even plans to use tamoxifen in an attempt to *prevent* the development of breast cancer in those women at greatest risk of the disease (see pages 258-8 for a discussion of risk factors). However, there are potential ethical problems: is it justifiable to give *any* drug to healthy women – especially one like tamoxifen which may interfere with their normal hormone production?)

Conclusions: what are your chances?

At this stage in the game it's impossible to predict which women with early breast cancer will live to a ripe old age and which ones will die from their disease. We know far too little about the way individual tumours behave even to guess. Nevertheless, some women do beat their cancer – though whether this is because of their treatment or because they happened to have a relatively less malignant form of the disease is far from clear.

Unfortunately, though, if you have breast cancer the odds are against you. Professor Michael Baum, one of the leading experts in the field, admits that a breast cancer patient's chances aren't all that good. And he is someone who takes a fairly optimistic view of the current medical scene. As he says in his book *Breast Cancer. The Facts*.[3]

It is reasonable to conclude that approximately 30 per cent of women presenting with 'early' carcinoma of the breast and subjected to mastectomy will have a normal expectation of life. Bearing in mind that little more than half of the cases of breast cancer that surgeons see fall within the 'early' stages of the disease, we are left with the rather depressing conclusion that overall only about 15 per cent of breast cancer cases referred to the clinics are 'cured' by conventional therapy. However, unlike cancer of the lung and cancer of the stomach, many of the women who may eventually be judged as incurable can be expected to live for a considerable number of years in comfort as a result of modern therapeutic strategy, which would at least allow them to see their children through school or be around to advise on the upbringing of their first grandchild.

So breast cancer is far from being an immediate death sentence – even if you're one of the unlucky ones. That may not be much consolation. But, at the very least, medical treatment may give you breathing space while you consider what else you could be doing about your cancer. And that's where alternatives come in. More about that later.

Cancer of the cervix

Cervical cancer very rarely kills – mainly because current cervical smear screening programmes are detecting the disease long before it becomes *invasive*, that is, capable of spreading to other tissues.

However, although there's no doubt that a regular smear is the best protection against this form of cancer, there's been some concern recently that some young women may develop cancer so quickly that even regular smears won't pick it up in time. It's even been suggested that the cancer in younger women is of a different, far more malignant, type. Opinions differ as to whether this is true. For example, a 1984 editorial in the *British Journal of Family Planning* stated, 'there is little or no evidence that the disease progresses more rapidly in young women or that there are two types of cancer, one in young and another in old women'. An editorial in the *British Medical Journal* in 1985 took the opposite view. Not surprisingly, therefore, there's also considerable controversy about whether we're screening the most vulnerable women often enough.

A 'positive' smear, that is, one which shows some abnormality, doesn't necessarily mean you have cancer. There are degrees of abnormality. The type of treatment depends both on the results of the smear and on additional tests done at the hospital. If the smear is abnormal, but there's no suggestion of cancer or of an infection, then all that may be necessary is for you to have more frequent smears for a time: a mild abnormality may go away on its own.

If cancer is suspected or diagnosed then the affected area must be removed. There are several ways of doing this. It may be burned or frozen (cautery), cut out or vaporized with lasers. The milder the abnormality, the more likely it is to be treated with lasers or cautery. Though some specialists believe that these more conservative techniques can be used to treat pre-invasive cancer, others consider that cervical conization is the best treatment for this form of the disease. This involves cutting a cone-shaped piece of tissue from all round the inside of the cervix.

The success rate of these techniques seems to vary. Conization is said by some specialists to cure 99 per cent of women, though others put it at a more conservative 80 to 90 per cent. Cure rates of 90 per cent have been reported for the other methods but – and this is certainly the case with lasers – there's some doubt as to whether your average gynaecologist is going to get such good results. Many surgeons still prefer to perform a conization because this is the best way to be sure that *all* the diseased tissue has been removed.

Conization does have drawbacks, however. It can scar your cervix so badly that giving birth normally becomes impossible and you may have to have your babies by Caesarian section. On the other hand, it may make your cervix incompetent (see page 214) so that you're more likely to have a miscarriage or premature baby. The more conservative treatments seem to give rise to fewer problems. Hysterectomy is also sometimes used as a treatment for cervical cancer. Generally, though, it's reserved for the invasive type. Pre-invasive cancer usually grows only slowly – and is not yet capable of spreading. So it doesn't merit such drastic surgery.

Endometrial cancer (cancer of the body of the uterus)

Hysterectomy is generally considered to be the only safe treatment for this form of cancer. (Though a few reports have suggested that, in premenopausal women, progestogen treatment may sometimes result in a complete regression of the disease.) Usually the ovaries and a small piece from the top of the vagina are removed at the same time. Radiotherapy may be used as well – both before and after the operation – to increase the chances of cure. If the cancer is confined to the body of the uterus then a woman has a 75 to 80 per cent chance of surviving for at least five years, though she can't be certain that her cancer has been eliminated until many years later. If the cancer has spread beyond the uterus, the outlook isn't nearly so good: only about 40 per cent of these women will be alive five years later.

CAN WE DO MORE TO PREVENT CANCER?

Orthodox and alternative approaches to prevention

Both orthodox and alternative practitioners believe that many cancers could be prevented. But there the similarities end. The orthodox view is that, although the scientific evidence gives us some general clues about cancer prevention, these are usually *only* clues: this, they say, means that we can't yet use the information in a practical way. Of course, for a few types of cancer, it's been possible to establish a definite link between the cancer and one of its main causes – for example, between smoking and lung cancer. However, for the vast majority of cancers, this hasn't been done. Though the evidence may point towards one or more specific causes, we're still a long way from being able to prove that a link really exists.

Alternative practitioners, on the other hand, feel that this sort of evidence is good enough. They argue that if we even suspect something of causing cancer or, for that matter, any other disease, then we should avoid it. But they go further. If we know something about what might cause cancer, they suggest, then we also have a tool to treat it. If, for example, certain types of food may trigger the development and growth of a cancer, it's reasonable to suppose – or so they believe – that those same foods may also make that cancer worse. Eliminate them from your diet and you increase your chances of beating it. Conversely, if certain substances appear to guard against cancer, then you need more of them once you've fallen victim to the disease.

From page 291 I'll discuss the alternative approach to cancer treatment in more detail. But first I want to look at the evidence in favour of cancer prevention because it's on this that the alternative practitioner bases much of his treatment.

Preventing cancer: research gives very general clues

Large numbers of studies of people in different parts of the world and in different parts of the same country have revealed that a person's chances of getting cancer vary considerably, depending on where he or she lives. In fact in some communities, remote from the Western world, people seldom if ever get cancer. In some cases, these differences may be due to genetics – certain forms of cancer, including that of the breast (see page 287) do sometimes seem to run in families and one would perhaps expect people of some races to be more susceptible to cancer than others.

However, researchers believe this is probably only a tiny part of the explanation. They've discovered that groups of people living in one part of the US, for example, get cancer far less often then very similar people living elsewhere in the country. And if a native of a country where a certain form of cancer is rare moves to one where it's common, he becomes much more likely to get it himself. Sir Richard Doll and Dr Richard Peto, two of the leading researchers in this area, give several examples in their book *The Causes of Cancer*.[4] One is of Indians who were particularly at risk of mouth cancer in their home country but not after they'd moved to Fiji or South Africa. In addition, Doll and Peto point out, black Americans share their cancer pattern not with the West African black population from whom they are descended but with the white Americans amongst whom they now live. The risk of some individual cancers such as breast cancer (see pages 288-90) also varies between similar people living in different countries.

From this sort of evidence, Doll and Peto conclude, 'it is reasonable to suppose that the proportion of cancers whose onset could have been avoided will be . . . more than 75 or 80 per cent in principle, but, they caution, perhaps less in practice for many years to come.' The reason for that caveat is that we haven't yet pinpointed exactly what it is about the way we live that makes some of us more prone to cancer.

Diet and cancer prevention

Everyone who believes that nutrition is at the root of cancer tells the story of the Hunza people in Asia. They're very healthy and they never get cancer. A long time ago now, Sir (then Dr) Robert McCarrison suspected that their diet might be the explanation for the Hunzas' miraculous health. So he fed the diet to rats and compared them with rats given other diets. The 'Hunza' rats remained healthy whereas the others got practically every disease under the sun – including cancer.

Modern research also suggests that diet has something to do with the development of cancer. For example, certain forms of cancer are much more common in countries where people eat a lot of fatty foods: the relationship seems a pretty direct one because the risk of cancer increases as the fat consumption goes up. But does that mean the one causes the other? We still don't know: there could be all sorts of additional differences between a 'low risk' country and a 'high risk' one. The fat might just be a red herring.

The argument in favour of the Hunza diet is more difficult to refute. What's problematical, though, is finding out what it is in the diet that has the magic anti-cancer properties. This is important because we in the West can't hope to copy the Hunza diet exactly. It includes lots of fruit, both fresh and dried – and, in particular, dried apricots – pulses, other vegetables, grains and milk – but very little meat. So the search is on to try to pin down individual foods that may protect against cancer in ordinary people – not just in isolated groups such as the Hunza.

Could it be green vegetables? According to a report in the *New Scientist* in 1984 a diet rich in greens *does* help guard against cancer. The report – of a huge Japanese study of more than 100,000 people – also suggested that this sort of diet could reduce the cancer risks associated with smoking, drinking and eating meat.

Other research, too, has suggested that generous amounts of vegetables make cancer less likely. There could be several reasons for this. First, if you base your diet on vegetables you're almost bound to eat less fat. Second, the diet will contain higher-than-average amounts of fibre. This may have a protective effect, particularly against bowel cancer – but perhaps also against other cancers. Third, vegetables contain, amongst other vitamins, A and C. Several studies have indicated that these may have a role in cancer protection.

You will have noticed that, throughout this section, I keep writing 'may' rather than 'do'. This is because, although there is evidence to support all these suggestions, there's also evidence against. Vitamin E, another supposedly anti-cancer vitamin, has even less going for it. In fact Doll and Peto conclude that 'clinical deficiency of [vitamin E] is so rare (and so easy to treat when diagnosed) that epidemiological [population] study of vitamin E deficiency is difficult'. Most alternative practitioners don't share these doubts. They believe that gaps in the research are less important than the positive results we already have. But are they right? To find out we need to take a critical look, ourselves, at some of the research.

The evidence in favour of vitamin A, or rather beta-carotene, a plant compound that is converted into vitamin A in the body, is particularly strong. Laboratory rats fed vitamin A and then given cancer-causing chemicals are less likely to develop cancer than similar rats who haven't had the vitamin. In many countries, a low intake of beta-carotene is associated with a higher risk of cancer. And a study of vitamin A in the blood showed that people with cancer had lower levels than healthy people.

However the conclusion isn't as obvious as it seems.

Though blood levels of vitamin A vary between individuals, other research has shown that giving someone extra vitamin A doesn't increase the amount in his blood. This suggests that vitamin A may have nothing to do with cancer. Something else – maybe in the diet but maybe not – could be different in cancer victims. The low vitamin A therefore may either be a fluke or merely associated with the real cause of the cancer, one which the researchers haven't yet discovered.

It's the same with vitamin C. Some studies have suggested that low vitamin C in human beings may increase the risks of cancer. But this finding could be due simply to the fact that, in our diet, vitamin C and vitamin A are often found together. If vitamin C levels are low, those of vitamin A will be, too, and it may be this which makes cancer more likely. There's also some worrying evidence, mentioned in the *New England Journal of Medicine* in 1984. This suggests that increased amounts of vitamin C may actually be dangerous – in animals it can make cancers grow faster.

As for vitamin E and selenium – several studies have shown that cancer patients have lower blood levels of both these substances but others have failed to find a link. It could be, some researchers believe, that someone with cancer doesn't eat all that much anyway: a reduced amount of vitamins and minerals would therefore be just a reflection of more general malnutrition. However, the authors of the *NEJM* article concede there may be something in the vitamin and mineral story and that further studies should be done.

Possible psychological causes: stress and the cancer personality

This is one of the 'growth areas' in cancer research. Quite a bit of the work done in the UK has concentrated on the possible effects of stress on the growth of breast cancer and I'll go into that later. Here I want to look at the general evidence to support the suggestion that the development of cancer is related to stress and that there is a type of person –

the so-called 'cancer personality' – who is particularly susceptible to the disease.

Experiments with rats and mice have shown that these animals are more likely to develop tumours if they're stressed – for example by giving them an electric shock. In humans, stress is generally a more subtle matter – not everyone finds the same things stressful. However, some experiences – for example losing a parent at an early age or splitting from one's partner – are always distressing for everyone. And there does appear to be a very strong link between this sort of trauma and the subsequent development of cancer.

The American psychologist Lawrence LeShan,[5] for example, examined 125 cancer patients and compared them with 125 'controls' who didn't have cancer. He discovered that 72 per cent of the patients had lost someone important in their lives – compared with only 12 per cent of the controls. He also found some other interesting differences. 47 per cent of the patients, but only 25 per cent of the controls, reported that they found it hard to express hostile emotions; and 38 per cent compared with 11 per cent respectively, of patients and controls, said that they'd suffered stress as a result of losing a parent.

LeShan also says that most of his patients shared a feeling of despair and seemed to have no goal in life. They were typically self-effacing characters who had always done what other people wanted. You could argue, of course, that someone with cancer is almost bound to feel sad and depressed. But LeShan's patients reported that they had *always* felt that way – apart, perhaps, from a few brief periods when their lives were going particularly well.

From other research, it appears that it may not be the stress as such – but rather the way she *reacts* to it – that makes someone susceptible to cancer. But stressful events in early life, such as losing a parent, may affect a person's psychological make-up so profoundly that she becomes less able to cope with stress when she's older. That, at least, is the picture that's beginning to emerge.

Some studies have indicated that depressed people are

more likely to develop cancer and this, too, would tie in with the idea that personality is a big factor. Others have suggested that cancer patients, as LeShan also found, tend to be emotionally inhibited and to have had bad experiences in childhood.

So there does seem to be such a thing as the cancer personality. What is less clear is why people with these particular traits are prone to cancer. There are a number of theories, to do with the way our moods affect our hormone levels and *vice versa*: it is possible that both stress and depression may make our immune systems less efficient and so less able to knock out those first few cancer cells when they appear.

The prevention of female cancers: what do we know about the causes?

BREAST CANCER

You're more likely to develop breast cancer if a member of your family – particularly your mother or sister – had it. This suggests that one of the causes of this form of disease is genetic and therefore can't be prevented.

We can't do much, either, about reducing the increased risk of breast cancer that's associated with an early menarche (onset of periods) and a late menopause. However, it also seems that having your first child fairly early (before the age of twenty-five) gives some protection. It used to be thought that it was breastfeeding, rather than child-bearing itself, which protected against cancer. There's a little evidence for this, but not much. Epidemiologists now think that a far more important factor is the length of time a woman is exposed to her natural female hormones and, in particular, the number of menstrual periods she has before she conceives for the first time.

But even though you may be more susceptible to cancer either because of your family history or because you've been menstruating for more than the average number of years, this certainly doesn't mean you're going to get the disease. The chances are that you won't. Cancer is what doctors call a *multifactorial* disease, that is, it's considered to arise from a combination of circumstances: if one or more occur together they increase the *statistical* risk of the disease. But cancer only develops when all the predisposing factors are present at the same time.

This is why it's important to look at some of the possible *preventable* causes of breast cancer.

Hormones

I mentioned that an early menarche and a late menopause increased the risks of cancer and that epidemiologists now believe that the key factor here is the length of time that a women is exposed to her natural female hormones.

Other evidence also supports the theory that hormones – in particular, oestrogen – play a crucial part in the development of breast cancer. Many breast tumours are known to be oestrogen-dependent (see page 277). And a study of women living on the island of Guernsey showed that those who got breast cancer had been excreting higher-than-normal amounts of oestrogen in their urine as many as ten years earlier. (This is also one of the reasons behind the planned trial of tamoxifen, mentioned on page 277.)

If high hormone levels are linked with breast cancer, it would be reasonable to expect that a woman on hormone replacement therapy or taking the contraceptive Pill might be at greater risk. And this does seem to be the case though the latest information suggests that the risks don't increase that much (see Chapters 6 and 9).

Diet

Vegetarian women are much less likely to get breast cancer than those who eat meat. But it's not just avoiding meat that has a protective effect. The increased incidence of breast cancer in affluent parts of the world such as Europe, New

Zealand and North America has been linked to a diet high in fat and low in fibre. It could be that the important features of vegetarian diets are their low-fat and high-fibre content.

Why should diets low in fibre and high in fat promote the development of breast cancer? For one thing, if you don't eat enough fibre you're likely to become constipated and constipation has been linked with certain breast abnormalities. These aren't cancerous but could lead to cancer, in time. It's also interesting that women who eat substantial quantities of fibre tend to have lower amounts of oestrogen in their blood and, as we know, high oestrogen levels may encourage the growth of breast cancer. A high-fat diet may compound this risk by altering hormone levels. The way in which it might do this is still uncertain but one suggestion is that fatty tissue, because it can make its own oestrogen (see page 299), may increase hormone levels. This could be important in post-menopausal women whose ovaries make very little oestrogen, and also could help explain why obese women are at increased risk of breast cancer.

But fat and low fibre may not be the only culprits. More recently, scientists have presented evidence that the increased incidence of cancer in the Western world may be linked to our high sugar consumption. Other research suggests that drinking alcohol may be involved as well.

Low levels of the vitamins A and E have been shown to be associated specifically with cancer of the breast as well as with the disease in general. In the study of women in Guernsey, mentioned earlier, low levels of beta-carotene (the vegetable compound that's converted to vitamin A) were discovered in the women who later developed cancer. They also had low vitamin E levels. The results of animal experiments point in the same direction: a report from the US showed it was possible to prevent mammary cancers in rats by giving them a low-fat diet, high in vitamin A. It could be that the two vitamins, which are found in large amounts in certain plants, could be at least partly responsible for the low incidence of breast cancer among vegetarian women.

Whatever the reasons, the influence of diet is clearly

profound. For those of us who haven't got the wholefood message, changing our diets to cut down fat and sugar and to increase fibre could well be worthwhile. One needs only to look at the fate of Japanese women who emigrate to the US to realize how important this could be. Women in Japan have very low rates of breast cancer. But when they emigrate to the States, their risk increases. Within a generation, they're just as likely to get breast cancer as other American women. Although other factors might be to blame, the adoption of a Western diet could well be responsible.

The 'breast cancer personality'

There doesn't seem to be any link between stressful events and the subsequent development of breast cancer. However there does appear to be a definite 'breast cancer personality'. And, as I explained above, such people may be the way they are at least partly because of previous stressful experiences, and they may respond to later stresses in a different way from healthy people.

The evidence, mainly, from a group of researchers at King's College Hospital, London, suggests that women with breast cancer are more likely to suppress their emotions – particularly anger. They're people who like to make a good impression. Not surprisingly, they react to stress slightly differently from healthy women. So far, the researchers haven't reached any conclusions about how this might be related to the development of cancer. But one idea is that women with cancer may produce different amounts of stress hormones and that these may promote cancer growth.

These results also help explain why it's not stress itself, but a person's ability to cope with it, that seems to increase her susceptibility to cancer.

CERVICAL CANCER

The Pill and sexual intercourse

Several studies have suggested that if you use the Pill, you're increasing your chances of developing cancer of the cervix. Despite this, many investigators are still not convinced there's a genuine link. This is partly because the risk seems fairly small – at most one and a half times that of women who've never used the Pill – and even that figure may not be accurate: the statistical methods used leave quite a large margin for error.

But there's also some evidence that cervical cancer is on the increase among young women – the very people who are most likely to use the Pill. However, the Pill itself may not be to blame, or so many researchers believe. Evidence is accumulating that a woman's sex life may be the real culprit (plus, possibly, her smoking habits – see below).

Clue 1. Nuns hardly ever get cancer of the cervix.

Clue 2. A woman who starts having intercourse in her teens and who has several sexual partners is more likely to develop cancer than one who begins her sex life later and sticks to one partner.

Clue 3. Even if a woman has only one partner, if *he* has had a wide sexual experience, then *her* chances of cervical cancer are increased.

Clue 4. Surveys have shown that the under-seventeens are twice as likely to be having sex now as compared with ten years ago.

These findings are unfortunate because they raise all sorts of moral implications: is cancer the penalty we have to pay for our less inhibited attitude to sex?

This possibility seems all too likely. Additional research has revealed a strong link between genital viral infections – particularly those caused by the wart and herpes viruses – and cervical cancer. Viruses *can* cause cancer and, of course, the more partners you have, the more likely you are to become infected. Younger women could be at added risk because their cervices are still developing and so more vulnerable to attack.

The reason for the apparent link with the Pill, then, may be that the more women use this form of contraception the less they're going to use barrier methods such as the cap or sheath. But these barriers shield the cervix from viruses – or anything else in a man's semen which may be capable of causing cancer. Some people, incidentally, believe that semen itself may be carcinogenic! I must confess, though, that I don't believe this theory – if it were true then surely cervical cancer would be much more common than it is.

I don't intend to draw any conclusions from this research. Certainly no one's suggesting that we should all become celibate! But it does throw new light on the possible advantage of barrier contraceptives.

Smoking

However wild or restrained your sex life, if you smoke you may be at additional risk. Smokers are more likely to get cervical cancer and research has shown that at least some of the constituents of cigarette smoke end up in cervical mucus. Whether these particular compounds are capable of causing cancer of the cervix isn't known. But it's quite possible that other substances in smoke – which *are* carcinogenic – also get through to the cervix.

Smoking also reduces our vitamin C levels and there's a little evidence that a vitamin C deficiency is associated with an increased cancer risk (see page 285).

ENDOMETRIAL CANCER

Hormones

This form of cancer usually appears after the menopause. There's a definite link between cancer of the endometrium and oestrogen-only HRT (see Chapter 9 on the menopause). Childless women are also more at risk. Very fat women seem to be, too, possibly because, after the menopause, most of our female hormones are made in our fatty tissues. So staying slim – which should be fairly easy if you eat the kind of healthy diet now recommended by most nutritionists – is one way you can guard against endometrial cancer.

ALTERNATIVE TREATMENT

Non-medical practitioners are not allowed by law to claim to treat cancer, let alone to claim to cure it. In practice, though, this claim is implicit in many alternative treatments. Even though they concentrate on improving a person's general health – by diet, extra vitamins and a variety of other techniques – if that person has cancer then he or she is looking for a cure, no matter what the practitioner may say.

But many alternative practitioners will refuse to take a patient on unless she consults a medical doctor, too. This is important for two reasons. Firstly, because ultimate responsibility for that patient rests with the doctor. Secondly, because, provided the doctor is happy for the patient to continue with alternative treatment she can have the best of both worlds.

You should consult only lay alternative practitioners who are members of one of the recognized professional associations (see Useful Addresses). In addition, try to find one who has a good relationship with his medical colleagues. Then, if necessary, he can refer you for hospital tests. And if, for any reason, he feels your condition is beyond his powers to treat – and that may well happen – he will feel able to pass you back to your own doctor. Be extremely wary of any practitioner who advises you to reject orthodox treatment. This suggests that he's just as narrow-minded as the doctors who won't entertain the idea that alternatives could conceivably help some of their patients. On the contrary, the two approaches *can* work side by side and are probably best combined.

Perhaps the ideal way to tackle your cancer is to consult a doctor who also practises alternative medicine or who can refer you to alternative practitioners he knows personally.

Often, no one treatment is enough and cancer help centres such as the one at Bristol, and the Association for New Approaches to Cancer (ANAC), recommend several different ones. They also have good links with both orthodox and alternative practitioners – and have helped to set up a number of self-help groups throughout the country where you can get advice and moral support.

The main methods

DIET

Great claims have been made for anti-cancer diets. Perhaps the most famous is the Gerson diet developed by Dr Max Gerson. It's based on fresh fruit and vegetables and is said to have cured many cancer patients. Obviously this diet contains many of the vitamins and minerals thought by some people to be important in the prevention of cancer. But while the results look good, we still don't have research findings to back these claims. It just isn't enough to put patients on a diet and then, if they improve, assert that the diet was responsible. All kinds of other factors may be involved – not least the medical treatment that the patients may have had or are still having. Even Dr Alec Forbes, former director of the Bristol Cancer Help Centre – where a diet similar to but less strict than the Gerson one is a major part of the regime – admits that more research is needed in this area.

Forbes estimates that fewer than one in three patients can stick to the Gerson diet long enough for it to do them any good. But even the Bristol diet has been modified recently: tomatoes, once banned, are now allowed and potatoes are on the menu more often than previously. One of the reasons for this is the Centre's growing conviction that a person's state of mind is the single most important influence on her health – and if she is miserable on a restrictive diet she'll be less likely to get well. (I'll explain this in more detail later.)

All the same, the diet is pretty rigorous. It's almost entirely vegan – apart from yoghurt – and mostly raw. Coffee, ordinary tea, and alcohol are forbidden, but patients can drink as much mineral water, herb tea and fresh fruit juice as they like. It's a diet which provides masses of vitamins and minerals and, because the food is fresh and organically grown, it contains no additives, no pesticides and, hopefully, few environmental pollutants. Though there's little evidence at the moment that the latter substances cause many, if any, cancers, even mainline orthodox researchers such as Doll and Peto agree that it might be a good idea to avoid them.

Vitamins

The Bristol diet also includes extra vitamin A in the form of the carotenoids found in carrot juice. This is said to be a much safer and more effective way of taking the vitamin than in tablet form. All the same, patients are advised to go easy and to report any side effects. A headache is a sign that you're overdoing it. On the other hand, yellow staining of the palms of the hands is considered normal provided you have no other symptoms – it merely shows that your body now has an adequate amount of this vitamin. Vitamin E is also recommended though, as I explained, the evidence to suggest that this vitamin helps fight cancer is fairly slim.

All alternative practitioners advised their patients to take vitamin C, because of its supposed (but still unproven) anti-cancer properties. Sometimes doses of up to 15 g a day – 500 times the recommended UK allowance – are recommended. Many orthodox practitioners question the wisdom of using such large doses. Forbes, however, points to research – mainly from the US – which has revealed that individuals need differing amounts of vitamins if they're to stay healthy (see also Chapter 2 on Eating for Health). 'A person is not just a statistical individual that you give fixed doses to,' he explains. 'Everybody is different – and so you get people with requirements for certain vitamins and minerals which are greatly in excess of the average statistical norm and also greatly below. So that you can get toxic doses more easily with some things, and some people need enormous doses. This concept is quite important to realize but, of course, it hasn't been looked at very seriously by orthodox practitioners.'

There is some research which suggests that vitamin C can help cancer patients[6] but, equally, there are studies which show it has no effect at all.[7] And though vitamin C is relatively non-toxic, large doses often cause diarrhoea. There is also evidence to show that, no matter how much of it you take, your body is incapable of absorbing more than about 2 grams.[8]

Evening primrose oil

This is increasingly becoming part of anti-cancer diets. Let me explain why. Many cancer cells appear to have lost one of their enzymes – one which makes a compound known as gammalinolenic acid (GLA). There's some evidence to suggest that GLA, which is found in abundance in evening primrose oil, can actually stop the cancer cells from multiplying. For example, this seems to happen when GLA is added to cancer cells growing in the laboratory. And when rats, with artificially induced mammary tumours, were given injections of evening primrose oil, within six weeks the lumps had shrunk to a third of their initial size.[9] It still remains to be proved that GLA can help human cancer victims – though this suggestion is now being tested in clinical trials. In the meantime, it might make sense for all cancer patients to take this supplement which, at worst, seems to be harmless.

Enzymes

One of the reasons for the emphasis on raw foods is that cooking destroys several of the vitamins thought to be important in cancer treatment. The other is that it also inactivates the natural enzymes contained in raw fruit and vegetables. Alternative cancer specialists consider that these enzymes are a vital part of the diet because they can attack cancer cells. Sometimes a patient may also be given additional enzymes in tablet form.

How do enzymes attack cancer? The theory is that cancer cells have a protective protein coat which prevents the body's immune system from recognizing them. Add an enzyme which can remove that coat and you leave the malignant cell exposed. This, incidentally, is why meat is excluded from the diet: it's suggested that if the enzymes in our body spend most of their efforts digesting the meat they'll have little spare capacity for chewing away the cancer.

It's a neat idea but one which, at the moment, doesn't stand up all that well. For a start, there's no evidence that cancer cells produce this protective coating, according to a leading cancer researcher I talked to. The second flaw in the enzymes argument is that if you take enzymes by mouth they're probably going to be inactivated once they hit the acid condition in the stomach. Of course, the stomach produces its own enzymes designed to work in an acid environment. But it's unlikely that other enzymes, especially those from plants, are going to survive. And if they did, there's no reason why they should be able to fight cancer.

Despite the lack of scientific evidence, Dr Forbes is convinced that enzymes can escape inactivation. In addition, he says, a German alternative cancer specialist, Dr Hans Nieper, claims to have treated a number of patients successfully, using enzymes in combination with other techniques. Forbes admits he doesn't know how enzymes work, but 'they seem to'.

Orthodox researchers concede there just might be something in the theory but they'll take a lot of persuading if they are to start looking into it. You just can't begin an expensive scientific study on the basis of so little evidence. They're also sceptical because so many other cancer 'treatments' have been proved to be so much scotch mist. The other problem is funding: most orthodox drug research is supported by pharmaceutical companies which, so far, have shown little interest in alternative treatments.

AMYGDALIN (LAETRILE)

This is the compound derived from the kernels of apricots which is said to attack cancer cells but not normal cells. Some of those who believe in it claim that amygdalin is the secret of the Hunzas' health. The Hunza diet, apparently, includes a lot of dried apricots which are eaten whole, stones and all.

A scientific study conducted in the US[10] has shown that amygdalin is worse than useless as a cancer treatment – not only did it fail to affect the cancer but it also caused toxic side effects. Dr Forbes, though, believes the trial's results shouldn't be taken too seriously. The researchers, he says, used the wrong sort of amygdalin: it was impure and therefore bound to be both ineffective and toxic. The patients were in the last stages of cancer and therefore unlikely to live long whatever treatment they had. They had also received extensive medical treatment, such as chemotherapy, which depresses the body's immune system and makes it less able to fight the cancer. In addition, Forbes points out, they weren't following the type of anti-cancer diet recommended by those practitioners who've obtained good results with amygdalin. Amygdalin in its pure form, Forbes told me, is a 'relatively non-toxic product'. The trouble is that the pure form is quite difficult to obtain.

At one time amygdalin formed part of the Bristol regime, although it's now been abandoned. Not because it's controversial, though it certainly is, but because Forbes has discovered that 'in the majority of people it doesn't work'. Amygdalin is supposed to attack cancer cells specifically because they're said to produce large amounts of an enzyme which normal cells make in only small quantities. This enzyme breaks the amygdalin into its constituent molecules, one of which is a poison. So the cells are killed. Though normal cells may split a little of the amygdalin and so release some of the poison, they have in addition, say alternative cancer practitioners, a further enzyme which neutralizes its efforts. Forbes suggests that the majority of people who don't respond to amygdalin don't produce enough of the enzyme which splits it.

The cancer researcher I consulted told me there was little evidence, anyway, that there's anything special about a cancer cell's enzymes. But, in view of the results obtained with GLA (see above), perhaps his judgement is a bit premature.

As you can see, the whole story of the 'metabolic' (as it's known among the cognoscenti) treatment of cancer is a confused one. There are clues, and explanations follow, but they often fail to stand up to scientific scrutiny. On the other hand, as the scientists freely admit, anything is possible. Just because we don't yet have the evidence to support a particular treatment doesn't mean that we never will have. *Something* is happening to those patients who improve on this sort of therapy.

TREATING THE BODY VIA THE MIND

When I spoke to Dr Forbes he made it clear that the arguments for and against anti-cancer diets, enzymes and amygdalin are really side issues in the treatment of cancer. 'What I want to talk to you about mostly,' he said, 'is the spiritual side and the psychological side – and changing people's attitudes.'

Relaxation, meditation and visualization

And, when I visited the Bristol Cancer Help Centre, that is what I heard most about. Patients are taught how to relax, how to meditate and how to look inside themselves to discover what sort of people they are. They are also advised on visualization techniques – the kind discussed in detail in *Getting Well Again*[11] by Carl and Stephanie Simonton. In essence this involves imagining your immune system winning the fight against cancer. Some people use very aggressive images – one girl, a keen gardener, saw herself stamping out the woodlice that plagued her flowerbeds. Others think of birds eating blackberries or mice eating cheese. The image itself doesn't matter too much – but you should use one you're happy with. One patient, for example, didn't like the idea of seeing cancer as an enemy. 'Your cancer isn't really your enemy,' she explained. 'It's part of you.' In such cases, Dr Forbes told me, 'we try to use a more peaceful form of assimilation. Your kindly white cells [which have a key role in attacking cancer] are doing a street-cleaning job, scavenging up the cancer cells, so they're being incorporated.'

There are probably almost as many images as there are patients but the object is the same – to kick the immune system into working harder. As I've already explained there's some evidence that our emotions can affect our immune systems and, although the visualization method is far from being proven, it makes sense. The Simontons report that out of 159 patients who'd been diagnosed as medically incurable, sixty-three were still alive more than two years later. Normally they'd have been expected to live for only twelve months. And of sixty-three, fourteen had no evidence of cancer, twelve still had a tumour but it was getting smaller, and in seventeen patients the cancer remained stable. In only twenty had the cancer actually got worse.

Relaxation and meditation may also help fight cancer because both methods reduce stress. (They're also recommended by the Association for New Approaches to Cancer.) Although stress itself may not cause cancer, it may be a particular problem to someone with a 'cancer personality' because they are less able to cope with it (page 285). These techniques may also help people who are depressed or unhappy.

Psychotherapy

This is rather a grand term for an integral part of alternative cancer treatment: talking to people, finding out about their hopes and fears and what makes them tick. Gemma Walker of ANAC told me: 'I want to know everything about them. Every one is wanting to get better in a physical, quite material world. But what I'm dealing with is spiritual emotions, the depths of the unconscious. That's where disease starts. If you're out of gear, at dis-ease with yourself, you're going to get ill.'

LeShan speaks of cancer patients as being people who've

never been able to 'sing their own song'. And when I joined a group session at Bristol a similar pattern emerged. Our first exercise was to write down ten answers to the question 'Who am I?' Many of the patients – especially the women – saw themselves primarily as appendages: 'John's wife' or 'Mary's mother'. Their feelings about *themselves* were very low down on the list.

Cancer patients, it seems, have got into the habit of not asserting themselves, possibly because they no longer know what *they* want. They have emotions but tend to suppress them for the good of everyone else. They are low on fighting spirit. Yet research suggests that the will to win may be one of the best ways of beating cancer. For example, the King's College Hospital group, in their work with breast cancer patients, has discovered that the women who vowed to beat their cancer did better than those who passively accepted their fate. In the study, sixty-seven women with early breast cancer were followed for five years after they'd had a mastectomy. At the end of that time, 49 per cent were alive and well with no sign of recurrence, 24 per cent were alive but had metastatic cancer and 27 per cent had died of their disease. However, a woman's attitude seemed to make a big difference to her prognosis. Of those women among the sample who refused to acknowledge their cancer or determined to fight it, 75 per cent were alive and well five years later. But of the women who had accepted their cancer stoically or despaired that anything could be done about it, only 35 per cent survived free from the disease.[12] Five years later again the differences were still there. 55 per cent of the 'deniers' and the fighters were still alive without evidence of the disease compared with only 22 per cent of the rest.[13]

The King's group is now looking into the possibility of giving women some group psychotherapy with a view to changing their attitudes to their disease. Several previous studies have suggested this could be useful. At the very least it seems able to change the way a woman sees herself and to help her if she's depressed or anxious. This could set her on the road to recovery. As LeShan says:

These techniques, in general, are designed to help the patient discover his true values – in terms of who he is, what kind of person he is, and what type of relationship would make the most sense and be the most rewarding and satisfying to him. For when a patient has denied his true values, and has sought to be loved only on other people's terms, then life inevitably comes to seem a series of endless frustrations and disappointments – disappointment not only with others but also with the self. And the will to live, smothered by self-contempt, can all too easily become enveloped in despair.

If the will to live is to flourish, the individual must live according to his own values, and seek to be loved for his own self.

Healing

This is usually an integral part of alternative cancer treatment. Some ANAC groups invite healers to their regular meetings and patients take it in turns to receive the laying on of hands. Any cancer help group should be able to put you in touch with one. Alternatively, you can consult the National Federation of Spiritual Healers.

Healing is seldom used on its own though Dr Forbes thinks it may be the best single treatment for people who are at the point of death.

OTHER THERAPIES USED IN ALTERNATIVE CANCER TREATMENT

Homoeopathy, herbs and acupuncture may all help. They're secondary, though, to the main approach based on diet and psychological therapy. This is because although homoeopathic and herbal remedies may alleviate symptoms, they're not generally thought to be able to combat an established cancer. However, there's some evidence that the homoeopathic remedy Iscador, prepared from mistletoe and given by injection, can cause regression of cancer in some cases.[14] Acupuncture may be used to relieve pain in people with advanced cancer.

Some specific remedies for cervical cancer

Although I said at the beginning of this chapter that alternative practitioners treat the person rather than her cancer, cervical cancer is a bit of an exception. Most gynaecologists will tell you that it's impossible to treat cervical cancer by anything other than medical methods. But there's evidence to show they're wrong. One woman doctor, practising in London, reports that thirteen of her patients have successfully treated their cancer with a combination of diet and the use of barrier methods of contraception.

A paper published in the *American Journal of Obstetrics and Gynecology* in 1981 also showed that condoms may be a good method of cancer treatment. Out of 139 patients who used the condom but received no conventional therapy, 136 had complete regression of their cancer! The authors of the paper suggest that the condom, by protecting the cervix from viruses in the man's semen, prevents further damage and meanwhile, the woman's immune system recovers sufficiently to fight the cancer off.

More evidence for the nutritional approach to this form of cancer comes from a report in the *American Journal of Clinical Nutrition*. Forty-seven young women on the Pill who had mild or moderate cervical dysplasia – conditions which aren't themselves cancerous but are thought possibly to progress to cancer if untreated – were given folic acid supplements. They were compared with a control group of women who received a placebo. The folic acid, the authors report, significantly improved the dysplasia.

COMBINING ALTERNATIVE AND CONVENTIONAL MEDICINE

Many cancer patients do use the two approaches together and, these days, more orthodox cancer specialists seem prepared to support their patients when they go on a diet or try relaxation and meditation – or other psychological approaches. At the very least, they argue, these can do no harm. One of them, Professor Kenneth Calman of Glasgow University, is reported as prescribing healing, herbal remedies and psychotherapy as well as all the usual drugs.[15]

Dr Forbes also believes that a combination may well give the best results. Dr Nieper, he points out, uses chemotherapy as well as metabolic therapy and claims to have extremely good results. Nieper, however, uses the chemotherapy in subtoxic doses so the side effects shouldn't be so bad.

> I think he's quite right [he adds]. I encourage people to have chemotherapy. All the people who go on our regime and work on it 'image' when they're going to have chemotherapy. We tell them to imagine that the chemotherapy is going to kill their cancer cells and not harm the rest of their body. And we ask them to imagine their hair follicles are holding onto their hair like mad [one of the side effects of this form of therapy is alopecia]. And because they're on heavy doses of vitamins and minerals they resist chemotherapy much better. Some of them don't lose their hair.

Vitamin E may be the important substance here. A report in the *New England Journal of Medicine* showed that alopecia was less common among patients taking vitamin E. (Incidentally, orthodox doctors sometimes use a special cap which keeps the scalp cool – with similar results.)

There seems to be very little other research examining the results of combining orthodox and alternative medicine. Dr Forbes, though, mentions one study of women with terminal breast cancer who were given the choice of having no treatment at all, either chemotherapy or psychotherapy alone, or both together. 'The "no-treatment" group,' he explains, 'survived seven months, the ones on chemotherapy approximately ten and the ones given psychotherapy about eleven. There was no statistical difference between the three groups. But the people who had both chemotherapy and psychotherapy survived for more than eighteen months and that difference was very significant. Very likely,' he concludes, 'doing both together will be better than doing either alone.'

THE DOUBTS REMAIN

Despite all the positive information coming in about alternative cancer treatment, we still don't know whether it really can cure the disease or whether the success stories that everyone talks about are examples of that medical 'miracle', the spontaneous regression. Or maybe the methods do work for a few people but not for the majority. Even some of those committed to the alternative approach doubt whether more than a minority of people ever gets better. Gemma Walker of ANAC reports: 'Cancers do go away but not very often. More common is that the cancer is contained. It's also common that they die, unfortunately.'

And a medically qualified alternative practitioner told me: 'Cancer is probably as well treated conventionally as it is unconventionally. I've a great dissatisfaction with some of the current things at Bristol. There are a lot of claims that they can only substantiate with one or two specific case histories which I find difficult to believe. I'm not convinced by my own clinical experience . . . I've seen enough to know that [alternative methods] aren't uniformly successful.'

However these views are at odds with the seemingly impressive results obtained abroad: some foreign alternative cancer specialists claim that up to 18 per cent of patients with terminal cancer and 80 per cent of those with the disease in its early stages get well again![16] Although orthodox treatment is sometimes used as well, the results are still better than one would expect with conventional medicine alone. We need to know if the success rate is really as good as it seems and, if so, why? Perhaps the time has come for orthodox specialists to take another look at alternative treatment.

In the UK this may be happening already. The Imperial Cancer Research Fund is now showing an interest in comparing Bristol patients with similar ones being treated more conventionally. The findings should be very revealing.

CANCER AS A TRANSFORMING EXPERIENCE

Whether or not alternative treatment helps patients to recover physically, it seems to bring other benefits which may be just as important. Gemma Walker explains: 'What I work towards is a healthy death so that a person dies at home with their loved ones with everything talked through and settled. So that they're able and ready to face their death in a much more open-hearted way.'

But the talking through, and the love and support given by cancer help groups, can do more than prepare for a peaceful end. It can change the way patients *live*, too. It may give them insights into themselves that they would never have had if cancer had not stopped them in their tracks. Pat Pilkington of the Bristol Centre speaks of cancer as a 'transforming experience'. Many patients, she says, have discovered new depths in themselves – a greater spirituality. They become more creative, turning to poetry and painting. Some of LeShan's patients also took up some form of art after psychotherapy.

I spoke to two Bristol patients – both had breast cancer. One is still battling with the disease six years later but is optimistic that she'll beat it. 'I have to be vigilant,' she explains:

I do my meditation and visualization techniques. I've enhanced my spiritual life. I'm a different person. Hopefully this kind of person does not act as a willing host for cancer. That's the idea, really. One is trying to transform oneself from being fertile soil in which cancer can grow. Sometimes having cancer is just to remind us what we ought to be doing.

The other, who now appears quite healthy, told me:

I don't think I would have made it without Bristol. It's three and a half years since I first started going. I was in a very bad state then. I've changed completely. Before, stress was a big thing in my life. But you're not looking at the world in the same way when you have cancer. What you learn is what's stressful and what's not. I take each day as it comes and don't worry about tomorrow. I've never wanted to live so much as I did when the doctor told me I was going to die. But now I don't think about death that much. What they show you at Bristol is the *quality* of *life*. And when that quality goes, you should be prepared to go, too.

If alternative treatment can do all these things, then it must be worthwhile.

12. Benign Breast Disease

Any lump in the breasts needs to be checked by your doctor, even though there's only about a one in ten chance that it will turn out to be malignant. If you're under thirty the odds are even more in your favour.

Cysts and fibroadenomas

Benign lumps come in several different varieties. Two of the most common are cysts, which are fluid-filled, and fibroadenomas, which are solid. Fibroadenomas, which are painless, are nearly always removed surgically. They're most common in women between the ages of fifteen and thirty-five and, at this age, cancer is very unlikely. But because it's usually impossible to tell, without examining the lump more closely, whether it's as innocent as the doctor suspects, it must be taken out.

Cysts may be painful or painless, depending on their size and where they are in the breast. A cyst may also tend to swell and become more painful just before your period. Solitary cysts are fairly easy to diagnose because of their different feel. Treatment is easy, too: a hollow needle is inserted into the lump and the fluid drawn off. Sometimes, though, a cyst may be so full that it feels quite firm – but again a simple needle aspiration to remove the contents is enough to clinch the diagnosis and, at the same time, rid you of your lump.

However, your specialist will want to give you a check-up a few weeks later to ensure that the cyst really has gone. He may also refer you for mammography (see page 272) to rule out any other abnormalities. Be prepared, too, for the strong possibility that you'll develop more cysts in the future. Cysts should always be treated. There's a very slight chance that they may contain some malignant cells, and some specialists believe that women who get recurrent cysts are more likely to develop breast cancer. Some of the latest evidence, though, in the form of a very thorough study published in the *New England Journal of Medicine* in 1985, suggests that neither women with fibroadenomas nor those with cysts are at increased risk of cancer.

Fibrocystic disease (painful, lumpy breasts)

This condition waxes and wanes with the phases of a woman's mentrual cycle, getting worse just before a period (see also page 62 on the premenstrual syndrome). It used to be thought that a woman with fibrocystic disease was more likely to get cancer. But these fears were largely allayed by the *New England Journal of Medicine* report I've just mentioned.

Some specialists now even doubt it's a disease at all. They point out that at least 50 per cent of all fertile women have symptoms of the condition and a further 40 per cent have similar but milder abnormalities – the sort which don't cause problems, but which can be seen when the breast tissue is examined under the microscope.[1] These findings, plus the clear link with natural hormone fluctuations, suggest, these experts believe, that fibrocystic 'disease' is simply the way the normal breast responds to changes in hormone levels. It is just that some breasts are more sensitive than others.

Of course, if you do have lumpy breasts you should ask your doctor to check them. But if the lumps – and pain – improve or get worse according to where you are in your menstrual cycle, the chances are that there's nothing wrong. 'Big deal,' I can hear some of you saying. 'But what about the pain? This is sometimes so bad that I can't bear to touch my breasts – let alone sleep on my stomach!' In practice, whether or not they believe that lumpy breasts are normal, most doctors do try to treat the pain.

MEDICAL TREATMENT

Diuretics

Your doctor may prescribe diuretics for you to take while you're premenstrual (see also page 64). The idea is to try to stop so much fluid accumulating in the breasts and therefore to reduce the swelling and pain. Diuretics make you produce more urine, so excess fluid in your body will be drawn out of the tissues and excreted. Diuretics do help some women, but not all. And those who benefit may find that, with time, the drugs become less effective and larger and larger doses are needed. With some of these drugs this may result in a potassium deficiency which could have a number of side effects ranging from fatigue to an irregular heart beat. So your doctor may prescribe a potassium supplement as well.

'. . . diuretics are only useful in the short-term,' writes PMS expert Dr Katharina Dalton, '. . . or in the mild case where [they're] used sparingly with the addition of extra potassium.'[2]

The other problem with diuretics – even those that don't deplete potassium levels – is that they can never *cure* your breast discomfort, merely alleviate it for the time being.

Hormones and anti-hormone drugs

Some authorities think that the breast pain is due to a hormone imbalance. There are several reasons for this belief. One is that the symptoms get worse just before a period – when fluctuations in hormone levels are particularly marked. The second is that women on the Pill (which irons out many of the dips and surges in our natural hormone patterns) seem to suffer less breast pain. The third reason is that the problem usually disappears during pregnancy and after the menopause – both times when hormone changes are at a minimum.

So, if you're not on the Pill, you may be advised to take it. But, as we've seen (Chapters 6 and 11), the Pill may bring its own problems. Alternatively your doctor may suggest an anti-oestrogen drug, such as tamoxifen or danazol. Tamoxifen is said to help about two-thirds of women and to cause few side effects. Danazol seems even more effective but it may stop you menstruating, make you put on weight or feel bloated. In addition, danazol does occasionally cause slight *virilization*, that is, a woman may develop some 'male' characteristics: an oily spotty, skin and excess hair growth. One recent report suggests that it may also cause a woman's voice permanently to deepen in pitch! Fortunately this last side effect seems extremely rare. The fertility drug bromocriptine works for some women. But it, too, can have side effects including nausea, faintness and headaches.

ALTERNATIVE TREATMENT

This is based on removing the causes of the problem rather than merely treating the symptoms.

Diet

A low-salt diet may help avoid the premenstrual accumulation of fluid – the cause of the increased breast pain. (This is discussed in a bit more detail in Chapter 3 on the premenstrual syndrome.)

Acupuncturists trained the traditional Chinese way may advise you to go on a diet which, they say, reduces the amount of mucus you produce. You'll be told to avoid raw and fatty foods, some types of nut, and a number of other things, particularly at certain times of the year. 'The best guideline,' an acupuncturist told me, 'is not to eat in winter the kind of food you would love in summer – tomatoes, for example.'

I can't tell you if such diets really work. This acupuncturist did however claim some success with a combination of diet and needling of the relevant points (see below).

Other foods and beverages to avoid

The main culprits are coffee, tea and chocolate. All of them contain compounds known as methylxanthines, of which caffeine is one example. Coffee, ordinary tea and cola drinks all contain caffeine. Even some herb teas do, too, so check the label before you buy them. Other methylxanthines are found both in tea and chocolate. If you steer clear of all these – or stick to decaffeinated drinks instead – you may well find your problems aren't so bad.

A 1979 study examined the effects of methylxanthines on forty-seven women with fibrocystic disease. Twenty of them eliminated all coffee, tea, cola drinks and chocolate from their diets. Within two to six months, thirteen reported that their symptoms had completely gone. Of the other twenty-seven, only one lost her symptoms entirely. A further study by the same researcher confirmed the initial results and also suggested that the level of methylxanthine is directly related to the severity of the symptoms. Of the forty-five women who cut out methylxanthines, thirty-seven recovered completely and seven reported less discomfort; only one found no change on the regime. Of the twenty-eight women who reduced but did not stop their methylxanthine consumption, seven found their disease disappeared, fourteen were less uncomfortable and seven experienced no change.

It seems, though, that the younger you are, the quicker the results. Women over the age of forty may have to wait one or two years before they notice any improvement. Of course this might be due not to the elimination of the caffeine but to the fact that they're approaching the menopause when the problem is quite likely to resolve spontaneously.

Penny Wise Budoff, an American doctor and author of *No More Menstrual Cramps and Other Good News*[3] writes: 'Though the numbers in this study are small, this observation, if substantiated by future better-controlled studies, may have wide repercussions for the coffee-drinking United States. Meanwhile I have been impressed enough to recommend that my patients with cystic breasts either stop their coffee, tea, cola and chocolate habits, or at least cut down.' This advice applies equally to the UK. How many cups of tea and coffee do *you* get through in one day?

Incidentally, a methylxanthine-free diet may also help women who don't have fibrocystic disease but who do experience breast tenderness premenstrually. It is not yet certain how methylxanthines exacerbate breast problems. The most likely explanation is that they inhibit an enzyme – one which breaks down *nucleotides*, natural substances which stimulate cell division. If this enzyme isn't working properly, the breast tissue may become overactive – and lumps are the result.

Vitamin E

'Vitamin E relieves most cystic breast disease,' proclaimed the headline on a *Medical News* report in 1980. The report described how, in a double-blind placebo-controlled trial (see page 32), 600 IU of vitamin E daily had abolished the disease in ten out of twenty-six patients and improved it in another twelve. These changes were accompanied by alterations in hormone and blood fat levels which the researchers couldn't really explain. However, they seemed harmless enough because the women didn't report any side effects. Most of the women who did get better responded pretty rapidly – within about two menstrual cycles.

Excellent news? Yes, but . . . a more recent study has found that vitamin E doesn't do any good at all![4] This was a much wider investigation – of 128 women. Again, the trial was placebo-controlled and again a substantial number – 55 per cent – of the women given 600 IU of the vitamin improved. But so did 55 per cent of the control group! Nor were the researchers able to find any differences in hormone levels between the two groups.

It's all rather mystifying. Which results are we to believe? The researchers involved in the second study point out that the women had taken the vitamin for only two months before being assessed. And they admit this may not be long enough.

However, since the earlier trial had suggested that most women should respond within this time, this explanation is rather unlikely.

It looks as though more work is needed before we can know for sure whether vitamin E really is a good treatment for fibrocystic disease. The other thing to remember is that this vitamin is potentially toxic. As I mentioned on page 284, serious vitamin E deficiency – the sort that might give rise to serious disease – is very rare. If fibrocystic disease *is* caused by a vitamin E deficiency, it must be a marginal one. Therefore, for some people, supplements might result in an overdose, particularly if taken over long periods. A dose of 600 IU *should* be safe but some authorities believe this is too much. In any event, it should only be taken under medical supervision. So if you want to try it, ask your doctor first. If he's not convinced, ask him to refer you to a doctor who's a member of the British Society for Nutritional Medicine (see Useful Addresses).

The psychological factor

In the vitamin E trial, the placebo helped more than half the women who took it. Why? Could it be that they got better simply because they thought they were taking the vitamin? Or even because the doctors were obviously taking their problems seriously? We can't dismiss this possibility. Some doctors do believe that breast pain could be – at least partly – psychological in origin.

This isn't just another 'women are the weaker sex' argument. Even *Women's Problems in General Practice*, a medical textbook which, on the whole, takes a reasonably feminist view of our problems, concedes that psychological factors can't be entirely ruled out. Drs Sheila Adams and Maureen Roberts, who wrote the chapter on breast disease, conclude: '. . . psychological reasons for pain have been suggested in the past. These are now largely discounted, but psychiatric help may be indicated for the occasional patient.'

Alternative practitioners, on the other hand, think that

emotional problems quite often cause physical symptoms, not only in the breast but also elsewhere in the body. That doesn't mean calling in the psychiatrist: few women with breast disease are actually mentally ill. Nevertheless, they may be unhappy or disturbed. One acupuncturist told me: 'There's a big emotional factor involved . . . either family or relationship problems; that's what the Chinese would say anyway.' And, in practice, acupuncturists will tend to treat the meridians that they believe may be affected by repressed emotions, particularly anger. Combined with the dietary measures mentioned above, this may work for some women. 'I had one very bad case,' she explained. 'Both her breasts were very lumpy and hard. With dietary changes and acupuncture, they lost their hardness. They still get lumpy occasionally but they're much, much better.'

Of course, it's impossible to tell which part of this particular treatment was the most effective. But tackling the problem from a psychological point of view – whether by acupuncture or a technique designed to look into the mind, such as psychotherapy – does make some sense. Some psychotherapists (especially those with feminist leanings – and they can be men!) believe that many women, by virtue of their conditioning, get into the habit of hiding their hostile feelings from other people. If you fail to express this basic part of your personality, it turns inward and can give rise to both physical and mental upset. (The way our emotions may affect our bodies is discussed in more detail in Chapter 11 on cancer, in Chapter 13 on migraine and in Chapter 14 on the mind.)

Osteopathy

Surprised that osteopathy can be used to treat breast problems? It can. Osteopathic manipulation of the spine relieves pressure on the nerves supplying the breast. 'You can often get the most amazingly good results just by dealing with the spine,' one osteopath told me.

Massage of the breast tissues can help get rid of some of the swelling. If you're unhappy with the idea of *any* practitioner, no matter how well qualified, massaging your breasts, ask him or her to show you how to do it for yourself. However, if your breasts seem to be inflamed then osteopathic treatment isn't suitable and you should consult your doctor.

13. Migraine

Although this chapter is about migraine, some of the alternative treatments you'll read about may be useful for other types of headache too. This may surprise you, especially if you're a migraine sufferer, because you'll have been told that migraine is different from the common-or-garden headache. You may also doubt – especially if you've tried powerful drugs without success – that anything short of decapitation could rid you of your headaches! Yet alternative remedies, such as acupuncture, cranial osteopathy and the herb feverfew do seem able to bring about almost miraculous results.

Migraine certainly is usually more vicious than the 'tension' type of headache that many of us get from time to time. It tends to be more severe and often occurs with almost predictable regularity. It's all the harder to bear because it usually comes with nausea, vomiting and sometimes diarrhoea as well. A full-blown migraine can keep you in bed for a day or more and leave you feeling exhausted. Some migraine victims also get an 'aura' beforehand: warning signs that an attack is imminent, such as not being able to see properly, or seeing flashing lights and spots.

But you'll notice the qualifications. There's no such thing as a 'typical' migraine attack. Some people get auras, some don't. Some vomit, others just feel sick. Some migraines last for only a few hours, others for several days. Even the word 'migraine' is misleading – it is derived from the Greek and, roughly translated, means 'half-head'. But although many migraines do affect just one side of the head, by no means all of them do.

Some migraine sufferers get what doctors called 'mixed' headaches: they have migraines *and* tension headaches. These may occur simultaneously or completely separately. Or a head pain that begins as a migraine may turn into a tension headache – and *vice versa*. Then there are the so-called migraine 'triggers'. Many victims have discovered that their headaches are sparked off by, for example, certain foods, alcohol and stress. But some people who *don't* have migraine do, nevertheless, get nasty headaches if they eat, say, hot dogs or Chinese food, drink red wine or get emotionally upset.

Nor is there necessarily anything special about some of the drugs used to treat migraine: aspirin or paracetamol sometimes work quite well. Anti-migraine remedies often contain caffeine – but so do many ordinary headache pills. And certain forms of anti-depressants and tranquillizers may be prescribed for *any* severe headache whether it is migrainous or not. So may propanolol, one of a group of drugs known as beta-blockers.

WHAT GOES ON DURING A MIGRAINE ATTACK?

Confusing, isn't it? Is migraine really so different from other sorts of headache? Well, yes and no. The *symptoms* are different – the nausea and vomiting, plus, in some people, the visual disturbances described above, are considered to be unique to migraine. And, unlike the more common tension headache, which arises in the muscles of the head, neck and scalp, migraine seems to be an affliction which affects the *blood vessels* in the head: they contract just before an attack and expand during it.

But some experts now consider that the symptoms and the blood vessel changes seen in migraine are simply the end results of some more basic changes in brain chemistry which are common to all headaches.[1,2] Migraine is, if you like, at one end of the headache spectrum, and the boring old 'ordinary' headache at the other. Not that there isn't *something* different about the migraine victim. A lot of research is being done to try to find out why the migraineur's blood vessels should respond the way they do. The favourite theory, which is backed by a growing body of evidence, is that there is an abnormality affecting the blood platelets. These are small cells in the blood which are responsible for making it clot when we cut ourselves. They also contain a chemical known as serotonin or 5-hydroxytryptamine.

The platelets of a migraine sufferer seem to be stickier than normal. Just before an attack this stickiness increases even further and the platelets form clumps, releasing the serotonin at the same time. This is then broken down and excreted in the urine.[3] These changes in serotonin could explain why the migraine victim's blood vessels behave in such an odd way. Serotonin makes blood vessels contract. If it suddenly floods into the blood, the vessels will rapidly shut down. On the other hand, once that serotonin has been flushed away, it will take some time for your body to make more and you'll be left, for the time being, with abnormally low levels of it. Your blood vessels will respond by expanding – perhaps until they're wider than they were to start with. And they'll stay that way until the serotonin levels return to normal. Researchers have also discovered that although the platelets soon replace the serotonin they've lost, they seem unable to release much of it for at least three days after a migraine attack.[3]

These findings tie in with the main features of a migraine attack: the changes in the blood vessels and the fact that, once you have recovered from one attack, it is usually several days before you get another.

MEDICAL TREATMENT OF MIGRAINE

Anti-migraine drugs

As I've already mentioned, many of the drugs used in

migraine may also be used to treat ordinary headaches. Aspirin is a painkiller and may also help prevent the platelets sticking together. Tranquillizers help calm you down and so reduce stress. Stress is thought to trigger off a migraine attack because it makes the body release chemicals which not only act directly on the blood vessels but also make the blood platelets more likely to stick together and release their serotonin. Why anti-depressants should be useful isn't so clear. Some researchers, though, believe that the same brain chemicals may be to blame for both headaches and depression.

The beta-blocker propanolol appears to work in two slightly different ways: it has a calming effect and also makes the blood vessels less sensitive. Clonidine seems to prevent the vessels overreacting to whatever it is that can trigger off an attack. Ergotamine preparations, which sometimes contain caffeine as well, shrink the blood vessels and so guard against the overexpansion that seems to be associated with the headache. Other drugs such as methysergide work by counteracting the effects of serotonin. Methysergide also shrinks the blood vessels.

Many of these drugs are used *prophylactically*, that is, their role is to prevent a migraine attack rather than to treat it once it has developed. There are two exceptions, though. One is aspirin which, because it may cause stomach problems, shouldn't be used for long periods. The other is ergotamine. This is often very successful in aborting attacks but mustn't be taken continuously (see below). Anti-sickness drugs are also often used in an acute migraine attack. These help reduce the feelings of nausea and the vomiting and also, of course, help you keep down other drugs long enough for them to work.

PROBLEMS AND SIDE EFFECTS

Any drug which affects the blood vessels is potentially dangerous. Propanolol and clonidine are used to treat high blood pressure as well, so you can see how powerful they are.

If you have migraine you'll be given a much lower dose than would be necessary if you had a blood pressure-problem, but side effects are still possible: for example, skin rashes, dry eyes, drowsiness and depression.

Methysergide shouldn't be used for longer than six months at a time and then only if your migraine won't respond to anything else. This is because it has been associated with several rare, but serious, side effects, resulting from obstruction of blood vessels elsewhere in the body. The risks are even greater with ergotamine; which is why its use is limited to treating the actual migraine attack.

Both these drugs – and caffeine too – may cause 'rebound' headaches if you take them too often. Though the headaches themselves are not dangerous, some people may misinterpret them as a sign that the drugs aren't working and take more and more of them to make the headache go away. This, of course, is very risky and the only remedy is to come off the drugs completely for at least a month – a sort of 'cold turkey' – to give your body time to recover.

HOW SUCCESSFUL ARE THESE DRUGS?

No one really knows, partly because practically any treatment for migraine – even a dummy tablet or placebo – seems to work in up to 40 per cent of all patients. This shows how little we know about the mechanisms at the root of migraine and also suggests that psychological factors such as stress may play a big part (see below).

Most of these drugs – either alone or in combination – seem to work for most people. Although they may not abolish the migraine entirely they will make life easier. It is estimated that only about one in ten patients have such frequent attacks that they need some form of prophylaxis and that, if you do get an attack, prompt treatment can, nine times out of ten, stop it within four hours. The question remains, though: do you want to take powerful drugs even if they work – and what can you do if you're one of the minority that they do nothing for?

IS MIGRAINE A FOOD ALLERGY?

Lots of people think so and avoid the food or foods they believe trigger off their attacks. However, in practice, these elimination diets seem only to help about 10 per cent of migraine sufferers. The rest still get their migraines just as badly. In any event, steering clear of foods that you may well enjoy – chocolate or red wine for example – is rather a dreary way of keeping migraine at bay. But if you do find this works, there may be another treatment that could help you – and allow you to follow a more normal diet. I'll return to it later.

WOMEN AND MIGRAINE

Hormones

Migraine is at least twice as common in women as in men. Could our hormones be to blame? The research points in that direction, certainly. Girls may start having migraines for the first time at puberty and then find that their headaches come most often either just before or during a period. Similarly, a woman who's never had a migraine in her life may start getting them when she goes on the Pill, and someone who already has migraines may find they're worse on this form of contraception. The migraines may also tend to come more frequently during those few Pill-free days each month. Conversely, migraines usually go away during pregnancy but return once the baby is born. All this suggests that fluctuations in our hormones levels may be one of the trigger factors.

Treatment

If you get migraines for the first time when you start taking the Pill, it is best to come off it straightaway. Usually once you've stopped the Pill the migraines stop too, though not, unfortunately, always. Migraines themselves don't seem to be dangerous but the fact that you get them on the Pill suggests that your circulatory system is changing and may be particularly sensitive to the extra hormones. In view of the known link between the Pill and circulatory disease (see Chapter 6) the headaches may be an early warning of more serious things to come and you should take them seriously. If you have migraines already, doctors believe it's safe for you to take the Pill provided they don't get any worse. However this seems to me to be adding insult to injury.

If you're not on the Pill, but get menstrual and premenstrual migraines, you could be in for a hard time. Doctors report that this sort of migraine is particularly difficult to treat, though the migraines you have at other times of the month may well respond to anti-migraine drugs. However, some researchers have claimed success with anti-prostaglandin drugs such as Ponstan, which are also sometimes used to treat period pains (see Chapter 4). These may not be the best way of tackling the truly premenstrual migraine, though: if you take them more than two days before your period is due you may find that bleeding is delayed. Another drug being tried by a few doctors is danazol. This seems to relieve premenstrual migraines as well as other PMS symptoms. However, in view of the possible side effects (see pages 311) this seems rather a sledgehammer remedy.

Whether you choose to take any of these drugs is, of course, up to you. But it may be well worth trying some of the more natural remedies for both migraine (see below) and PMS (discussed in Chapter 3) first. They're unlikely to cause side effects and they may well help.

Other possible causes of migraine in women

THE EFFECTS OF UPBRINGING ON OUR PSYCHOLOGY

It is all too easy to see hormones as the explanation for the increased prevalence of migraine among women. But it doesn't quite add up. While changing hormone levels help to explain why a woman with migraine may well get more *attacks* when she's premenstrual, it doesn't explain why she is more likely than a man is to have the *condition* in the first place. So what else is it about us that makes us more prone to migraine? Could it be our different psychological make-up? There is some evidence for this.

A number of studies – of both men and women – have shown that migraine victims tend to be more obsessional, more anxious and less able to cope with stress than other people (but *not*, incidentally, more intelligent – sorry!) Other research has suggested that migraine has its origins in childhood: it is more likely to appear in children whose parents expect them to 'grow up' too quickly: to be restrained, obedient, well behaved and to work hard. To win their parents' approval they therefore have to suppress their natural inclinations – to be affectionate, spontaneous and carefree. This, the researchers argue, so overloads their nervous systems that, in the words of psychologist Dr Peter Lambley, they're 'like a loaded gun, waiting for just one more thing – one more upset – to go off'.[4]

Add to this the fact that such children are desperate for recognition, says Dr Lambley, and you can see why they get migraines – either then or later, in adolescence. A migraine is a fairly dramatic thing; it makes people – especially parents –, sit up and take notice. This isn't to say that the child is faking or deliberately trying to bring on an attack. No, the migraines are genuine enough and a sign that that person has had more than he or she can take.

So far so good. But where do women fit in? Well, the theory goes, little girls have to suppress their emotions even more than little boys. They're under even greater pressure to conform. They have to be better behaved and are discouraged from dashing about, making too much noise and getting dirty. Many parents regard such childish exuberance as fairly normal for a boy – but unfeminine in a girl. As she gets older, the girl learns even more about quelling her emotions, about being helpful and unselfish, and not showing too much of the aggression that is so often admired in both boys and men.

This may strike you as somewhat out of date. Surely we all know enough by now to allow our children – boys and girls – a freer rein. Well, maybe some of us do. But how many of us can say, hand on heart, that we treat our sons and our daughters *exactly* the same? Don't we tend to pat our daughters on the head when they're showing their caring, nurturing 'feminine' side – while frowning on their temper tantrums and selfishness? And when they're adolescent, don't we worry more about our daughters than our sons: vet their friends more closely and try to put greater restrictions on their activities? It's natural for us to want to protect them from harm and to teach them to be a success in the world outside. But, the psychologists say, we may be doing this at the expense of their mental wellbeing.

I think it makes quite a bit of sense, especially when you remember that many more women than men suffer from mental illness, too (see Chapter 14 for further information on this). Are they inherently weaker or are they simply reacting to their conditioning? I know which explanation I prefer. And the fact that psychotherapy has been able to help some women with migraine when all other treatments have failed (see below) suggests there may well be something in this theory.

CANDIDA

Candida albicans, the organism that causes vaginal thrush, has also been implicated in migraine. Although most orthodox doctors would deny that there's any connection, there's now quite a bit of evidence that Candida can practically take over the whole body, may precipitate food allergies and may also be one of the causes of premenstrual tension. I discuss the role of Candida in more detail elsewhere (Chapter 5). But I'm mentioning it here because sometimes an alternative treatment designed to treat the

Candida problem is amazingly successful at abolishing the migraines, too (see page 332).

ALTERNATIVE TREATMENTS FOR MIGRAINE

Treatment for the temporomandibular syndrome

I mentioned that some migraines start off as tension headaches. If this seems to happen regularly to you, there's a fair chance that muscular tension is your main trigger. So anything that relieves that tension may help. However, before turning to techniques such as relaxation (see below), it may be a good idea to visit your dentist!

There's growing evidence that an imbalance in the jaw joint (temporomandibular joint or TMJ) can cause all sorts of aches and pains,[5] the most common being a headache. A dentist who specializes in the treatment of the TMJ syndrome will probably be able to tell at a glance if this is your problem. More important, he'll be able to correct it, first by prescribing a special appliance which fits over your teeth and helps to bring your jaw back into alignment and then by doing orthodontic work so that eventually you'll be able to manage without the device. He'll also recommend certain exercises which will encourage your jaw muscles to relax and work properly – perhaps for the first time in years.

One cause of the TMJ syndrome, incidentally, is grinding your teeth – something you may not be aware of as you probably only do it during your sleep. So ask your partner: the chances are he or she will have noticed but been too polite to say anything!

Treatment is often very successful. Judi Goodwin, an inveterate teethgrinder, reported in the *Daily Telegraph*: 'It has not solved my problems completely but there has been a 75 per cent reduction in the pain and discomfort and for that I am more than grateful.' However she adds: 'It follows a distressing nine months of trying to get proper treatment from dentists who had no experience of the condition and little sympathy.'

If you suspect that the TMJ is the cause of your headaches and your own dentist can't help, contact either the Migraine Trust or the British Dental Migaine Study Group for more information (see Useful Addresses). This group reports that treatment is particularly successful for premenstrual migraine.

Biofeedback and other relaxation techniques

For brief details see Chapter 1. These probably won't help you unless your migraine is associated with muscle tension. A review of biofeedback research published in the *Journal of Psychosomatic Research* in 1983 concluded that there was no evidence that it worked in migraines. And though it *was* an effective treatment for tension headaches, it was no better than simple relaxation without the frills.

Relaxation, as I've already explained, comes in all sorts of different packages of which biofeedback is only one. But whether you try autogenic training, yoga, meditation, listen to tapes or learn to relax from a book, your success is in your own hands. If you neglect to practise, none of them will work. And it's no good getting rid of your headaches and then abandoning your relaxation because you think you're cured. You aren't and you'll slip back into your old tense-making habits. This shows that, whatever the technique, relaxation isn't really addressing the source of the problem: what makes you tense in the first place. To do that you need a treatment which goes far deeper than the physical level and psychotherapy is the obvious choice.

Psychotherapy

Whether or not you're aware of being tense, psychotherapy may be able to help you. This is because, though some of us respond to stress by contracting our muscles – and giving ourselves muscle-tension headaches – others internalize the

stress to such an extent that we *don't even know it's there*.
Often these hidden strains are a result, as I explained, of
childhood experiences. And because these experiences hurt
us so much at the time our conscious minds protect us by
burying the pain deep in our subconscious, where it festers.
Later on it may surface as some form of mental illness – or at
the very least, emotional disturbance. But that doesn't always happen. Sometimes our conscious minds are in such
control and we're 'coping' so well that we don't allow
ourselves to feel mental anguish. But that pain has to go
somewhere. And it may well pop up in the only way left to it:
as a physical disease or simply as a pain.

This at least is the theory favoured by many psychologists.
The repressed child I mentioned above may get, instead of
migraines, tummy aches – and recent research backs the view
that children who have a difficult childhood are more prone
to stomach pains.[6] So why not migraine too? Maybe the child
copes well until she's adolescent – or even until she marries
and has children. Then new stresses crop up. These may
prove the last straw. The hidden pain is reactivated and
migraines start.

You may remember your childhood as particularly rosy
and your parents as kind and caring. Maybe, now that you're
an adult – possibly with children of your own – you believe
that your parents made a pretty good job of raising you. So
why turn to psychotherapy? Admittedly, you may not
benefit. But it's worth pointing out that if you *did* suffer
emotional pain as a child, you will have probably forgotten it.
It's still there, somewhere, though. It's just that your mind is
making damned sure that you won't remember it.

Psychotherapy can help you get back in touch with parts of
your real self, the bits you may have left behind long ago. It
doesn't offer any easy answers or promises of cure. And it
may be a long time before you even notice any progress. All
the same, if your migraine has failed to respond to any other
treatment – orthodox or alternative – it's definitely worth
trying.

Take this report from *Women and Migraine*,[7] a self-help

pamphlet which includes several other accounts of migraine sufferers' experiences of psychotherapy:

Migraines are one of the most common symptoms of stress in our society. They particularly afflict women. I believe that they are the reflection of tension between our repressed emotions, wants or energies, and our internalised conditioning which tells us that we must *not* express those emotions or those energies, that we must play the role ascribed to us as women – coping, hardworking, cheerful, unprotesting, undemanding of ourselves, competent to live our daily lives and look after others. When I get a migraine, I have found that by deliberately exploring my emotions and letting myself express them and release the energy I'm holding in, I can get rid of a migraine in two or three hours whereas previously they sometimes lasted days. Other women may not want to approach migraines as I have done – they do get worse before they get better, and my motive was to find out about myself as much as to get rid of the migraines – but in case it may help others I have started to describe here what I have learnt about migraines in this way . . .

It was not until I started doing some therapy on a small scale – out of a book with a friend – that I began to realise that my headaches were connected with feelings I was not expressing . . . During therapy I had begun, almost for the first time in my life, to express my feelings directly – letting myself cry, be angry, feel hurt, etc., instead of keeping a brave face to the world of being cheerful, together and 'coping' as I had been taught to do since childhood . . . now my migraines are rarer . . . though [they] are painful, I have learnt to value them in some ways: they are a concrete sign of my body rebelling against the policeman in my head; they bring an acute openness to messages from my body and from the world around me; and they teach me about the ways I am repressing and abusing my body in my daily life. Working with them has for me been part of the process of dismantling the patterns of socialised behaviour which I have learned since my childhood, and reclaiming my own emotions, body pleasure, energy and power.

Other alternative treatments

Not all migraines are due to such complex psychological factors – or even to muscle tension. Some sufferers, after years of unsuccessful drug treatment, find their headaches respond well – even, sometimes, miraculously – to quite simple alternative treatment. However, you have to remember that migraines are usually due to a variety of factors and few alternative practitioners are in a position to deal with all of them. Nevertheless, they're able to tackle at least some – and this can make a big difference to the number of migraines you get.

TREATMENT OF FOOD ALLERGY

The usual treatment is the elimination diet – which though it may work is not, as I explained, a very satisfactory way of avoiding migraine. Far better would be some way of treating that allergy so you could eat more or less what you wanted but still keep the migraines at bay. And quite recently there have been one or two reports that this can, in fact, be done. Though qualified medical doctors are involved in this research, this is very much a new area and is a long way from being adopted by most migraine specialists. The idea is to damp down the body's reaction to the foods that trigger off the migraine so that in time these foods can be reintroduced into the diet.

One method is to *desensitize* the patient by giving her either drops, or an injection, of a diluted dose of the offending foods. (This treatment is also discussed in Chapters 1 and 5.) The other is to give her, by mouth, *sodium cromoglycate*, which prevents the release of substances such as histamine which are involved in the allergic response. Neither treatment *cures* migraine but, when used regularly, both may prevent attacks in some people.

As I explained in Chapter 1, desensitization is still considered scientifically dubious. Sodium cromoglycate, on the other hand, is a medically accepted way of tackling allergic reactions; it is also used in the treatment of asthma. Despite quite promising results, though,[8,9] many orthodox researchers doubt whether migraine in adults is a true food allergy while agreeing that in children it may well be.

NATUROPATHY, OSTEOPATHY AND CRANIAL OSTEOPATHY

A conventional osteopath, especially if he is also a trained naturopath – which many of them are – will concentrate primarily on your diet. So in that sense, there's nothing particularly 'alternative' about the treatment. In addition, though, he may identify mechanical problems in your neck which may be triggering your headaches, and try to correct them by manipulation and advice on posture. (In this way the osteopath is doing for your neck what the dentist does for your jaw joint. A good osteopath may even refer you to a dentist first, just to be sure that you're not suffering from the TMJ syndrome.) It is quite likely that your osteopath will be able to reduce the *number* of migraines you have but they are unlikely to go away altogether – or so I was told. And once you're in the middle of an acute attack, drug treatment may be the only answer.

Cranial osteopathy seems to give better results – although osteopaths who don't practise it are still doubtful whether the technique is really as effective as is claimed by its supporters. However I spoke to two women who had had migraine for years. Both had discovered that drugs didn't help them for very long. Cranial osteopathy, however, had produced dramatic results. Sandra told me: 'I first went to see my osteopath about five months ago. I only went about three or four times and I haven't had a migraine since. I was staggered. Before that I was having migraines once a week: I was in bed and not beginning to feel well again until a couple of days later. I would have paid anyone £1 million to get rid of my headache.'

Eleanor started getting migraines when she became engaged and went on the Pill. Three children later she still had them. Now after cranial osteopathy, plus the homoeopathic remedy Bidor: 'I can't remember when I last had a migraine.' She is still taking propanolol, too, but has reduced the dose considerably and hopes to wean herself off the drug altogether.

Sceptics would point out that migraine often goes away without any treatment at all. But was it really just coincidence that both these women – who had suffered for years – should have started to improve almost as soon as they started this form of alternative treatment?

Yet another treatment advocated by some naturopaths and osteopaths is aimed at attacking the Candida overgrowth I discussed in Chapter 5. Diet is the key (for details of anti-Candida diets see also Chapter 5), followed by stomach massage. The reason for this is that the practitioners believe that the Candida stops one of the main valves in the intestine from working properly. This allows backflow of toxins from the bowel into the small intestine, where they get absorbed into the blood stream. After the combination of diet and massage has corrected this problem, the migraines should stop.

I haven't been able to find out very much about this technique – not all osteopaths appear to have heard of it. But one practitioner I contacted claims that out of the 2000 patients he has treated for migraine only four have failed to get better! Unfortunately, as is the way with so much of alternative medicine, we have to take these apparently amazing results on trust: practitioners don't go in much for publishing reports of their treatment so that they can be submitted for scrutiny either by their peers or by orthodox medical researchers. Although I've no reason to doubt these claims, it seems strange that such a successful treatment should remain relatively unknown. Could this really be the answer to migraine? If it is, it makes any other treatment superfluous. On the other hand, why should other, completely different, therapies also work – at least to some extent? Further research on the Candida problem may provide some clues.

ACUPUNCTURE

'I think acupuncture is marvellous,' says Claire. 'It can actually shift my migraine when it's coming on.' She also has regular 'maintenance' treatment to prevent attacks. 'It certainly reduces the likelihood of an attack.'

Acupuncture is one of the better researched alternative therapies and there's good scientific evidence that it does relieve pain. So you would expect it to be one of the best treatments for migraine. And some practitioners claim an 80 per cent success rate. Unfortunately, this doesn't stand up to close scrutiny.

One problem with researching acupuncture – or any other alternative headache treatment – is that you have to control for the placebo effect: remember that any treatment – no matter how useless or bizarre – will help 40 per cent of patients, at least for the time being. And when you compare acupuncture with a placebo, the results don't look so good. The results of one trial published in the journal *Pain* in 1985 revealed that, at best, acupuncture was 20 per cent more effective than placebo. But there was no statistical difference between the two treatments – in other words, that 20 per cent could have been a fluke. The researchers conclude: '. . . headache is very sensitive to placebo therapy, but it is possible that acupuncture has a real therapeutic benefit of approximately 20 per cent over placebo.' Not terribly convincing, is it? However, I understand that since that trial was completed the patients who had the acupuncture have had less trouble with their migraine than those given the placebo treatment.

There's no getting away from the fact that the placebo effect probably has a lot to do with acupuncture pain relief. Acupuncture also tends to relax you – yet another way in which it may help a headache. Maybe it doesn't matter too much *why* it works, just that it does.

HERBS AND HOMOEOPATHY

I've already mentioned the homoeopathic remedy Bidor. Another apparently excellent migraine treatment is the herb feverfew which, according to the results of one scientific trial, can help about 70 per cent of sufferers. Most eat one large or three small leaves a day, chopped up in a sandwich with honey or sugar to disguise the bitter taste. Eaten regularly, these can prevent or reduce the number of attacks. The drawback, though, is that it doesn't cure migraine any more than drugs do. Stop taking it and the migraines return.

Very recent research has suggested that the active ingredient of feverfew may indeed be quite a potent drug.[10] This isn't so surprising as quite a number of modern medicines including aspirin, digoxin, and some anti-cancer drugs, are derived from plants. Feverfew extract, the scientists have discovered, stops the blood platelets from releasing those excessive amounts of serotonin which appear to be the cause of migraine attack. Though this finding has worried some people because it suggests that herbs may be more powerful – and therefore more dangerous – than they're often given credit for, I find it reassuring. Not only does it work but we know why! Moreover, say medical herbalists, feverfew has a much gentler effect that usual anti-migraine drugs.

However, we don't yet know for certain that taking feverfew for long periods is safe although, as a 1985 report in the *British Medical Journal* – which again demonstrated the beneficial effects of the herb – pointed out: '[It] has been used by large numbers of people for many years.' But there is a possibility that it may be dangerous in pregnancy – nor should you take it if you're breastfeeding.[11]

There is also a homoeopathic version of feverfew: goodness knows why it should work, but it seems to. It is readily available in either tablet or liquid form from most health food shops. As with all homoeopathic remedies, it appears completely safe, but again, it's worth remembering, particularly in pregnancy, that *none* of them has been *proven* to be so.

14. Peace of Mind?

THE HUMAN SPIRIT

Nobody understands the human spirit though everyone has a stab at it: the laboratory scientist who dissects our brains when we're dead and the psychologist who probes them while we are still alive; all of us who, at one time or another, have pondered on the meaning of life.

It is the spirit (or, if you prefer, the mind – which describes the same concept but without the religious connotations) which makes us human and makes each of us unique. It includes our emotions – in the way we experience and react to the world we live in. But it is the mind – what we *are* – that interprets those experiences and tells us what to make of them.

No one has yet been able to define the spirit, much less cut it out and look at it. (Some people have used faith as a path to the human spirit and to give their lives meaning. It is one answer. But unshakeable faith isn't granted to many. The rest of us are still searching.) True, we're learning more and more about emotional *states* – that certain chemicals are released during fear and anger and that, in turn, these chemicals can affect our mood. Evidence suggests that the tendency to mental illnesses may, to some extent, be passed on in our genes. And psychologists tell us that the way we are in the present is very often a result of what went on in our past. All these findings are valid as *windows*, if you like, on the mind. But the windows are minute – they allow us only the tiniest of glimpses. What we know of the way the mind works is infinitesimal compared with what we don't know.

Many researchers believe that we will never fully understand the mind because, in studying it, we become entangled in a paradox. The object of the research – the mind – can't examine itself without inevitably changing in the process! This means that, no matter how many *parts* of the mind we may eventually be able to analyse, the whole will always be greater than all the parts when put together.

It also helps to explain why so many different techniques and therapies – orthodox and alternative – may be used with varying degrees of success to treat mental problems. They may be directed at the whole mind or at any rate as much of it as we have access to; psychotherapy comes into this category. Or they may be aimed at specific parts of the brain: for example, mood-altering drugs or nutritional therapy, both of which are intended to correct imbalances in brain chemistry.

THE UNQUIET MIND: MENTAL ILLNESS OR SPIRITUAL DIS-EASE?

This chapter is about stress, anxiety and depression and about some of the ways you can combat them. Stress is more acceptable than either anxiety or depression because it is seen as part of the normal human condition. We're all under stress. If we work we're stressed, if we don't – if we're unemployed – we're under even greater stress. Raising a family is stressful. But let's face it, just the business of being alive, of surviving and of maintaining relationships, on whatever level, isn't easy.

Of course, stress isn't all bad. It can, in the right circumstances, spur us on, help us to perform better. The job's difficult? We try harder and with any luck produce better results. The children are driving us up the wall? We try to see things from their point of view so we talk to them more – and they understand us better, too. Our relationship with our husband or lover is going through a rough patch? Again, we talk about it, perhaps get professional help. Maybe things improve or maybe we decide that the relationship is best ended. Either way, the stress pushes us to seek a solution and, with that solution, some of the stress is relieved. Whether or not we can relieve tensions of this sort, most of us don't mind admitting to them. Stress is OK. We can mention it to other people and know that they share at least some of the same feelings.

Anxiety and depression are different. I'm not, of course, talking about the 'normal' anxiety and depression we all feel from time to time in response to certain events which everyone regards as stressful. It's normal to feel anxious when our children are unexpectedly late coming back from school or when we're about to take an examination. It's normal to feel depressed when somebody we love has just died or when we're made redundant.

But when we're depressed or anxious most, or all, of the time, that is 'abnormal'. It isolates us from the rest of society. Society takes the view that stresses come and go but that life is something with which a 'normal' person can cope. If you suffer from continual anxiety or depression, you're not coping; you're going under, you're ill.

But this, some psychologists believe, just isn't so. Your anxiety or your depression is your particular response to a difficult, stressful situation. That other people may not recognize the stresses doesn't mean they're not real. (Some authorities, notably R. D. Laing, take this concept to its extremes and suggest that 'mad' people aren't insane at all but are coping in the only way they can with a life situation which they experience as unbearable.)

In fact psychotherapists, who treat anxious and depressed clients by trying to examine their inner conflicts, usually come to the conclusion that none of them is ill. Their minds are unquiet, they're at dis-ease, they're unhappy. But for myriad reasons – including childhood experiences, present social pressures or a sense of the purposelessness of life – their distress is perfectly understandable. 'Those of us who break down or face a crisis are usually amongst those closest to sanity or authenticity,' writes Emmy van Deurzen-Smith.[1]

This is also the view of David Smail, Honorary Special Professor in Clinical Psychology at Nottingham University.

I'll quote him at some length because he seems to me to have captured the essence, and the dilemma, of the human condition:

> Despite our readiness to consider them at, as it were, a distance (for example in literature and popular entertainment), our cultural mythology has it that negative experiences such as psychological anguish, self-doubt, anger and hatred towards others (particularly family members), helplessness and inadequacy – the kinds of feelings in which 'symptoms' tend to be embedded – are not things which trouble 'normal' people over-much. And yet the true nature of society is such that it is virtually impossible to get far through life without feeling any of these things. But because of our institutional myths, we find when we do feel them that there are very few means at our disposal whereby we might take them seriously. Instead, we are confronted by standards of how we *ought* to be: our parents should love and protect us and we should love and respect them, we should succeed at school and at work while cooperating amicably with others, we should be sexually 'normal', have happy marriages, earn the respect of those with whom we come in contact, and in general conform to what is expected of us in the context of our particular place in society. We are born, it seems, into an absolutely real and unalterable world which cannot be expected to bend as we come up against it, so that we must therefore adapt to it . . .
>
> After a time, you may well become aware that the particular world you occupy departs in some respects from the ideals and the values of the wider society or that you do not seem to match up to what seems to be valued . . . when you fail you will find almost no one ready to take your failure seriously, and no conceptual structure, no language, in which to consider it – you will just be exhorted to try even harder to succeed . . .
>
> Our values are not such that they *could* be positively achieved by everybody or even by most people: they are *bound* to generate failure and distress more than comfort and happiness.
>
> Most people, metaphorically, walk round under the baleful gaze of a relentless judge – the 'generalized other' who measures you with a cold eye and, almost inevitably, finds you wanting. No

wonder so many people find themselves, for example, cowering in their homes, sick with dread if they have to venture out into the world beyond their own four walls (and worse, by succumbing to their fear, relegating themselves to a new class of failures – the 'agoraphobics'). And yet, I wonder whether people such as these really are failures, or whether between us we have managed to create a society in which cruelty has got out of hand. It may perhaps be that the person whose anxious dread has shattered the mythical reality in which we are taught to believe has caught onto a truth which the rest of us are desperate not to acknowledge, and for which there are almost no words to provide an understanding.[2]

And Dorothy Rowe, a clinical psychologist who has written several books on depression, sees this 'illness' too as a perfectly explicable response to natural yet unresolvable spiritual turmoil:

By the time I was ready to write a book about my work I could no longer refer to depression as an illness, and so I called my book *The Experience of Depression*. I had begun talking to people – all patients at a psychiatric clinic – about their attitudes to their immediate reality, their ideas about themselves, their family, their environment, but . . . I found that we soon left discussions of immediate reality and instead we talked about the issues of life and death, that is, about the purpose of life, the supposed existence and nature of God, the possibility of annihilation or life after death, guilt, sin, punishment and reward, expiation and propitiation, fear and courage, forgiveness and revenge, anger and acceptance, jealousy and sharing, hate and love. The issues that these depressed people and I discussed were those that have exercised the minds of philosophers and theologians for thousands of years, and the solutions that my clients had espoused had led them inevitably to the prison of depression . . .

. . . if we want to understand why a person behaves as he does, then we should seek to discover how that person sees the purpose of life and the nature of death.[3]

Mental misery, spiritual anguish, call it what you will, is *real* and a normal part of being a thinking, feeling, experiencing individual. We can't escape it.

But we can, perhaps, make it easier to bear. Not only because none of us wants misery as a permanent companion. But also because, if our minds are troubled, this affects our bodies too. We may not believe we're ill in the accepted sense of the word but we *feel* ill nevertheless. And we may find that the continual mental strain brings genuine physical ailments in its wake: there's now substantial evidence, as we have seen throughout this book, that an increased susceptibility to infections, migraine, cancer and many other conditions is linked to our mental state.

ORTHODOX AND ALTERNATIVE MEDICINE ARE NOT SO FAR APART

This isn't to say that *all* mental 'illness' of this type is due to psychological factors. There's also evidence that the food we eat or don't eat may give rise to symptoms of anxiety and depression. Some physical diseases also produce these symptoms as a side effect. But my aim is to give you some idea of how complicated the whole subject is and how no one theory can have *all* the answers. This also means, of course, that the treatment of mental problems is seldom clear-cut and you may have to try a number of different approaches before you find one – or more – that helps you to live more comfortably with your *self*.

In most of the other chapters I've been able to point to the divisions between the orthodox and alternative approaches to a particular condition. Here the differences are less obvious. Many orthodox practitioners accept the benefits of, and will sometimes use, alternative therapies in addition to, or instead of, drugs. And although practitioners in two branches of alternative medicine – nutritional therapy and clinical ecology

– tend to favour their particular approach, they still, to a greater or lesser extent, recognize that stress-reduction techniques and psychotherapy have a role to play.

WHY WOMEN ARE MORE VULNERABLE

Surveys have shown that women are twice as likely as men to have psychological problems. At least, twice as many of them are *diagnosed* as suffering from mental disturbance. And a 1977 study of general practitioners in Oxfordshire revealed that over 20 per cent of women between twenty-five and forty were on mood-altering drugs. At the time in our lives when we're supposed to be most settled – free from adolescent hang-ups, established in career and marriage, not yet menopausal and with old age still on the distant horizon – one in five of us is sufficiently miserable to ask for medical help!

It may be that men are equally afflicted but that they're more likely to seek solace in their work or in non-medical remedies such as drink and cigarettes, or – and better for them – a vigorous game of squash. Or it may be that their mental conflicts are more likely to be expressed in a physical form – as an ulcer or heart attack, for example. What we do know, though, is that on average they die younger than we do, while more of us end up with a prescription for tranquillizers and anti-depressants.

No doubt we share some of the same stresses but react to them in different ways. No doubt, too, that men have stresses which tend to be peculiar to their sex. One of these is that, from a very early age, they're encouraged to suppress their emotions much more than we are. Hence, or so some authorities believe, their increased susceptibility to stress-induced diseases. And hence the reason why women seek help for anxiety and depression more often: they are more in touch with their feelings and so recognize their emotional problems more easily. (This also helps explain, as I'll discuss a bit later, why male–female relationships are so often unsatisfactory from the woman's point of view.)

However, it seems that women are more *at risk* of mental 'illness' in the first place. And it's not *just* because of our hormones. In Chapters 9 and 13 I explained why that theory doesn't hold much water. So what else is different between the sexes?

Well, many psychologists argue that women are trained from early childhood to be submissive, to take second place. They're taught to be caring, nurturing, and not to show aggression. They are brought up to see their future in terms of marriage and motherhood. This is a generalization, of course, and with the growing awareness – among members of both sexes – that women are, first and foremost, *people*, maybe our daughters will be spared some of this destructive conditioning. But, unless our parents were exceptional, there was probably a lot of that in our own upbringing. Or maybe, for some of us, the conditioning went the other way and the message we received was about doing well at school and going for a rewarding career.

Either way, we ended up confused. On the one hand, most of us did want to get married and have children but, at the same time, we wanted to realize the other parts of our personality: our wish to assert ourselves, and to make good use of whatever brains we'd been given.

Come adulthood, what did we do? First came the pressures of the mating market. Everyone thinks that a woman should be half a couple. A thirty- or even a forty-year-old bachelor is looked on as simply postponing marriage while a thirty-year-old woman has, in many people's eyes, left it too late! (I'm not including gay people in this scenario because they have their own special pressures.) Sexual attractiveness is considered to decline far more quickly for women than for men, despite the fact that we live longer. So we have to grab our chances while we've still got our looks!

Once married, what about having children? Ostensibly, we have three choices. (In practice it's not a question of 'choice' but of the impossible task of trying to identify our real selves amidst the effects of conditioning and biological drive.) We can either go along with the motherhood scene; we can reject it entirely and throw ourselves into a career; or we can try to compromise and do both at the same time. Not always, of course, *exactly* at the same time – perhaps we delay getting married and/or having children until our careers are established or maybe we do it the other way round. The end result, though, is the same: we become either part-time wives and mothers and earn money full-time, or we put paid work into second place while we devote our main energies to our families.

It's a no-win situation: the rejection of either family life or career can leave large parts of us unfulfilled. The compromise isn't much better – divided loyalties make us feel guilty. To say nothing of the sheer fatigue of trying to do two jobs well.

In the meantime, how is our relationship with that mate, that partner with whom we chose to share our lives? We find we're living with someone who most probably has only the vaguest idea of what makes him tick – let alone us! Men themselves are dimly becoming aware of their emotional inadequacy, as shown in Phillip Hodson's book *Men. An investigation into the emotional male*.[4] Men, says Hodson, 'couldn't pass an O-level in describing their own feelings. That is why they often become violent – it is the only way we can convey our passions while somehow denying the importance of them.' 'Failure to generate intimacy,' says Hodson later in his book, 'is one of the primary causes of divorce.' A woman wants her partner to *be there* for her and very often he's not. Oh, he's there in body, all right, but with his emotions under lock and key. And, as Hodson points out, more often than not it is the woman who starts divorce proceedings: the man hangs on in there, vaguely wondering what he's done wrong.

Lillian B. Rubin gives several eloquent examples of this emotional inequality between the sexes in her book *Intimate Strangers*,[5] and argues persuasively that men and women are looking for something different in their relationship with each other. And again these differences go back to our very earliest experiences. Babies of both sexes, explains Rubin, begin by identifying with the person who is literally the centre of their world – the one who cares for them and meets *all* their needs. This, of course, is nearly always the mother. But whereas a girl, as she grows, can incorporate this into her own sense of self, the boy can't:

> Since [the girl] need not displace the internalized representation of the loved mother, there's no need to build defenses against feeling and attachment, therefore, no need for the kind of rigid boundaries a man develops as a means of protecting and maintaining those defenses . . .
>
> It is in this part of the developmental scenario that we see the birth of the empathetic capacities for which women are so justly known. The context within which separation takes place and identity is forged means that a girl never has to separate herself as completely and irrevocably as a boy must. Her sense of self, therefore, is never as separate as his; she experiences herself always as more continuous with another; and the maintenance of close personal connections will continue to be one of life's essential themes for her.

In contrast, Rubin points out, the little boy must repress his identification with his mother:

> With the repression of the identification with mother, therefore, the attachment to her becomes ambivalent. He still needs her, but he can't be certain any more that she will still be there, that she can be trusted.
>
> To protect against the pain wrought by this radical shift in his internal world, he builds a set of defenses that, in many important ways, will serve him, for good or ill, for the rest of his life. This is the beginning of the development of ego boundaries that are fixed and firm – barriers that rigidly separate self from other, that circumscribe not only his relationships with others but his connection to his inner emotional life as well.

And, in therapy, Rubin, like many other psychotherapists, has discovered that men aren't simply hiding their feelings – they're not aware that they have them:

Repeatedly, when therapy begins, I find myself having to teach a man how to monitor his internal states – how to attend to his thoughts and feelings, how to bring them into consciousness. In the early stages of our work, it's a common experience to say to a man, 'How does that feel?' and see a blank look come over his face. Over and over, I find myself listening as a man speaks with calm reason about a situation which I know must be fraught with pain . . .

Programmed as he is, a man will quite likely bring this same 'calm reason' into emotional encounters with his partner and then wonder why she gets more upset! Rubin also shows how a woman's need to talk about her feelings clashes with a man's wish for some sort of silent 'communion':

For [a woman], intimacy without words is small comfort most of the time. It's not that she needs always to talk, but it's important to her to know what's going on inside him if she's to feel close. And it's equally important for her to believe he cares about what's going on inside her . . . For a man, it's reassuring just to be in a woman's presence again – to know that, like the mother of infancy, she's there and available when and as she's needed. Then, in that distant past, he didn't need words to feel soothed and comforted; mother's presence was enough. To recreate that experience in adulthood is to heal some of the pain of childhood. Words, therefore, are less important than proximity itself.

The Hite Report on Male Sexuality,[6] which represents the results of a survey of more than 7000 men, confirms these findings. Most of the men conformed to the 'strong silent' stereotype (although many had worries about it) and though most craved close emotional contact with a woman they usually felt that this was only possible – or acceptable – through sex:

The psychological/emotional reason most gave for liking and wanting intercourse was the feeling of being loved and accepted that intercourse gave them. . . . In fact, in many of the replies, there is less a feeling that men enjoy intercourse than that they *need* it, sometimes almost desperately. Sometimes there is a feeling that the implications of the act, combined with the affection, the laying on of hands, add up to a kind of acceptance, affirmation, and even benediction which almost transcends words.

Would it be too obvious to conclude, yet again, that men are seeking to recreate that intense, wordless, and primarily *physical*, relationship that, as babies, they had with their mothers but which they had to reject to become men?

So, yes, it's true. Women are more emotional than men in the sense that they are more in touch with their feelings and have a greater need to express them verbally. It's also revealing that men seem to thrive more on long-term relationships than we do. 'All the research available,' Rubin writes, 'shows that married men live longer, healthier lives than those who are single. The reverse is true for women; those who never marry live longer and with fewer physical and emotional problems than their married sisters. Widowhood may be difficult for both, but the life span of a woman is not affected by the death of her husband, even if she doesn't remarry. The same is not true for men, whose lives are in serious jeopardy if they do not marry again quickly.'

Clearly many of us are giving more than we receive; is it any wonder that our emotions, denied an outlet, then turn inward against ourselves?

TREATMENT

I'm going to start by discussing some therapies – orthodox and alternative – that may help many people suffering from emotional problems, irrespective of whether they're anxious and/or depressed or think they're 'simply' under stress. If you've stayed with me so far, it won't come as a surprise to learn that – with one or two possible exceptions that I'll come to a bit later – the same therapy can often be beneficial in a number of different conditions. Stress is a big component of both anxiety and depression; prolonged stress can lead to anxiety and unrelieved anxiety can result in depression. Most patients diagnosed as either 'anxious' or 'depressed' usually have symptoms of *both* conditions. This, of course, is why tranquillizers – anti-anxiety drugs – are prescribed so often.

Drugs: benefits and drawbacks

TRANQUILLIZERS

The most commonly prescribed drugs are the so-called 'minor' tranquillizers, the benzodiazepines: for instance chlordiazepoxide (e.g. Librium) and diazepam (e.g. Valium). (Librium and Valium – and a number of other well-known brand names are no longer available on the NHS as their *generic* equivalents, which are exactly the same, are cheaper.) These drugs relax you, they relieve anxiety and they also help you to sleep better at night. Unfortunately, they also have a number of side effects. They can make you feel dopey, wobbly and forgetful, and sometimes they may make you act more irrationally than you might otherwise.

The main problem with these drugs, though, is that people often find it difficult to give them up: they become addicted to them. There's some controversy over whether this is a *physical* addiction – that is, that our bodies become dependent on them – or whether it's a *psychological* one – that anxious people simply can't cope with the anxiety that returns once they stop taking their tranquillizers. In some respects, or so many specialists believe, a psychological dependence is the more worrying. 'The moral argument [against tranquillizers] is that [they] may be the new opium of the people, since they suppress emotional symptoms while the underlying social and political causes remain unchanged,' two psychiatrists recently wrote in the *British Medical Journal*.

Ironically, it is still not certain whether tranquillizers do all the good they're supposed to. The authors of the *BMJ* article conclude that for many patients they may be acting simply as a placebo! Which adds weight to the argument that though an anxious brain may be chemically awry, that's the result of the anxiety and not the cause of it. For the causes we must look elsewhere – outside of ourselves and at the world around us.

I'm not going to say much more about these tranquillizers here – except to add that most doctors now believe that they should be reserved for short-term use, if they're used at all. They may help you if your anxiety comes from an obvious and specific problem which is likely to be short-lived: an exam, for example, or some other temporary stressful change in your life. You may also want to take them if your anxiety is preventing you from seeing your way out of your distress. They'll calm you down sufficiently to allow you to be more objective and to look at some of the other ways of solving your problems. But tranquillizers on their own won't cure you. For more information read *The Tranquillizer Trap* by Joy Melville.[7]

Beta-blockers, which are also used to treat high blood pressure, are sometimes prescribed for anxiety – when a person is particularly troubled by palpitations and shakiness. These aren't habit-forming but they do have side effects, such as faintness and wheezing. And again, they treat the symptoms, not the causes.

FOR DEPRESSION

As I've explained, tranquillizers are often used to treat depression as well. They relieve the anxiety symptoms that so many depressed people get and may help them sleep better (disturbed sleep is a symptom of both anxiety and depression).

Other drugs – the tricyclic anti-depressants and the monoamine oxidase inhibitors (MAOIs) – aim to treat the chemical imbalances that have been discovered in the brains of depressed people and which are thought by some authorities to be one of the causes of depression. The virtue of the tricyclics – drugs such as imipramine, clomipramine and doxepin – is that they only work if you're depressed. If you're not, they don't have any effect at all. So it seems you can't get hooked on them. Once your depression has gone, you don't need them any more. In fact, in most cases, you'd get better without them but a short course – say six weeks – will make life more bearable while your body heals itself. However they do have some side effects such as a dry mouth, blurred vision and constipation. Unfortunately, it's quite common for people to start getting the side effects several weeks before they notice any benefits from the drug.

MAOIs take time to work and have side effects, too. They may give you a 'high' which you become dependent on and so they may be habit-forming. In addition, MAOIs are dangerous if you eat certain foods because they interfere with the breakdown of a substance called tyramine found in cheese, yeast, beans, alcohol and several other foods. An excess of tyramine can cause severe headaches, breathlessness and sometimes even a heart attack or a stroke. So if you're taking these drugs you'll be warned to modify your diet considerably.

WHO NEEDS ANTI-DEPRESSANTS?

Many specialists believe that the people who benefit most from anti-depressants are those with *endogenous* depression, that is, those who are depressed for no apparent reason.

Reactive depression, on the other hand, is seen as a response to a depressing event or set of circumstances such as a death in the family, splitting from your partner or losing your job. The suggestion is that endogenous depression most probably arises from biochemical causes – disturbances in brain chemistry – whereas reactive depression has its roots in purely psychological problems. It is argued that though anti-depressants may help people with reactive depression they may be working primarily *via* the placebo effect. The biochemical imbalance of endogenous depression, on the other hand, responds *directly* to these drugs.

That's one theory. However, some psychologists think

that even endogenous depression – particularly in women – has psychological causes if we know where to look for them. I've already mentioned that men, by and large, are not very skilled at delving into the female mind. And most doctors are men. The majority of their patients, on the other hand, are women. As Dorothy Rowe points out:

> . . . it is the doctor, not the patient, who decides whether the patient has a reason for being depressed. It is a man who decides whether or not a woman has reason to be depressed. He, not she, judges whether she would ordinarily be content with her life. If so, then when she gets depressed it must be endogenous depression. This would be all right if men assessed women's lives in the way that women do, but they don't. There are still many men who believe that all a woman needs to be happy is a husband, a home and children. They do not understand that a woman can have, and love, these and still want something more – such things as companionship and the right to be herself.

'Thousands of women,' writes Dr Rowe, '. . . [are] trapped by what society expects of them and what they expect of themselves.'[8] They are treated by drugs, by electro-convulsive therapy (ECT – an electric shock applied to the brain) and yet still they're depressed. There is also evidence that though depressed people do sometimes show alterations in brain chemistry these may well be the result of the depression and not its cause.

Of course, anti-depressants do help many people – often quite dramatically. But not every depressive is a victim of faulty brain chemistry. Whatever the diagnosis – reactive or endogenous – she may equally well be a victim of *life*.

ALTERNATIVE APPROACHES TO MENTAL DIS-EASE

Towards a quieter mind

STRESS-REDUCTION AND BREATHING TECHNIQUES

Although the techniques discussed in this section are usually regarded first and foremost as aimed at stress, they can also be used to treat anxiety and depression. This is because stress, somewhere along the line, is an inevitable part of both these problems.

The methods include relaxation, meditation, biofeedback and autogenic training (for brief details, see Chapter 1). All of them will help you to relax. You'll learn to stop your muscles becoming tense and to breath in a more controlled fashion. This is important because the symptoms of anxiety are often made worse by muscular tension and faulty breathing. In fact, there's some evidence that people who suffer from *panic attacks* (with or without the phobias that so often go with them) can be greatly helped by breathing *retraining*.

Researchers have observed that people who panic tend to 'overbreathe' or *hyperventilate*. That is, they breathe shallowly and quickly, using only the upper part of their chests. This changes the levels of a number of chemicals in their blood; the most important change seems to be an increase in the level of sodium lactate, a chemical which, if infused into the bloodstream of people who are prone to panic, often provokes an attack.

A study at St Bartholomew's Hospital, London, investigated the effects of breathing retraining – where the patients were taught to breathe properly using their diaphragms and stomach muscles – on agoraphobics. The usual treatment for agoraphobia is *behavioural therapy* – either *desensitization* or *flooding*. In desensitization the patient learns to relax and is then gently and gradually encouraged to take longer and longer trips outside, initially with the therapist. Flooding goes to the opposite extreme: the therapist takes the patient into the street and stays with her while she works through her panic and eventually calms down. The idea is that as the patient realizes that nothing terrible is going to happen to her – that her panic comes from within herself – she will overcome it. Flooding, which is also known as 'real-life exposure' generally gives quicker results than desensitization but, as it can be very traumatic, it's not suitable for everyone. And some evidence suggests that although behaviour therapy does indeed help phobics live a more normal life, it doesn't necessarily make them less anxious or stop them from panicking. They may merely learn that each panic attack goes away on its own and so they manage to live with it.

At Bart's, the agoraphobics were divided into two groups. Both groups had real-life exposure therapy but one set of patients had breathing retraining as well. Both groups improved at first but those who had had only the behavioural therapy gradually worsened once the ten-week course of treatment was over. The patients in the 'breathing' group, though, carried on improving.

'I think this is a breakthrough,' one of the Bart's researchers is quoted as saying. 'Breathing retraining is not the whole answer but it should be looked at and treated first. It relieves agoraphobics of that horrible feeling of loss of control.'[9] They can then begin to use other therapies to deal with the psychological factors that may underlie their phobia. Breathing retraining can be used in conjunction with biofeedback – as is now being done at Barts. A belt round the patient's stomach is wired up to a lamp which is automatically switched on when she's breathing correctly.

Anxious people – not just phobics – typically overbreathe so this technique could help them too.

YOGA

This seems to me to be one of the ideal ways of tackling emotional problems. Yoga combines posture work, which tones up the whole body, with instruction about proper breathing, plus relaxation and meditation. It is also based on a philosophy which may help heal the spirit. The whole works in one package! However, not all teachers offer such a comprehensive range. Some concentrate on postures and relaxation but spend little time on breathing and meditation. Obviously you should make sure your teacher is properly qualified but, unfortunately, that doesn't necessarily mean that he or she is sufficiently experienced in the techniques of most importance to you. It's usually a question of hunting around until you find a teacher who suits you; if you have difficulty, try contacting the Satyananda Yoga Centre or the Yoga Biomedical Trust (see Useful Addresses).

The meditational side of yoga works best for some people. If practised regularly, it definitely helps calm the mind. Some experienced meditators say it does more than that, that it's actually a form of psychotherapy, and that during meditation you gain insights into yourself. This, though, can be at odds with the conventional view that meditation is always a peaceful experience!

'I've had very dynamic, very affronting things happen in meditation,' one woman who beat her anxiety and depression through yoga and now teaches it, told me. 'People think of it as being this very peaceful and tranquil state. It isn't unless you're very peaceful and tranquil inside and most people who start meditation are far from that.' This woman also found that the yoga philosophy gave her some of the answers she desperately needed and which she had failed to find elsewhere. Her past life had been unhappy and she had lost some of the people she loved. 'My life's crises are always partly religious,' she explained. 'The meaning of life and so on . . . Yoga gave me the most rational answers I hadn't found in Christianity.'

Results are usually quite gradual. Though many people find yoga gives them an instant 'lift', it may take several years before they can say they're totally recovered. Of course it might be argued that by then they might have got better anyway. But I doubt if this is the explanation. The evidence suggests that tranquillizer 'junkies' need help to break the habit and yoga seems able to free people from both their drugs *and* their misery.

PSYCHODYNAMIC PSYCHOTHERAPY

It is generally accepted that behavioural psychotherapy (see above with phobias and also below, under hypnotherapy) is often an appropriate treatment for phobias. The trouble with behavioural psychotherapy, or so its critics claim, is that it teaches people different reactions. It doesn't change them *inside*. Nevertheless, certain forms of behavioural therapy, such as assertiveness training, may be useful for dealing with certain forms of anxiety that occur in specific situations. For example, someone who is scared to death of speaking in public but whose job demands that she often give lectures may be helped to overcome her fear.

Psychodynamic psychotherapy, on the other hand, looks at the *reasons* for anxiety and depression – at the deep-seated inner conflicts, perhaps buried a long time ago, that may be involved in a person's present unhappiness. I'm only going to mention it briefly here because by now you'll have a fairly good idea of what it's all about. And there's little controversy about it – nearly all the practitioners I spoke to, whatever their affiliation, agreed that most people could benefit from a course of psychotherapy.

At its most basic, psychotherapy is simply talking to someone about your problems and having them listen. You don't need any special qualifications to be sympathetic and to be a good listener. When you pour your heart out to a friend or to your partner, they're giving you psychotherapy. When your GP says: 'Tell me about it,' he's practising psychotherapy. But if you're considering this form of treatment, you've got beyond this stage. Talking to your best friend, your lover or your doctor hasn't helped. You need more concentrated attention from someone who is trained specifically to understand the workings of the mind.

Formal psychotherapy comes in all shapes and forms. You can receive therapy individually, with your partner or in a group. Then there are different psychotherapeutic *schools* whose therapists start from slightly different assumptions about the origins of psychological conflict and who use somewhat different techniques to elucidate them. It's a vast subject and one to which I couldn't possibly do justice in such a small space. The aim, though, is the same: to help the client towards an acceptance of herself as a whole and special person with wants and needs that have to be expressed and fulfilled.

If you want to find out more – and I suggest you do before you embark on a course of treatment – there are a number of excellent books available and I've included some of them in the Bibliography. Then ask if you can have an assessment interview with a psychotherapist: this will give you an opportunity to ask about his/her methods and will allow him/her to determine whether or not you're likely to benefit.

Unfortunately, you may find it hard to get the kind of psychotherapy you need on the NHS. The obvious way to go about it is to get your doctor to refer you to a psychiatrist. But not all of us want the label that goes with that. Nor is a psychiatrist necessarily the ideal therapist. Many psychiatrists are still immersed in the 'medical' model of mental illness and favour drugs rather than talk. And they're mostly men. Some psychiatrists do practise formal psychotherapy but, because it's so time-consuming and because they have so many patients in their care, they can't spend the time on it that they might like. However, you might be lucky enough to live in an area where you can see a clinical psychologist who is also trained in psychotherapeutic methods.

In general, the easiest way to find an experienced psychotherapist who can give you the intensive therapy you'll probably need is to go to the private sector. This, of course, is a very expensive option, especially as therapy is often a long drawn-out process spread over months or years. But that way you can choose your therapist: on the NHS it's a matter of taking pot luck.

Many women have found that group therapy is an excellent compromise. It's cheaper, and in an all-female group the contact with the other women who are also battling with life helps remove the main stigma of emotional distress – the feelings of isolation and 'abnormality'.

HYPNOTHERAPY

Hypnosis can be used to relax someone. That alone may help you if you're feeling tense and nervous. But it can do more than that. A medically qualified hypnotist explained: 'When you're relaxed, you're not anxious and, when you're not anxious, things can be suggested to you which perhaps you can see in a more reasonable, more logical light. When you're relaxed in hypnosis with anxiety removed, you can think more clearly . . . But most of us believe there's a little more to it and that by having this two-way closed circuit of communication between the therapist and the patient, one also has access to what we know as the unconscious mind . . .'

So under hypnosis, with the unconscious mind working on your problems, you may be able to resolve them more easily than when you're in a normal conscious state. It can certainly be a very effective treatment for anxiety. Another doctor told me that patients who were encouraged to probe their unconscious minds while under hypnosis were likely to get better more quickly and less painfully (ordinary psychotherapy can be a very disturbing experience) than if they were treated with psychotherapy alone. 'Usually,' he said, 'the improvement is very quick indeed. Often after the first treatment there's some improvement.'

The great thing about hypnosis is that treatment can continue *between* sessions because the patient is taught to hypnotize herself. This is, apparently, very easy: nearly all of us are susceptible to hypnosis and once we've been taught the induction techniques we can 'go under' on our own.

What do the patients have to say? Dianne Doubtfire, a novelist, wrote about her experience in *Vogue* in 1978. She explained how she had turned to hypnosis in an attempt to relieve bad nervous tension which had afflicted her for years. She had taken tranquillizers and sleeping pills but they made her drowsy and affected her ability to think clearly – disastrous for a writer. In addition, she had suffered from bouts of depression and a number of physical ailments, including headaches, backache, dizziness and indigestion.

Hypnosis changed her life dramatically. After three sessions she was able to abandon her drugs. That was in 1972. Six years later she was still managing without them and hadn't had a headache for more than a year. In the article, Dianne admitted she still wasn't entirely free from tension. Nor had all her health problems gone. But, provided she practised self-hypnosis regularly, she could keep them at bay.

She had learnt self-hypnosis at the beginning of her therapy, she reported, so that she'd never felt in danger of becoming dependent on the hypnotist: she eventually needed to see him only twice a year for a 'booster' session. He'd given her a post-hypnotic suggestion that, whenever she told herself to 'Let Go' and counted backwards, she would go into a trance. While hypnotized and deeply relaxed she could then think more positively about her difficulties. When Dianne contacted me, she told me that 'the benefits are even greater now than when I wrote the article. I practise self-hypnosis for ten to fifteen minutes twice a day (if I'm good!) But if I miss out, I really notice tensions creeping back.'

Veronica turned to hypnosis as a last resort after weaning herself off the tranquillizers she'd been taking for twelve years. She had suffered from anxiety for a number of years before that but became really desperate after the birth of her daughter in 1969:

I suffered from very severe depression. My doctor began to prescribe tranquillizers for me in 1971 and I remained on these – in quite high dosage – until, after much misery and horrible withdrawal symptoms, I managed to get myself off them twelve years later (I had so many different tranquillizers that I almost feel peeved now if someone mentions one that I haven't had!).

I was still feeling desperate after stopping the tranquillizers so I saw a different doctor on the panel and he offered me training in auto-hypnosis [self-hypnosis] . . . I have to admit that it sounded like so much hokum but I was willing to try anything. It has helped me enormously, so much so that I would recommend it to anyone with the same sort of problems as myself . . .

It is wonderful to feel like a person again and I really wouldn't have believed it possible. I still have anxiety feelings from time to time, but then most people do . . . and a totally unexpected bonus was that I faced my last visit to the dentist with equanimity!

Hypnosis is also used to treat phobias. The patient is first hypnotized and then invited to imagine the situations that make her panic. An agoraphobic will visualize a trip to the bus stop, for example. Because she is hypnotized, this experience will seem real to her but because, under hypnosis, she's relaxed and calm, she'll learn that she *can* face it without fear. So, after a number of sessions she should be able to do the same exercise in real life. Used in this way, hypnotherapy is very similar to the desensitization technique mentioned on page 351 but less traumatic for the patient.

A warning, though. Hypnotherapy is a dodgy business in the wrong hands. Though it helped Veronica, it's clear that her doctor had already recognized that her anxiety was at least as important as her depression. Where depression is the overriding problem, hypnosis, by relieving any accompanying anxiety, may make the depression worse. It could even drive the patient to suicide. Some medical hypnotists believe that hypnosis is best reserved for people with obvious symptoms of anxiety, whether or not they happen to be depressed as well.

That's why it is vital that you consult a properly trained hypnotist – and one who's either a medical doctor or a qualified psychologist. A lay hypnotist won't be able to accurately diagnose your condition or to predict the effects that hypnosis is likely to have on you. The other thing to bear in mind is that even reputable hypnotists are not all equally successful. One I spoke to said he had treated anxiety but had found the results 'very disappointing'. Success also depends on *you*. If you're determined to stay off drugs – despite the withdrawal symptoms – hypnosis is more likely to work than if you're half-hearted about beating the tranquillizer habit.

Hypnotherapy, like psychodynamic psychotherapy, is not usually available on the NHS unless, of course, your own doctor happens to practise it.

Other approaches

IS YOUR DIET TO BLAME?

Correcting dietary deficiencies

'We know that psychological disturbances are some of the earliest symptoms of nutritional inadequacy,' writes Dr Jeffrey Bland.[10] He backs this claim by citing a number of scientific studies linking our understanding of brain chemistry with the effects of giving nutritional supplements to patients with various kinds of mental problem.

Our brains need feeding just as much as the rest of us. But there's one important difference: the brain is protected by what is known as the blood-brain barrier. Its effect is partly to shield the brain from toxins, bacteria and other harmful substances. Obviously, being a highly sensitive and sophisticated organ, it mustn't be exposed to just any old trash which happens to be floating around in our bloodstream. This barrier has its disadvantages, too, however. It means that the brain has to make a special effort to grab the nutrients it needs out of the blood. That's why nutritional deficiencies hit it first.

To make *neurotransmitters*, the chemicals that conduct nervous impulses across the gaps between nerves, the brain needs a number of different starting products, all of which must come from the blood and therefore, ultimately, from the food we eat. Two of the best-researched are the amino acids tryptophan and tyrosine. In the brain, tryptophan is converted to the neurotransmitter serotonin. Tyrosine is the starting product for neurotransmitters of the *catecholamine* family, including dopamine, noradrenaline and adrenaline.

Deficiencies of tryptophan and tyrosine may therefore affect the levels of neurotransmitters and lead to depression. In fact there's good evidence that neurotransmitter levels are lower than normal in at least some cases of depression: anti-depressant drugs work because they increase the amount of neurotransmitters available, either by preventing their being taken up too quickly by the nerves after they've been released or by slowing the rate at which they're broken down.

The problem can be tackled from the other end, though, by providing more tryptophan and tyrosine. And indeed tryptophan does help some depressed people – even con-ventional doctors prescribe it for this purpose. The evidence for tyrosine is less convincing – so far – but what there is sug-gests it may be useful for older people with depression who seem to be unable to produce enough of the catecholamine neurotransmitters.

Depression is also sometimes associated with low blood sugar (hypoglycaemia). The brain is very dependent on the level of sugar reaching it in the blood because it can produce very little of its own. The trouble is that the modern, refined diet can often result in hypoglycaemia. Our bodies were not designed to handle sugars and refined starches (see Chapter 2 on eating for health): digestion and metabolism are intended to be fairly slow processes so that, in between meals, we have enough blood sugar to keep us going. If we give our bodies too easy a job – by providing them with simple substances that they can deal with quickly, our blood sugar may fall quite rapidly and the poor brain doesn't have the chance to get hold of much of it.

The answer, then, is to eat a wholefood diet rich in both protein and complex carbohydrates which the body takes several hours to process, and to eat frequent small meals each day rather than two or three large ones so that the blood sugar level never drops too low.

Other aspects of your diet and lifestyle

Continual stress – and some of the things you may have been using to combat it, such as alcohol and coffee – tend to make hypoglycaemia worse. Although they initially raise blood sugar, the body, in its attempt to return things to normal, may overcompensate so that blood sugar levels fall too low. They may also deplete the body of some vitamins and minerals. So may smoking.

As you can see, the nutritional approach to mental health involves more than just taking supplements. You have to take a hard look at practically every aspect of your life and you may well need to use some form of stress reduction, and kick your bad habits as well, before you notice some improvement. It must also be said that good nutrition isn't *the* solution to mental disorders any more than drugs are. Both depend for their effects on brain biochemistry and, as we've seen, this is only part of the story.

Cerebral allergy

This is the technical term applied to food sensitivity affecting the brain. Clinical ecologists, who are experienced in this field, say that food sensitivity can cause all sorts of mental disturbances including anxiety, depression, lack of concentration and those vague physical complaints that so often plague people who are miserable but which doctors tend to dismiss as psychosomatic.

'I have suffered for over three years with extreme food allergies,' Sheila wrote, 'and was only able to eat pineapple, mangoes and other exotic fruit. *Anything* else would cause almost immediate symptoms. Earache, dizziness, nausea, severe headaches and, over a far longer period, depression, tiredness, inability to concentrate and make decisions, fear of going out in the car and severe pains in the joints. I then found out by accident, after going the rounds of the brain specialists etc., that it was food causing all these symptoms.'

Everything fell into place for Sheila when she saw a TV

programme on food allergy. She consulted a clinical ecologist and discovered that she was sensitive not only to many foods but to some chemicals as well, including natural gas! She was given desensitization treatment (see page 136) and it worked.

Sheila's specialist believes that many mental problems are due to allergies. She says that although psychological factors definitely play a part – and that psychotherapy may therefore be useful – she thinks that many people, because of their allergies, are more vulnerable to psychological stress. Most of us, she points out, go through stormy periods in our lives but we don't all succumb to anxiety or depression.

This is rather a simplistic view and one which is far from being accepted by mainstream medicine. Even clinical ecologists seem divided. Some claim that allergies are at the bottom of most of our modern ills. Others are more cautious. 'We simply don't know what percentage of psychological or psychiatric disturbance is precipitated by food or chemical sensitivity,' admit Drs George Lewith and Julian Kenyon, medical doctors who now spend most of their time practising alternative medicine, including clinical ecology, 'but it is obviously not the complete explanation for all such problems.'[11]

OTHER ALTERNATIVE THERAPIES

Since a nutritious, wholefood diet is the starting point for nearly all these therapies it's difficult to know whether the specific therapy has any additional beneficial effects. A good practitioner will also be a good – albeit informal – psychotherapist!

I received mixed reports about *acupuncture*. 'Acupuncture is very good in anxiety and depression,' said one practitioner. 'But it has to be accompanied by a chat. I've treated a number of people for panic attacks and anxiety with a reasonable amount of success. I've used acupuncture in phobias but I do a fair bit of saying: "Let's look at this", too. Depression,' she went on, 'is the hardest. It's about how people live their lives and that's not easy to change.' Many acupuncturists, she told me, won't attempt to treat emotional problems.

Another practitioner – a medically qualified one – was also less than enthusiastic even though, he said, there was some evidence that acupuncture affects serotonin levels and so might be expected to be beneficial in depression. 'I've used it for depression but without incredible success.' And he added that he wouldn't use acupuncture on someone who was severely depressed. 'If they wouldn't accept a safe-ish anti-depressant in small doses . . . I would get a psychiatrist to see them pretty rapidly, because these people sometimes kill themselves.' However, acupuncture might be useful for people with milder forms of depression, particularly if they were also tense and anxious, he said.

A number of *herbs*, including valerian and verbena, have calming effects. These, a herbalist explained, are far better than their medical equivalents because they calm you without sapping your energy. Herbs may also be a useful stop-gap while you're coming off tranquillizers. But if a herbalist suspects there are psychological reasons for your problems, he will probably suggest that you see a psychotherapist as well.

Homoeopathic remedies may help. The practitioner will choose one that best fits your 'picture' – the symptoms you describe, your past history, your feelings towards other people and so on. For example, Phosphoric Acid is indicated if the patient's main symptom is one of indifference to everything, and someone who's very irritable and anxious may respond to Arsenicum Album. But as we've seen, mental disorders are seldom easy to categorize – least of all by the patient herself. So if you try to treat yourself, the chances of success are slim.

Practitioners of *cranial osteopathy* say that sometimes unexplained depression – of the endogenous type – may be due to back and neck problems. This affects the flow of the cerebrospinal fluid which bathes both the spinal cord and the brain – hence the depression.

One patient who regularly had bouts of depression had had

a series of falls on the base of her spine. And when the osteopath examined her, she discovered that her sacrum – at the bottom of the spine – was 'jammed solid. The whole flow of the cerebrospinal fluid was inhibited and that leads to a slow-down of the whole system. From the first time I treated her and freed up her sacrum . . . she did not have her depression again.'

CONCLUSIONS

The causes of mental distress are still imperfectly understood, so there's no panacea. Nevertheless, there are now a number of promising alternative treatments. My own view is that if you can avoid drugs, it is probably better to do so, although if your anxiety or depression is severe you may need them at least temporarily. They may calm your mind enough for you to explore the other possibilities.

References

Introduction

1. McPherson, A. 'Why women's health?' in *Women's Problems in General Practice* (Oxford University Press, 1983).
2. Roberts, H. *The Patient Patients* (Pandora Press, 1985).

1. Alternative Therapies

1. Quoted in *Here's Health* (April, 1985).
2. Boyd, H. 'Homoeopathic medicine' in Lewith, G. T. (ed.) *Alternative Therapies* (William Heinemann Medical Books, 1985).
3. Keysell, G. R., Williamson, K. L. and Tolman, B. D. 'An investigation into the analgesic activity of two homoeopathic preparations, Arnica and Hypericum' in *Communications No. 11, Midlands Homoeopathy Research Group*, February 1984).
4. Waxman, D. *Hypnosis* (Unwin Paperbacks, 1984. First published by Allen and Unwin, 1981).
5. Lett, A. *Treatment of the Reflex Zones of the Feet* (British School – Reflex Zone Therapy of the Feet).
6. Marcer, D. 'Biofeedback and Meditation' in *Alternative Therapies, op. cit.*

2. Eating for Health

1. Colgan, M. *Your Personal Vitamin Profile* (Blond and Briggs, 1983).
2. Bland, J. *Your Personal Health Programme* (Thorsons, 1984 – published by arrangement with Harper and Row, New York).
3. Bender, A. *Health or Hoax? The Truth about Health Foods and Diets* (Elvendon Press, 1985).
4. Davis, R. D. 'Nutritional needs and biochemical diversity' in

Bland, J. (ed.) *Medical Applications of Clinical Nutrition* (Keats Publishing Inc., 1983).

5. Eaton, S. B. and Konner, M. 'Paleolithic Nutrition: A consideration of its nature and current implications', *New England Journal of Medicine, 312* (1985), 283.

6. Marshall, C. W. *Vitamins and Minerals: Help or Harm?* (George F. Stickly Company, 1983).

3. The Premenstrual Syndrome

1. Dalton, K. *Once a Month* (Fontana Paperbacks, 1978).

2. Cited by Sanders, D. 'Premenstrual Tension' in *Women's Problems in General Practice, op. cit.*

3. Cited by Jones, M. M. 'The premenstrual syndrome: Part 1', *British Journal of Sexual Medicine, 10,* No. 99 (August, 1983), 9.

4. Horrobin, D. F. 'The role of essential fatty acids and prostaglandins in the premenstrual syndrome', *Journal of Reproductive Medicine, 28,* (1983), 465.

5. Reid, R. L. 'Endogenous opioid activity and the premenstrual syndrome', *Lancet, 11* (1983), 786.

6. *Ibid.*

7. Abraham, G. E. 'Nutritional factors in the etiology of the premenstrual tension syndrome', *Journal of Reproductive Medicine, 28,* (1983), 446.

8. Brush, M. G., Watson, S. J., Horrobin, D. F. and Manku, M. S. 'Abnormal essential fatty acid levels in plasma of women with premenstrual syndrome', *American Journal of Obstetrics and Gynecology, 150,* (1984), 363.

9. Horrobin, D. F., *Journal of Reproductive Medicine, op. cit.*

10. Dalton, K., 'Pyridoxine overdose in premenstrual syndrome', *Lancet, 1* (1985), 1168.

4. Menstruation and Problem Periods

1. Anderson, A. and McPherson, A. 'Menstrual Problems' in *Women's Problems in General Practice, op. cit.*

2. Smith, T. *A Woman's Guide to Homoeopathic Medicine* (Thorsons, 1984).

3. 'Anorexia effects can be permanent', *General Practitioner*, 16 December, 1983, 47.

4. Healy, D. L., Fraser, H. M. and Lawson, S. L. 'Shrinkage of a uterine fibroid after sub-cutaneous infusion of a LHRH agonist', *British Medical Journal, 289* (1984), 1267.

5. Cited by Charnock, M. 'Dysfunctional Uterine Bleeding' in Chamberlain, G. (ed.) *Contemporary Gynaecology* (Butterworths, 1984).

5. Vaginal Infections and Cystitis

1. 'Asymptomatic herpes can be infectious', *General Practitioner*, 9 August, 1985, 3.

2. Barlow, D. 'Vaginal Discharge' in *Women's Problems in General Practice, op. cit.*

3. Clayton, C. *Thrush. How it's caused and what to do about it* (Sheldon Press, 1984).

4. Truss, C. Orian. *The Missing Diagnosis* (Published by the author, 1983); and Chaitow, L. *Candida Albicans. Could Yeast be Your Problem?* (Thorsons, 1985).

5. North, B. B. and Crittenden, P. P. *Stop Herpes Now!* (Thorsons, 1985).

6. Kilmartin, A. *Cystitis. A Complete Self-Help Guide* (Hamlyn Paperbacks, 1980).

7. Cheraskin, E., Ringsdorf, W. M. and Sisley, E. L. *The Vitamin C Connection* (Bantam Books, by arrangement with Harper and Row, 1984).

6. Contraception

1. Guillebaud, J. *The Pill* (Oxford University Press. First published 1980; third edition 1984).

2. Grant, E. *The Bitter Pill* (Elm Tree Books, 1985).

3. 'Sexual arithmetic proves man outstrips rabbit', *Daily Telegraph*, 30 August, 1985.

4. Bromwich, P. and Parsons, T. *Contraception: the Facts* (Oxford University Press, 1984).

5. Flynn, A. M. and Brooks, M. *A Manual of Natural Family Planning* (George Allen and Unwin, 1984).

6. Drake, K. and Drake, J. *Natural Birth Control* (Thorsons, 1984).

7. Roberts, C. and de Trafford, J. 'Cold hands, conception and contraception', *New Scientist*, 10 January, 1985, 22.

8. Short, R. V. 'Breast Feeding', *Scientific American, 250* (1984), 23.

7. Pregnancy and Childbirth

1. Wright, J. T. *et al.* 'Alcohol consumption, pregnancy and low birth weight', *Lancet, 1* (1983), 663.

2. Grisso, J. A. *et al.* 'Alcohol consumption and outcome of pregnancy', *Journal of Epidemiology and Community Health, 38* (1984), 232.

3. Anonymous. 'Misconceptions about preconceptual care', *Lancet, 11* (1985), 1046.

4. Wald, N. J. and Polani, P. E. 'Neural tube defects and vitamins: the need for a randomized clinical trial', *British Journal of Obstetrics and Gynaecology, 91* (1984), 516.

5. Cited by McMichael *et al. Early Human Development* (1982), 59 (Elsevier Biomedical Press); by Passwater, R. A. and Cranton, E. M. *Trace Elements, Hair Analysis and Nutrition* (Keats Publishing, 1983); and by Ghosh, A. *et al.* 'Zinc deficiency is not a cause for abortion, congenital abnormality and small-for-gestational age infant in Chinese women', *British Journal of Obstetrics and Gynaecology, 92* (1985), 886.

6. Bryce-Smith, D. 'Environmental Influences on Prenatal Development' in *The Next Generation. Avoiding Damage Before Birth in the 1980s* (Foresight, 1983).

7. *Ibid.*

8. Macfarlane, A. and Mugford, M. *Birth Counts* (HMSO, 1984).

9. Sperryn, P. N. *Sport and Medicine* (Butterworths, 1983).

10. 'Morning sickness is a "healthy sign"', *General Practitioner*, 5 April, 1985, 7.

11. 'Strange case of the disappearance of morning sickness', *New Scientist*, 30 June, 1983, 928.

12. Gibb, D. M. F. *et al.* 'Prolonged pregnancy: is induction of labour indicated? A prospective study', *British Journal of Obstetrics and Gynaecology, 89* (1982), 292.

13. Harrison, R. F. *et al.* 'Is routine episiotomy necessary', *British Medical Journal, 288* (1984), 1971; and Sleep, J. *et al.* 'West

Berkshire perineal management trial', *British Medical Journal*, *289* (1984), 587.

14. Welburn, V. *Postnatal Depression* (Fontana Paperbacks, 1980).

8. Infertility

1. Stanway, A. *Why Us?* (Thorsons, 1984. First published 1980).
2. Howe, G., *et al.* 'Effects of age, cigarette smoking and other factors on fertility: findings in a large prospective study', *British Medical Journal*, *290* (1985). 1697.
3. Day Baird, D. and Wilcox, A. J. 'Cigarette smoking associated with delayed conception', *Journal of the American Medical Association*, *253* (1985), 2979.
4. Hellhammer, D. H. *et al.* 'Male infertility: relationships among gonadotropins, sex steroids, seminal parameters and personality attitudes', *Psychosomatic Medicine*, *47* (1985), 58.
5. Oakley, A., McPherson, A. and Roberts, H. *Miscarriage* (Fontana Paperbacks, 1984).
6. Mowbray, J. F. *et al.* 'Controlled trial of treatment of recurrent spontaneous abortion by immunization with paternal cells', *Lancet*, *1* (1985), 941.
7. Broome, Annabel and Wallace, Louise (eds.) *Psychology and Gynaecological Problems*, (Tavistock Publications, 1984).
8. Humphrey, M. 'Infertility and Alternative Parenting' in *Psychology and Gynaecological Problems, op. cit.*
9. Bland, J. *Your Personal Health Programme, op. cit.*
10. Hargrove, J. T. and Abraham, G. E. 'Effect of vitamin B_6 on infertility in women with premenstrual tension', *Infertility*, *2* (1979), 315.
11. Pfeiffer, C. C. *Mental and Elemental Nutrients* (Keats Publishing, 1975).
12. Collins, J. A. *et al.* 'Treatment-independent pregnancy among infertile couples', *New England Journal of Medicine*, *309*, 1201.

9. The Menopause

1. Reitz, R. *Menopause. A Positive Approach* (Unwin Paperbacks, 1981).
2. Anderson, A. and McPherson, A. 'The Menopause' in *Women's Problems in General Practice, op. cit.*

3. Cooke, D. J. 'Psychosocial Study of the Climacteric' in *Psychology and Gynaecological Problems, op. cit.*
4. Anderson, A. and McPherson, A. *op. cit.*
5. Mohun, J. 'New study overturns theories on oestrogen', *General Practitioner*, 4 May, 1985, 4.
6. Mohun, J. 'New HRT regime avoids withdrawal bleeding', *General Practitioner*, 15 March, 1985, 15.
7. *Your Personal Health Programme, op. cit.*
8. Meredith, S. 'Recent advances in oral contraception', *British Journal of Sexual Medicine, 11*, No. 100 (September 1983), 38.
9. Padus, E. *The Woman's Encyclopedia of Health and Natural Healing* (Rodale Press Inc., 1981).

10. Double Trouble. Uterine Prolapse and Incontinence

1. Malvern, J. 'Incontinence of urine in women' in *Contemporary Gynaecology, op. cit.*
2. Noble, E. *Essential Exercises for the Childbearing Year* (John Murray Ltd, 1980. First published 1978).
3. Swami Muktananda Saraswati and Swami Satyananda Saraswati. *Nawa Yogini Tantra* (Bihar School of Yoga, Bihar, India, 1983).

11. Female Cancer

1. Kidman, B. *A Gentle Way with Cancer* (Century, 1983).
2. Fisher, B. *et al.* 'Five-year results of a randomized clinical trial comparing total mastectomy and segmental mastectomy with or without radiation in the treatment of breast cancer', *New England Journal of Medicine, 312* (1985), 665.
3. Baum, M. *Breast Cancer. The Facts* (Oxford University Press, 1981).
4. Doll, R. and Peto, R. *The Causes of Cancer* (Oxford University Press, 1981).
5. LeShan, L. *You Can Fight for Your Life* (Thorsons, 1984. First published in the United States in 1977).
6. Cited by Moertel, C. G. *et al.* 'High-dose vitamin C versus placebo in the treatment of patients with advanced cancer who have had no prior chemotherapy: a randomized double-blind comparison', *New England Journal of Medicine, 312* (1985), 137.

7. Moertel, C. G. *et al*, *op. cit.*

8. Cited by Marshall, C. W. *Vitamins and Minerals: Help or Harm?*, *op. cit.*

9. Booyens, J. and Katzeff, I. E. 'Cancer: a simple metabolic disease?', *Medical Hypotheses, 12* (1983), 195.

10. Moertel, C. G. *et al*. 'A clinical trial of amygdalin (Laetrile) in the treatment of human cancer', *New England Journal of Medicine, 306* (1982), 201.

11. Simonton, C. O. and Matthews-Simonton, S. *Getting Well Again* (Bantam Books, 1980. First published 1978).

12. Greer, S. *et al*. 'Psychological response to breast cancer: effect on outcome', *Lancet, 11* (1979), 785.

13. Pettingale, K. W. 'Coping and cancer prognosis', *Journal of Psychosomatic Research, 28* (1984), 363.

14. Leroi, R. 'Fundamentals of mistletoe therapy', *Krebsgeschehen, 5* (1979), 145.

15. Schwarz, W. 'The doctors who feel threatened by the fringe healers', *Guardian*, 21 November, 1984.

16. Cited by Forbes, A. *Cancer and its Non-toxic Treatment* (Cancer Help Centre, Bristol).

12. Benign Breast Disease

1. Love, S. M. *et al*. 'Fibrocystic "disease" of the breast: a non-disease?', *New England Journal of Medicine, 307* (1982), 1010.

2. Dalton, K. *Once a Month*, *op. cit.*

3. Wise Budoff, P. *No More Menstrual Cramps and Other Good News* (Angus and Robertson, 1980).

4. London, R. S. *et al*. 'The effect of vitamin E on mammary dysplasia: a double-blind study', *Obstetrics and Gynaecology, 65* (1985), 104.

13. Migraine

1. Pearce, J. M. S. 'Migraine: a cerebral disorder', *Lancet, 11* (1984), 86.

2. Anonymous. 'Headache and depression', *Lancet, 1* (1984), 495.

3. Hanington, E. 'Migraine: a platelet disorder', *Lancet, 11* (1981), 720.

4. Lambley, P. *The Headache Book* (W. H. Allen, 1980).

5. Gelb, H. and Siegel, P. M. *Killing Pain Without Prescription* (Thorsons, by arrangement with Harper and Row, 1983, first published 1980).

6. Hodges, K. *et al.* 'Life events occurring in families of children with recurrent abdominal pain', *Journal of Psychosomatic Research, 28* (1984), 185.

7. *Women and Migraine* (obtainable from 7 St Mark's Rise, London E8, price 60p + 20p postage).

8. Munro, J. A. 'Food allergy in migraine', *Proceedings of the Nutrition Society, 42* (1983), 241.

9. Munro, J. *et al.* 'Migraine is a food-allergic disease', *Lancet, 11* (1984), 719

10. Heptinstall, S. *et al.* 'Extracts of feverfew inhibit granule secretion in blood platelets and polymorphonuclear leucocytes', *Lancet, 1* (1985), 1071.

11. *Feverfew* (Leaflet published by the British Migraine Association, 1985).

14. Peace of Mind?

1. van Deurzen-Smith, E. 'Existential Therapy' in Dryden, W. (ed.) *Individual Therapy in Britain* (Harper and Row, 1984).

2. Smail, D. *Illusion and Reality. The Meaning of Anxiety* (J. M. Dent and Sons, 1984).

3. Rowe, D. *The Construction of Life and Death* (John Wiley and Sons, 1982).

4. Hodson, P. *Men . . . An investigation into the emotional male* (British Broadcasting Corporation, 1984).

5. Rubin, L. B. *Intimate Strangers* (Fontana Paperbacks, 1985. First published by Harper and Row, 1983).

6. Hite, S. *The Hite Report on Male Sexuality* (Macdonald Futura, 1981).

7. Melville, J. *The Tranquillizer Trap and how to get out of it* (Fontana Paperbacks, 1984).

8. Rowe, D. 'Men's Theories, Women's Pain', in press.

9. Sattaur, O. 'Breathing correctly stops agoraphobic panic', *New Scientist*, 28 February, 1985, 22.

10. Bland, J. *Your Personal Health Programme, op. cit.*

11. Lewith, G. T. and Kenyon, J. N. *Clinical Ecology* (Thorsons, 1985).

Bibliography

Balaskas, A. and Balaskas, J. *New Life* (Sidgwick and Jackson, 1979).

Balaskas, J. *Active Birth* (Unwin Paperbacks, 1983).

Barlow, D. *Sexually Transmitted Diseases. The Facts* (Oxford University Press, 1981).

Bland, J. *Hair Tissue Mineral Analysis* (Thorsons, 1983. First published in the US by Northwest Diagnostic Services, 1981).

Boyd, H. *Introduction to Homoeopathic Medicine* (Beaconsfield, 1981).

British Herbal Pharmacopoeia (British Herbal Medicine Association, 1983).

Campbell, D. M. and Gillmer, M. D. G., (eds.) *Nutrition in Pregnancy* (Royal College of Obstetricians and Gynaecologists, 1983).

Chaitow, L. *Osteopathy* (Thorsons, 1982).

Clover, A. *Homoeopathy. A patient's guide* (Thorsons, 1984).

Davies, S. and Stewart, A. *Nutritional Medicine* (Pan, 1987).

Dominian, J. *Depression* (Fontana Paperbacks, 1976).

Ernst, S. and Goodison, L. *In Our Own Hands. A Book of Self-Help Therapy* (The Women's Press, 1981).

Faulder, C. *Breast Cancer* (Virago, 2nd edition 1982).

Flaws, B. *Path of Pregnancy* (Paradigm, 1983).

Forbes, A. *The Bristol Diet* (Century, 1984).

Fulder, S. *The Handbook of Complementary Medicine* (Coronet Books, 1984).

Harvey, D. *The Power to Heal* (Thorsons, 1983).

Health Education Council. *Pregnancy Book* (1984).

Inglis, B. and West, R. *The Alternative Health Guide* (Michael Joseph, 1983).

Iyengar, B. K. S. *Light on Yoga* (Unwin Paperbacks, 1976, first published by Allen and Unwin, 1966).

Kaptchuk, T. J. *The Web That Has No Weaver: understanding Chinese medicine* (Congdon and Weed, 1983).

Kitzinger, S. *The Experience of Breastfeeding* (Penguin, 1979).

Kitzinger, S. *The Experience of Childbirth* (Penguin, 4th edition, 1978).

Kitzinger, S. *Pregnancy and Childbirth* (Michael Joseph, 1980).

LeShan, L. *How to Meditate* (Thorsons, 1983. First published in the US, 1974).

Lesser, M. *Nutrition and Vitamin Therapy* (Bantam Books, 1981. First published by Grove Press, 1980).

Macdonald, A. *Acupuncture: from Ancient Art to Modern Medicine* (Unwin Paperbacks, 1984. First published by Allen and Unwin, 1982).

Mackarness, R. *Not all in the mind* (Pan, 1976).

MacManaway, B. with Turcan, J. *Healing* (Thorsons, 1983).

Marquardt, H. *Reflex Zone Therapy of the Feet* (Thorsons, 1983).

Nazzaro, A., Lombard, D. and Horrobin, D. *The PMT Solution* (Adamantine Press, 1985).

Newman Turner, R. *Naturopathic Medicine* (Thorsons, 1984).

Paterson, B. *The Allergy Connection* (Thorsons, 1985).

Price, W. A. *Nutrition and Physical Degeneration* (The Price-Pottenger Nutrition Foundation, 1945. Tenth printing 1979).

Priest, R. *Anxiety and Depression. A practical guide to recovery* (Martin Dunitz, 1983).

Rowe, D. *Depression. The way out of your prison* (Routledge and Kegan Paul, 1983).

Shone, R. *Autohypnosis: a step-by-step guide to self-hypnosis* (Thorsons, 1982).

Shreeve, C. *Depression* (Thorsons, 1984).

Shreeve, C. *The Premenstrual Syndrome. The Curse that Can be Cured* (Thorsons, 1983).

Stanway, P. and Stanway, A. *Breast is Best* (Pan, 1978).

Turin, A. C. and Coleman, V. *No More Headaches!* (Robert Hale, 1985).

Tyrer, P. *How to Cope with Stress* (Sheldon Press, 1980).

Vithoulkas, G. *The Science of Homoeopathy* (Grove Press, 1980).

Weller, S. *Easy Pregnancy with Yoga* (Thorsons, 1983).

Wilkinson, M. *Migraine and Headaches* (Martin Dunitz, 1982).

de Winter, J. *How to Die Young at Ninety* (The Jan de Winter Cancer Prevention Foundation, 6 New Road, Brighton, BN1 1UF, 1983).

Witkin-Lanoil, G. *Coping With Stress. A practical self-help guide for women* (Sheldon Press, 1985).

Useful Addresses

This section includes a number of professional organizations representing practitioners of alternative medicine. Most will supply a list of members (enclose stamped, addressed envelope; some also charge a small fee for this service). Most of the doctor-only organizations, however, will not – in theory, at least – release names of members to the general public as this could be construed as advertising. In such cases, the only way to find a practitioner is to ask your own doctor to refer you – which can be a problem if he or she is antagonistic to alternative medicine. A few medical associations, while adhering in general to this rule, will sometimes send you a list of members on the proviso that, again, you are referred by your doctor (though in practice of course, once you have the name of a practitioner there's nothing to stop you from contacting him or her direct). Others, though they don't release members' names, will arrange for one to get in touch with you.

UNITED KINGDOM

Alternative Therapies

GENERAL

The British Holistic Medical Association
179 Gloucester Place
LONDON NW1 6DX
Telephone 01 262 5299

Doctors only. List available to members and associate members only. Associate membership open to the general public at a subscription of £10 a year. Information and referral service. Doctors advise by post and on the phone one day a week.

Council for Complementary and Alternative Medicine
  10 Belgrave Square
  LONDON SW1X 8PH
  Telephone 01 235 9512

Concerned with professional standards and training. Founder members are the British Acupuncture Association and Register, the British Chiropractic Association, the British Naturopathic and Osteopathic Association, the College of Osteopaths, the National Institute of Medical Herbalists, the Register of Traditional Chinese Medicine and the Traditional Acupuncture Society. Also an information service, run by the Koestler Foundation, at the same address. Telephone 01 235 4912

The Institute for Complementary Medicine
  21 Portland Place
  LONDON W1N 3AF
  Telephone 01 636 9543

Research Council for Complementary Medicine
  Suite 1
  19A Cavendish Square
  LONDON W1M 9AD
  Telephone 01 493 6930

Primarily a research body but will answer very general inquiries from the general public and refer you to the relevant organization.

ACUPUNCTURE

British Acupuncture Association and Register
  19 Prebend Street
  LEICESTER LE2 OLA
  Telephone 0533 556366

The register also includes those of the two other major schools of acupuncture: the Register of Traditional Chinese Medicine and the Traditional Acupuncture Society. Some doctor-members.

British Medical Acupuncture Society
67-9 Chancery Lane
LONDON WC2 1AF

Doctors only.

CHIROPRACTIC

British Chiropractic Association
5 First Avenue
CHELMSFORD
Essex CM1 1RX
Telephone 0245 358487

CLINICAL ECOLOGY

Action Against Allergy
43 The Downs
LONDON SW20 8HG
Telephone 01 947 5082

Can put you in touch with a practitioner.

HEALING

National Federation of Spiritual Healers
Old Manor Farm Studio
Church Street
SUNBURY-ON-THAMES
Middlesex TW16 6RG
Telephone 09327 83164

HERBAL MEDICINE

National Institure of Medical Herbalists
PO Box 3
WINCHESTER
Hampshire
Telephone 0962 68776

HOMOEOPATHY

Society of Homoeopaths
    11A Bampton Street
    TIVERTON
    Devon
    Telephone 0884 255117

Non-medical

British Homoeopathic Association
    27A Devonshire Street
    LONDON W1N 1RJ
    Telephone 01 935 2163

Will supply a list of medically qualified homoeopaths.

HYPNOTHERAPY

British Society of Medical and Dental Hypnosis
    42 Links Road
    ASHTEAD
    Surrey KT21 2HJ
    Telephone 03722 73522

Doctors and dentists only. No list of members but if your own
doctor seems unwilling or unable to help, the Society may agree to
contact one on your behalf so that he or she can then discuss your
case with your doctor.

British Society of Experimental and Clinical Hypnosis
    PO Box 133
    CANTERBURY
    Kent CT2 7YS

NATUROPATHY AND OSTEOPATHY

British Naturopathic and Osteopathic Association
    6 Netherhall Gardens
    LONDON NW3 5RR
    Telephone 01 435 8728/7830

NUTRITIONAL MEDICINE

British Society for Nutritional Medicine
   (Information Officer: Dr Alan Stewart)
   5 Somerhill Road
   HOVE
   East Sussex BN3 1RP

Doctors only.

OSTEOPATHY

College of Osteopaths
   110 Thorkhill Road
   THAMES DITTON
   Surrey KT7 0UW
   Telephone 01 398 3308

General Council and Register of Osteopaths
   1-4 Suffolk Street
   LONDON SW1Y 4HG
   Telephone 01 839 2060

British Osteopathic Association
   8 Boston Place
   LONDON NW1 6QH
   Telephone 01 262 1128

Medically qualified.

REFLEX ZONE THERAPY

British School of Reflex Zone Therapy of the Feet
   25 Brooks Mews
   LONDON W1
   Telephone 01 629 3481

RELAXATION, STRESS REDUCTION, MEDITATION, YOGA, ETC.

British Association for Autogenic Training and Therapy
   (BAFATT) c/o The Centre for Autogenic Training
   LONDON (see below).

For names and addresses of trained AT teachers.

British Psychological Society
   St Andrew's House
   Princess Road East
   LEICESTER LE1 7DR
   Telephone 0533 549568

British Wheel of Yoga
   Mrs Di Kendall
   Grafton Grange
   Grafton
   YORK
   Telephone 09012 2404

Centre for Autogenic Training
   101 Harley Street
   LONDON W1N 1DF
   Telephone 01 935 1811

Relaxation for Living
   Dunesk
   29 Burwood Park Road
   WALTON-ON-THAMES
   Surrey KT12 5LH
   Telephone 0932 227826

Satyananda Yoga Centre
   70 Thurleigh Road
   LONDON SW12
   Telephone 01 673 4869

Siddha Meditation Centre
   SYDUK
   Campenton
   Riverside Temple Gardens
   STAINES
   Middlesex TW18 3NS
   Telephone 0784 8164962

Yoga Biomedical Trust
   PO Box 140
   CAMBRIDGE CB1 1PU
   Telephone 0223 65771

PREMENSTRUAL SYNDROME

Premenstrual Tension Advisory Service
  PO Box 268
  HOVE
  East Sussex BN3 1RW
  Telephone 0273 771366

INFECTIONS

Herpes Association
  41 North Road
  LONDON N7 9DP
  Telephone 01 609 9061

CONTRACEPTION

The Family Planning Information Service
  27-35 Mortimer Street
  LONDON W1N 7RJ
  Telephone 01 636 7866

Natural Family Planning Centre
  Birmingham Maternity Hospital
  Queen Elizabeth Medical Centre
  BIRMINGHAM B15 2TG
  Telephone 021 472 1377 extension 102

PREGNANCY AND CHILDBIRTH

Active Birth Movement
  PO Box 740
  LONDON W9 1BA
  Telephone 01 286 9655 and 01 794 2354

The Association for Postnatal Illness
  7 Gower Avenue
  LONDON SW6
  Telephone 01 741 5019

Expectant Mothers' Clinic
   British School of Osteopathy
   1-4 Suffolk Street
   LONDON SW1Y 4HG
   Telephone 01 930 9254

Foresight
   The Old Vicarage
   Church Lane
   Witley
   GODALMING
   Surrey GU8 5PN
   Telephone 042879 4500

National Childbirth Trust
   5 Queensborough Terrace
   LONDON W2 3TB
   Telephone 01 221 3833

Pre-eclamptic Toxaemia Society
   Dawn James
   33 Keswick Avenue
   HULLBRIDGE
   Essex SS5 6JL
   Telephone 0702 231689

INFERTILITY

CHILD
   'Farthings'
   Gaunts Road
   Pawlett
   NR BRIDGWATER
   Somerset
   Telephone 0278 683595

Miscarriage Association
   18 Stoneybrook Close
   West Bretton
   WAKEFIELD
   Yorks WF4 4TP
   Telephone 0924 85515

National Association for the Childless
  Birmingham Settlement
  318 Summer Lane
  BIRMINGHAM B19 3RL
  Telephone 021 359 4887/2113

PROLAPSE AND INCONTINENCE

Chartered Society of Physiotherapists
  14 Bedford Row
  LONDON WC1R 4ED
  Telephone 01 242 1941

Yoga Biomedical Trust
  (See page 380)

CANCER

Association for New Approaches to Cancer
  c/o the Seekers' Trust
  Addington Park
  MAIDSTONE
  Kent ME19 5BL
  Telephone 0732 848336

British Association of Cancer United Patients
  and their families and friends (BACUP)
  121/123 Charterhouse Street
  LONDON EC1M 6AA

BACUP's Cancer Information Service is on 01 608 1661

For information on the disease, its orthodox medical treatment and how to cope.

Bristol Cancer Help Centre
  Grove House
  Cornwallis Grove
  Clifton
  BRISTOL BS8 4PG
  Telephone 0272 743216

Cancerlink
  46 Pentonville Road
  LONDON N1 9HF
  Telephone 01 833 2451

Information service (on the disease and its orthodox treatment.
People inquiring about alternatives will be referred to the relevant
organization).

Clinic for Cancer Prevention Advice
  6 New Road
  BRIGHTON B1N 1UF
  Telephone 0273 727213

Walk-in clinic for advice on cancer prevention.

Mastectomy Association
  26 Harrison Street
  LONDON WC1H 8JG
  Telephone 01 837 0908

Women's National Cancer Control Campaign
  1 South Audley Street
  LONDON W1Y 5DQ
  Telephone 01 499 7532-4

Information service. List of well-woman clinics for cervical smear
and breast examinations.

MIGRAINE

British Dental Migraine Study Group
  6 Union Road
  New Mills
  STOCKPORT
  Cheshire SK12 3ES

British Migraine Association
  178a High Road
  Byfleet
  WEYBRIDGE
  Surrey KT14 7ED
  Telephone 09323 52468

City of London Migraine Clinic
  22 Charterhouse Square
  LONDON EC1M 6DX
  Telephone 01 251 3322

Migraine Trust
  45 Great Ormond Street
  LONDON WC1N 3HD

PEACE OF MIND

Association for Humanistic Psychology in Britian
  62 Southwark Bridge Road
  LONDON SE1 0AM
  Telephone 01 928 8254

Interpersonal therapy e.g. Gestalt, Rogerian, co-counselling. Most practitioners are London-based.

British Association for Counselling
  37A Sheep Street
  RUGBY
  Warwickshire CV21 3BX
  Telephone 0788 78328

British Association of Psychotherapists
  121 Hendon Lane
  LONDON N3 3PR
  Telephone 01 346 1747

Members mostly in London and the home counties.

Institute of Psycho-Analysis
  63 New Cavendish Street
  London W1M 7RD
  Telephone 01 580 4952

Freudian and Kleinian. Mostly in London. Long waiting list.

Lifeskills
  3 Brighton Road
  London N2 8JU
  Telephone 01 346 9646

Relaxation tapes and books.

The Society of Analytical Psychology
  1 Daleham Gardens
  Hampstead
  LONDON NW3 5BY
  Telephone 01 435 7696

Jungian.

Women's Therapy Centre
  6 Manor Gardens
  LONDON N7
  Telephone 01 263 6200

Yoga Biomedical Trust
  (See page 380)

AUSTRALIA

Alternative Therapies

Those organizations marked ** are national organizations, or the national head office, and as such can give contacts in other states and territories (enclose s.a.e. when inquiring).

GENERAL

**Australian Natural Therapists Association Ltd
  8 Thorpe Road
  WORONORA NSW 2232
  Telephone 02 521 2063

Association of Self-Help Organizations & Groups
  39 Darghan Street
  GLEBE NSW 2037
  Telephone 02 660 6136

Australian Vegetarian Society
  25 Ainslie Street
  KINGSFORD NSW 2032
  Telephone 02 349 4485

Collective of Self-Help Groups
  65 Gertrude St
  FITZROY VIC 3065
  Telephone 03 417 6266

Dorothy Hall College of Herbal Medicine
  558 Darling Street
  ROZELLE NSW 2039
  Telephone 02 818 4233

Western Institute of Self-Help
  80 Railway Road
  COTTESLOE WA 6011
  Telephone 09 383 3188

ACUPUNCTURE

**Acupuncture Association of Australia
  5 Albion Street
  HARRIS PARK NSW 2150
  Telephone 02 633 9187

**Acupuncture Ethics and Standards Organization
  5th Floor
  620 Harris Street
  ULTIMO NSW 2007
  Telephone 02 212 5250

CHIROPRACTIC

**The Australian Chiropractors Association
  1 Martin Place
  LINDEN NSW 2778
  Telephone 047 531 013

**United Chiropractors Association of Australasia Ltd
  PO Box 679
  POTTS POINT NSW 2011
  Telephone 02 358 6688

CLINICAL ECOLOGY

Institute for Orthomolecular Research
  41 Boundary Street
  RUSHCUTTERS BAY NSW 2011
  Telephone 02 357 5474

HERBALISTS

**National Herbalists Association of Australia
  2 Duffy Ave
  KINGSGROVE NSW 2208
  Telephone 02 787 4523

HOMOEOPATHY

**Australian Centre of Homoeopathy
  41 Murray Street
  TANUNDA SA 5352
  Telephone 085 63 2932

**Australian Institute of Homoeopathy
  PO Box 122
  ROSEVILLE NSW 2069
  Telephone 02 407 2876

HYPNOTHERAPY

**Australian Society of Clinical Hypnotherapists
  3 Trelawny Street
  EASTWOOD NSW 2122
  Telephone 02 85 1276

Australian Society for Clinical and Experimental Hypnosis
  PO Box 237
  RANDWICK NSW 2031
  Telephone 02 349 2671

NUTRITIONAL MEDICINE

Hyperactivity Association (NSW)
  29 Bertram Street
  CHATSWOOD NSW 2067
  Telephone 02 411 2186

OSTEOPATHY

United Osteopathic Physicians Guild
    332 Oxford Street
    WOOLLAHRA NSW 2025

REFLEX ZONE THERAPY

**All Australia Register of Massage Therapists Organization
    756 Pacific Highway
    GORDON NSW 2072
    Telephone 02 498 1997

RELAXATION, STRESS REDUCTION, MEDITATION, YOGA

Australian Meditation Centre
    175 Elizabeth Street
    SYDNEY NSW 2000
    Telephone 02 267 6274

A Course in Miracles
    47 The Point Road
    WOOLWICH NSW 2110
    Telephone 02 817 2635

Hopewood Health Centre Pty Ltd
    Greendale Road
    WALLACIA NSW 2750
    Telephone 047 73 8401

International Meditation Society
    8 Bannerman Street
    CREMORNE NSW 2090
    Telephone 02 909 3199

Swami Sarasvati Rejuvenation Centre
    185 Pitt Town Road
    KENTHURST NSW 2154
    Telephone 02 654 9030

Woman's Stress Resource Centre
112 West Botany Road
ARNCLIFFE NSW 2205
Telephone 02 59 4251

PREMENSTRUAL SYNDROME

Women's organizations and hospitals

CONTRACEPTION, PREGNANCY AND CHILDBIRTH

**Australian Federation of Family Planning Assoc. Inc.
24 Campbell Street
SYDNEY NSW 2000
Telephone 02 211 1944

(There are family planning clinics in all States and Territories)

**Childbirth Centre
The Suite 4
29 Cowper Street
PARRAMATTA NSW 2150
Telephone 02 633 5899

**Homebirth Australia
PO Box 107
LAWSON NSW 2783
Telephone 047 59 2014

**Nursing Mother's Association of Australia
5 Glendale Street
NUNAWADING VIC 3131
Telephone 03 877 5011

Homebirth Access
Sydney PO Box 66
BROADWAY NSW 2007
Telephone 02 95 6137

Pregnancy Counselling & Support Strathfield
    56 Mosely Street
    STRATHFIELD NSW 2135
    Telephone 02 745 2972/02 745 2904

CANCER

**Australian Cancer Society
    155 King Street
    SYDNEY NSW 2000
    Telephone 02 231 3355

**Cancer Information & Support Society
    14 Herberton Ave
    HUNTERS HILL NSW 2110
    Telephone 02 817 1912

Sydney Square Diagnostic Breast Clinic
    Breast Clinic Division
    2nd Floor, St Andrews House
    Sydney Square
    SYDNEY NSW 2000
    Telephone 02 264 7388

PEACE OF MIND

Institute of Private Clinical Psychologists of Australia
    135 Macquarie Street
    SYDNEY NSW 2000
    Telephone 02 241 1688

New South Wales Association for Mental Health
    194 Miller Street
    NORTH SYDNEY NSW 2060
    Telephone 02 929 4388

NEW ZEALAND

Alternative Therapies

Mr Ken McIver
New Zealand Clinic of Acupuncture
  First Floor
  APC House
  24 High Street
  AUCKLAND

Dr Ben Y Yan
Peking Chinese Acupuncture Institute
  506 Queen Street
  AUCKLAND

New Zealand Chiropractic Association
  PO Box 2858
  WELLINGTON

Dr Taylor
Chiropractic First New Zealand Ltd
  PO Box 33.674
  Takapuna
  AUCKLAND 9

Australasian College of Herbal Studies
  Hillside Road
  OSTEND
  Waiheke

Suzanne Woods
New Zealand Association of Medical Herbalists
  ASB Chambers
  139 Queen Street
  AUCKLAND

Homoeopathy Department
  Lincoln Grove Health Centre
  292 Lincoln Road
  HENDERSON

Dr Parker
New Zealand School of Hypnotic Science
　PO Box 15.170
　NEW LYNN

Mr Peter Herrick
Psychological and Hypnotic Therapeutics Institute of New Zealand
　PO Box 2054
　AUCKLAND

South Pacific College of Naturopaths and Therapeutics
　10 Arthur Street
　Ellerslie
　AUCKLAND 6

Other

Dr Margaret Tillott
Alice Bush Family Planning
　214 Karangahape Road
　AUCKLAND 1

Professor Nanson
Cancer Society of New Zealand
　41 Gillies Avenue
　AUCKLAND 3

Mr Ian McCormick
New Zealand Psychological Society
　PO Box 4092
　WELLINGTON

Epsom Counselling Services
　676 Ranfurly Road
　Epsom
　AUCKLAND 3

SOUTH AFRICA

Homoeopaths, naturopaths, osteopaths and herbalists fall under the umbrella of:

South African Homoeopathic Association
 PO Box 10255
 STRUBENVALE 1570
 Telephone Johannesburg 011 565121

Chiropractors fall under:

Chiropractic Association of South Africa
 701 Poyton Building
 Gardener Street
 DURBAN 4001
 Telephone Durban 031 3044200

Anyone wishing to contact their nearest practitioner can get in touch with these associations which will provide them with addresses of registered practitioners.

Index

Katharina Dalton

ONCE A MONTH

Once a month, with demoralising regularity, over fifty per cent of women feel tired, confused, irritable and incapacitated due to the effects of premenstrual tension. Many others are indirectly affected – husbands, children, colleagues, workmates and friends.

Premenstrual syndrome is responsible for the timing of half of all criminal offences in women, for half of all suicides, accidents in the home and on the roads, hospital admissions, incidents of baby battering and alcoholic bouts. These are the calculable effects – how much greater are the less obvious changes in a woman's daily life, in her behaviour, appearance and health?

The problems might seem insurmountable – but are they? This book is a popular and easily understood account of menstrual difficulties by a doctor with many years of professional and research experience in their causes and treatment. Katharina Dalton shows that in most cases women can treat themselves, and that in severer cases progesterone treatment can be highly effective. It is a book which many readers – male as well as female – will find informative, sympathetic, helpful and above all practical in relieving the suffering caused by premenstrual syndrome.